Waves Astern

A Memoir of World War II and the Cold War

by

E. Spurgeon Campbell

authorHOUSE™

1663 Liberty Drive, Suite 200
Bloomington, Indiana 47403
(800) 839-8640
www.AuthorHouse.com

© 2004 E. Spurgeon Campbell
All Rights Reserved.

No part of this book may be reproduced, stored in a retrieval system, or transmitted by any means without the written permission of the author.

First published by AuthorHouse 10/27/04

ISBN: 1-4184-9892-0 (sc)
ISBN: 1-4184-9893-9 (dj)

Printed in the United States of America
Bloomington, Indiana

This book is printed on acid-free paper.

If men could learn from history, what lessons it might teach us! But passion and party blind our eyes, and the light which experience gives is a lantern on the stern, which shines only on the waves behind us!

Samuel Taylor Coleridge

Table of Contents

Preface ix

Acknowledgements xi

Chapter 1 "It's Another Boy" 1

Chapter 2 Decision Time 6

Chapter 3 Gallups Island 10

Chapter 4 My First Ship 29

Chapter 5 Sea Duty 39

Chapter 6 Henry Bacon 64

Chapter 7 Marriage 90

Chapter 8 Post War Adjustments 103

Chapter 9 Changes 115

Chapter 10 Eniwetok 120

Chapter 11 You Can Go Home Again 137

Chapter 12 One Night and One Day in Thule .. 144

Chapter 13 Washington 161

Chapter 14 Portugal 176

Chapter 15 Darmstadt 211

Chapter 16 Munich 220

Chapter 17 Retirement 245

Chapter 18 The Happy Ending 288

Preface

I was born Earnal Spurgeon Campbell in Eldridge, Alabama on December 28, 1921, into the family of George and Martha Campbell, their sixth son and ninth child. They would eventually have three additional children, making a family of six male and six female children.

I was known as Spurgeon, the surname of an eighteenth-century Baptist minister in England, who was admired by my mother. My siblings shortened it to "Spud" and I still am known by this nickname. During many years while living abroad I was called "Ernie" which was derived from Earnal.

That was 82 years ago in 2003 and what happened to me in the meantime was mostly routine, but sometimes unusual and even, on occasion, somewhat dangerous. My life has spanned many innovations from the beginning of radio broadcasting to the present age of cyberspace.

Since my retirement from Radio Free Europe/Radio Liberty in 1982, my days have been filled with the joys and frustrations of golf, and spending time with my lovely wife, Bea, and with immediate and extended family and friends, and with watching my grandson, Chris Sparks, from his birth in 1983 through primary and secondary school and into college as he grows into manhood. Bea and I have also enjoyed adventures traveling to other countries and in the US.

The last ten years have brought many reminders of long forgotten events of World War II when I served in the US Merchant Marine. The forced remembering of some horrible days in the winter of 1945 has at times inflicted on me nightmares and days of vertigo, resurrecting memories which I had wished to be left undisturbed. On the other hand, this resurrection of a long lost story has brought Bea and me, along with son Steve and his wife, Nan, many interesting and enjoyable adventures in touring Norway, Scotland and the US as we participated in reunions and documentary productions concerning the ship SS *Henry Bacon*. But more about that later. In the mid 1990s I had to face these memories. I had always avoided talking about them and even thinking of them.

So why am I now sitting here at my computer doing what I swore not to do—planning to create a written record of my life? Many people have suggested to me that certain events with which I was involved should be documented. My old friend, Bill Brewer, a schoolmate from Gallups Island Radio School in Boston, who now lives in Jacksonville, Florida, has been after me for years to get down to writing. I have always declined for various reasons, not the least of which is the fact that I do not seek attention. I've had more than enough of that as some things have been written about me in books and media articles and covered by TV interviews and documentaries. A recent series of events may have changed my mind.

Grandson Chris had requested information on my life as he did a college course paper on an interview with "someone you have admired." "Grandpa," he said, "you have had the most interesting life of anyone I know." (Certainly not an objective opinion, but one I liked) Then recently our son Steve, after reading my brother Julian's well written and crafted memoirs which have now been printed into a book, has asked me to at least put things down in a form which would carry forward my "story."

So this is for you Chris and you Steve, along with my dear Bea, daughter Lynda and daughter-in-law, Nan. And if anyone else is interested—well I suppose it isn't classified material.

Acknowledgements

The replay button of my memory was triggered by a 1992 trip that Bea and I took to Washington. There I met many people including Ian Millar who was largely responsible for convincing the Russians to present medals to people who delivered the material which helped to stem the Nazi advance on Moscow in World War II. Ian had written an article, "The Murmansk Run," about the SS *Henry Bacon* and other ships that made the treacherous voyage during that war. This forced me to remember many things I had deliberately forgotten.

Several people have been helpful to me as I have tried to recreate the major events of my life of some 82 years. Among those to whom I am indebted is Bill Brewer, a good friend and classmate from Gallups Island Radio School in Boston during 1941 and 1942. During many conversations with him over the past 10 years, Bill has encouraged me to write my remembrances as he did with his memoir, "*Trumpet in the Dust*." Bill was also kind enough to read the "Gallups Island" chapter and to give me his comments and suggestions. My Cullman friend, Sonny Drain, also encouraged me to write down my memories.

My memory has been augmented by recent contact with other Gallups Island classmates: Coleman Barber, Bill Ishee, Sam Notaro, Art Shedden, James Smart and others whose stories have been included in the Gallups Island Radio Association (GIRA) book, *We Came From All Over, We Went Everywhere,* which was edited by my friend Stan Jennings. I have kept in contact via e-mail with many of my friends from that time. Frank Hetzler, who shared many common experiences during World War II and now lives in Sweden, informed me of a new Merchant Marine exhibit at Lofoten, Norway's new Krigsminnemuseum (War Museum) where the SS *Henry Bacon* story was featured with some pictures I sent to him.

Wartime experiences on the SS *Henry Bacon*, have been vividly resurrected in my memory by many events of the past dozen years. Among the most helpful were discussions with surviving shipmates

Chuck Reed, Dick Burbine, Bill Herrmann and the Norwegian survivors, as well as the complete story of the ship's fate by Donald Foxvog and Robert Alotta in their book, *The Last Voyage of the SS Henry Bacon.* Thanks to Dr. Alotta for reviewing this manuscript and making many helpful comments. My contacts with Harald Hendriksen and others during the filming of Hendriksen's excellent documentary, *Convoys to Russia,* refreshed my memory, as did the Scottish crew of Elly Taylor, director of the documentary, *Through Hell and High Water.* My trip with Bea and Steve to Loch Ewe, Scotland, where I talked with Jack Harrison and other veterans of the Russian convoy experience, provided invaluable information. Communications with Len Phillips, who was on the rescue ship HMS *Opportune* when the Royal Navy picked us out of the arctic water, have been extremely helpful to me as I tried to remember events after the disaster. Thanks to C.B. Tye of the North Russia Club for our meeting at Loch Ewe and to the Peter Harrison family for being such generous hosts at their hotel. Many thanks to Baard Haugland of Rasta, Norway for his interest and many communications. And to the whole country of Norway for making us feel so welcome during our two visits.

The experiences on the other ships and of the war have depended largely on my own memory. This is also the case of my time at Eniwetok and at Thule, Greenland. It would be interesting if I could compare my memories with those of others. I would welcome contact with any of the people I knew at those times. If anyone with such knowledge should read this book I can be reached by e-mail at spud@cneti.com.

My continuing contact with Russ Poole who recently retired as Vice President, Administration of Radio Free Europe/Radio Liberty has been very interesting and helpful. I also thank Russ for reviewing the first draft of the Munich chapter.

As I have tried to focus my mind on a particular time I have found it very helpful to review newspaper headline stories of the time. This I have been able to do on the internet, by the various library archives and in the book, *The New York Times PAGE ONE.* My ancient edition of the *Encyclopædia Britannica* and its yearbooks, and other books of the Cold War years have been very helpful to remind me of dates and details of world events during those turbulent years.

My friend and neighbor, Dr. Howard Williamson has helped by reviewing some parts of this story where his expertise was needed. My twelve-year classmate, Billie Hamner Malone supplied pictures and her memory of some events. (No Billie, I will not "tell on you" for breaking my new red crayon in the 1st grade.) Bill Fuller's pictorial record of the Campbell reunions and my brother Julian's memoirs have been referenced and were invaluable.

However, this tale would have remained untold except for the encouragement and assistance of my immediate family.

Major credit I give to my son, Steve, who made the suggestion, and persistently pursued it until I decided to give it a try. Then he continued his support by taking each chapter as I e-mailed them to his Denver home for backup on his computer and reviewed the draft with suggested changes and additions. Steve also did the design, layout and picture insertions, a task which I can scarcely imagine. His knowledge and assistance, as he fitted it into his busy life as an environmental consultant with an educational background in engineering, law and economics, has been essential.

Steve's wife, Nan, has been the delightfully enthusiastic editor as she used her talent, training and experience to make my sometimes too technical and amateurish syntax more readable.

Daughter Lynda has vast knowledge of language which was useful as she read portions and made suggestions. Chris, my grandson, has been helpful with getting me through some computer glitches and by our discussions over the years and lately on the golf course.

My wife, Bea the humanitarian, has been my inspiration as she accompanied me through most of these adventures and as she read and reread every word with valuable help from her memory and her great sense of style and proportion.

Chapter 1
"It's Another Boy"

I'm sure that is what someone sighed when a squealing kid with a full head of dark hair slid helplessly from his mother's womb. If I had been more aware at the time, I probably would have thought that my arrival failed to create great shock waves or even a hint of celebration in the neighborhood of the little town of Eldridge in Walker County, Alabama. I can visualize my brother Julian, who was nearly two, standing by and thinking, "This kid is a threat to my territorial domain and sustenance." Well, he could have relaxed because it was not to be. Except for taking over what previously was his source of milk, I didn't disturb his established routine.

I understand I was a healthy kid with few needs not supplied by my parents and the many siblings in our household. When one grows up in a family of eight or ten as the case was with us at the time, one learns to get along with little personal attention. Early on, I began to lean toward learning how to understand the world around me and how things worked.

I was three when we moved from Eldridge to an even more rural place. It was to Arley in Winston County, where the recently established high school of Meek was located. My father wanted his

Figure 1. It's Another Boy

large family to be educated in a farming community with a good school, and that was not easy to find at the time.

By this time, my brother Julian and I had developed a ritual of fun and games mostly designed by the one who was almost twice my age and was bigger and stronger. We had fun with all of our mostly self-invented routines, and I was even then beginning to tire of being dominated by one who was always quick to let me know he was my senior. (We continue this play at our local golf course of Terri Pines in Cullman, Alabama). We began growing up as friends, buddies and partners, and we tried to disguise the undercurrent of sibling rivalry. But it was always there in the background.

Some of my earliest clear memories are of the time when Julian was six and went off to school at Meek. He read his primer, *The Little Red Hen*, in the evening as I lay in bed trying to get some sleep. As he read aloud, he would often get stalled and ask an older sibling to help with the unknown word. I had heard the story many times, and my young uncluttered mind had mostly memorized it. Once, as he paused for help on a word, I blurted out the answer from memory. Needless to say, this business of an illiterate four-year-old correcting a six-year-old scholar didn't sit well with Julian and he vented his fury by thrashing my tail the next day.

Two years later it was finally my time to enter those hallowed halls and begin my education. Julian was reading and doing mathematics and I was both impressed and fearful for my immediate future. On the first day as I was getting ready for the bus I suddenly got cold feet and ran to my Mom. "Mama, I don't know enough to go to school," I sobbed. But she said I should go anyhow and maybe I could somehow begin at the beginning.

I remember Miss Mollie Barron met us at the door of the building where I was to spend much of the next 12 years. There began the great adventure of learning to read. This was a magical discovery, and it opened a whole new world to me. Soon I was trying to read the daily newspaper which came to our house, the Bible and any books I could find. We didn't even have our first radio at that time and my knowledge of life outside our family and the small community was virtually limited to what I was able to pick up from listening to adult conversation.

My class was small, about 20, and came from many of the more stable families of the area—Hamner, Cox, Murphy, Cook, Fuller, and Evans were there and continued together for the next 12 years when I graduated from high school. Others would have been with us for all those years but for that lean year during the Depression when school at Meek only held for half the year due to insufficient funding. The following year, half of each class continued to the next level and half repeated. So we left some behind and were joined by some older students from the year ahead.

During these formative years, I was a serious student and was competitive with the two best students. They were girls—Billie Hamner and Jewel Cox. Unfortunately, as I reached puberty some years later, I slipped into the accepted male tendency of exhibiting a certain disdain for academics.

About this time our father brought home a radio. It was in the days before we had electricity, which came to Arley in the early 1930s as the TVA system developed. The battery-powered radio was the greatest marvel I had ever encountered. I remember how I spent hours listening and trying to imagine what people were about in places like Cincinnati, Nashville and Del Rio, Texas. My inquisitive mind tried to imagine how a voice was carried from one place to another. I mailed off a coupon to a technical school and asked for sample lesson materials. I studied these papers and found other boys who had a smattering of knowledge of the subject. I got myself into trouble by opening the radio and checking out all the parts. Luckily, after much experimentation, I was able to get it working again. Otherwise I would really have been in trouble. My sister Mary, in a recent letter, reminded me that at the time my mother said, "Don't worry, he will get it back together." This little box was the spark that set in motion my future life and career.

It was the content of information from the radio that helped to continue my quest for knowledge about people outside our little community. Many of the voices had different accents, and most seemed to speak faster and with better grammar than mine. This also gave me incentive to study English and grammar with the hope that I could improve my speaking ability. I also heard languages other than English, and I wondered if one could ever learn to speak two different tongues. Most of these questions went unanswered because I was hesitant to bring them up with anyone. I just had a desire to get out into the world and explore and learn about things I could only imagine in the little place where we lived.

As I sat in a class of beginning English and grammar, my mind would wander to other things. "How does this precision in talk and writing relate to the mysteries of the inner workings of electrons circling inside an atom, and how one could control it to make radio talk, and does it help me to explore this big old world and its many varied people and to understand the magic of the universe?" And, "Why can't I question my strict Baptist training of someone's understanding of the Bible and my faith in God?" I quit trying to relate these thoughts to others because of the strange looks I got in return.

How could one as naive as I was foresee: going into a world war and experiencing survival of a ship sinking and living to celebrate with the ship's foreign survivors; participating in the testing of atomic and hydrogen weapons; living and working in a most severe climate while supervising the work on a vital project monitoring the possible launching of enemy missile attacks; and spending 20 years in a job matching wits with a cold war enemy while working alongside thousands of people who spoke a couple of dozen different languages.

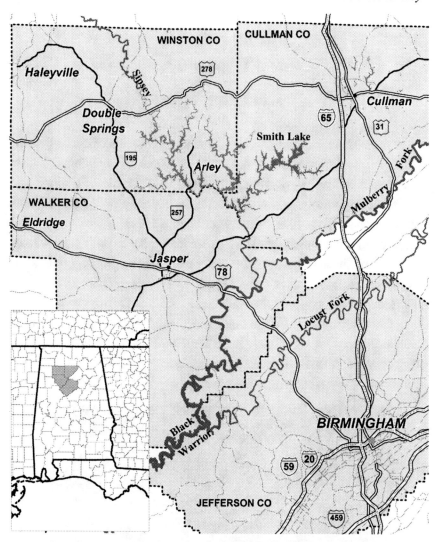

Figure 2. Winston, Walker and Cullman Counties, Alabama

Chapter 2
Decision Time

My class of 13 (seven boys and six girls) consisted of some very good students in my senior year at Meek High School. Many of us had become more or less "paired off." Barney Hamner and Hollis Melear were close friends. Wyatt Murphy and Cortis Fields were close, and my best friend had become E.B. Barron, who had joined us in the seventh grade after attending the little feeder school at Helicon. The remaining boy was Frank Evans, and he was a bit of a loner, although this didn't seem to bother him at all. On the girls' side, it was Billie Hamner (Barney's cousin) paired with Jewel Cox (daughter of our Ag teacher, Dad Cox), Myrl Evans and Hazel Cook, Margie Jones and Bessie Fuller. Someone once asked me if I was ever romantically interested in a classmate, and I answered, "of course not, they all seemed like sisters."

Figure 3. Meek High School Class of 1940 (left to right: Myrl Evans, Margie Jones, Wyatt Murphy, Bessie Fuller, Barney Hamner, Hollis Melear, Cortis Fields, Hazel Cook, Jewell Cox, Spud, Billie Hamner, E.B. Barron, Frank Evans)

Decision Time

My motivation for study had gradually decreased, and I ended my high school career with average grades and with a tendency to live up to my reputation of finding ways to get into trouble with the teachers. However, when we were given our evaluation in an exam given by the Alabama Department of Education (I suppose it was a Stanford-Benet test), our high school principal told us we did very well compared with other schools in Alabama and other states. He said while he could not tell us how each person scored, the results came out pretty much as he expected, but glancing at me he added "except for a case or two." Later I was contacted by both the University of Alabama and Auburn (Alabama Polytechnic Institute at the time) and both stated that my percentile rating among all high school seniors was above 97, and both of the state universities offered some scholastic aid if I would apply to their school. I felt that I should pursue the opportunity for more education, but I was unable to find the way to do so.

Figure 4. Spud in 1940

This was 1940, the Depression was still with us and the war in Europe was on everyone's mind. Hitler had already defeated much of the European continent and was threatening England. Our government had committed to defend the free world by beginning the lend-lease program of support to the Europeans and the rebuilding of the armed forces. We had begun building merchant ships for delivering this aid to our friends abroad, and there was already talk of a military draft of males over 19.

That summer of 1940, as I helped my father plant crops, we had many serious talks. Papa, as I called him, was the one person I could always talk with when I had a problem. He was kind and loving as he thanked me for staying with him that year. The five brothers who preceded me had left after high school, or sooner in the case of Tommy, who left before he graduated. Papa was approaching retirement age without a retirement plan, and I was his only male support on the farm. He also had a wife and three daughters who were still in high school. We discussed my future, and he said that while he wanted me to stay on the farm with him, he also could see that my needs and the war situation probably made that impossible. He was one who believed in getting a good education, and he would have helped me if he could, but I understood that he could not.

So, instead of enrolling at Tuscaloosa or Auburn as I would have loved to do, after the crop was finished in the fall of 1940, I went to Birmingham and spent some time with my sister Evelyn and her husband, Arvel Waldrep. They had a young daughter, Betty, and since their house had only two bedrooms, I slept on the couch in the living room. Evelyn served great meals and the couple always was helpful to me without any expectation of my paying rent. I have always been grateful and fond of that family until this day.

That fall, I learned of a government program, National Youth Administration. This program offered training to youth not in college. I signed up for it and almost immediately was assigned the technical course in radio theory and Morse code. I spent two weeks per month in this class throughout that winter, and in the spring something happened that set my career course for life.

The NYA School was visited by a US Coast Guard officer who told our teacher, Carl Martens, that he was recruiting candidates for a school, located on an island in Boston Harbor, which was training young men to become radio officers in the US Merchant Marine. The recruiter was picking one, two or three from each state of the union, and he said that he was very selective. First the candidate should have a good academic background in high school and an interest in learning radio theory. Each student should have impeccable loyalty to our country. (I later learned that some of the radio officers on ships had been removed due to questionable loyalty.) The qualifying candidates were to be given an intense 12 months of instruction and training, after which they would each go aboard a separate ship and be able to take complete control of communications. No other member of the crew would have enough knowledge of the job to be helpful.

When I was selected along with Fred Digesu, another guy from Birmingham, I was thrilled and agreed immediately although I hadn't the slightest idea what this entailed as I had never been aboard a ship. This kid from Arley, Alabama, had found his niche. See the world, learn the mysteries of electronics and serve your country. My college education could come later. I couldn't wait to get home to tell my father and mother.

Mama cried like a baby and Papa took me by the arm as we went for a walk over the 40-acre farm. As we strolled over the newly plowed field and saw the corn beginning to sprout and the preparation for planting some 15 acres of cotton, we talked about how my decision could change both our worlds. He tried to hide his worry and concern for his finances but began to talk of his fear for my safety. This was the first hint I had of the possibility that this could be a dangerous adventure. But I was 19 and the word "dangerous" only made the adventure more appealing. I remember that I did ask about his financial situation and offered to help by sending half of any pay I would receive over the year I was in school. (I had no idea at the time how that promise would affect my social life at school as I began at $21 per month and it ballooned to $36 and eventually to $54 over the next year).

Being one not able to handle situations which contained too much sentiment, I hurriedly said goodbye to a tearful Mother and to Papa, who gave me a firm handshake and looked me squarely in the eye as he said, "Good luck Spurgeon." I had no idea that it would be another 17 months before I would see anyone from home again.

Chapter 3
Gallups Island

As Fred Digesu and I boarded a train in Birmingham that spring day in 1941, Fred's father and mother and other family members saw him off and my sister Evelyn gave me a goodbye hug and wished me well. I remember she brought her one-year-old daughter Betty with us to the train station. I thought I detected a tear or two on Evelyn's cheek, but she was always somewhat of a stoic person, so I am not sure. I gave young Betty, to whom I had become attached, a little kiss even though I was so excited that I felt almost giddy to be on my way into the great unknown. Little did I know.

Neither Fred nor I was an experienced traveler, and we were quite concerned as the train headed south. I was thinking that this was a strange way to get to Boston which I knew was "up north." But we soon remembered we had been told that we were going first to Tampa, Florida to be with other students at a Civilian Conservation Corps (CCC) camp for a week or so.

The train car was loaded with people talking about their lives and plans. One family of five said they were going to Florida for a month at the beach. They were from Indiana and seemed to me to be wealthy. I listened to their conversation which sounded like the radio announcers I had heard on WLW in Cincinnati, Ohio. Finally Fred ventured a comment to them, and we both told them something of ourselves and our plans. But we were hesitant to give the details of our activities. The war threat was already causing people to be careful what they said.

Some of the young men aboard the train seemed to be military recruits, and they were interested in talking about the possibility of the US getting into the European war. The name "Hitler" was mentioned often. Everyone expressed hatred and some fear of the man who had been so successful in quickly crushing many small countries and some larger ones like Poland and France. The Russians, led by Joseph Stalin, had already made a pact with Hitler to divide up some of the many countries of Eastern Europe. However, they both were so greedy that this agreement rapidly fell apart, and in May 1941, Hitler's *blitzkrieg* forces struck to the east and overran everything in the way to the Russian border. That must have taught the Soviet leader a lesson in not trusting anyone whose moral credo so closely resembled his own.

All of this news and discussion was interesting to me as I pondered how I might eventually fit into the scheme of things. That talk only occasionally diverted my attention from looking out the window as the train crossed the farm lands of Alabama and into the sandy, flat land of northern Florida. We stopped in many small burgs and some towns and some larger cities such as Montgomery and Tallahassee. I noticed how the trees and other vegetation began to change from what I had known in northern Alabama. There were fewer deciduous trees, and the pines were mostly long leaf and stately. Often the oaks were large at the base but short and were filled with a gray, parasitic looking moss. I soon learned they were live oaks which stayed green all year and were covered with Spanish moss. (Funny how one's memory retains such small details of the distant past and has a problem with yesterday's events.)

It was a long day's trip and I was a bit tired from all the exciting activity when we arrived around midnight at the station in Tampa. I thought it was an hour earlier but soon learned that I was now in the Eastern Time Zone for the first time in my life. That knowledge relieved me of some concern that my inner clock had malfunctioned. You see, I had never had the luxury of wearing a watch but had been able to develop a "dead reckoning" ability to know when to do certain activities like eat and sleep.

We were met by a driver with a vehicle (I seem to remember it being a truck with all of us standing in the bed at the back). We were driven some miles north of Tampa where we were to spend the next couple of weeks. It was a camp where young men were living and working on rural and forest projects for our government. It turned out to be a CCC camp. Like the NYA which I had left in Birmingham, CCC was a New Deal project. These two programs were intended to aid young people in getting training in preparation for many different careers.

This little CCC camp was called Camp De Soto and was hewn out of a tropical jungle. It had tents, a few buildings and many trails leading in all directions, it seemed. The buildings and other facilities were fashioned from native materials by some unknown amateur artist in a way that preserved the natural appearance of the jungle. I enjoyed being there for those two weeks as I met a few of my future classmates. We also were given tours to Sulphur Springs where we swam in a pool and met local people.

Digesu and I had wondered if Camp De Soto would be like a boot camp in the military. It was not that at all. We did have to launder our clothes, but this was not a big problem. I had only brought one change of the basics and probably washed them about once a week. We had been told that we would be outfitted in a complete wardrobe at Gallups Island near Boston. The leaders of the camp led us in some routines of calisthenics and running. Some of the guys were not in shape and they had trouble with soreness the next day, but it didn't seem to bother me very much.

The food was good and we were given the opportunity to tour the area including the beach which was only a few miles away. One of my friends remembers that I had trouble on the beach when I discovered how sand spurs affect bare feet. But it was like a paid vacation for me. After all I had not seen an ocean before.

There were about two dozen guys from various southern states. Some had been with me at the CCC camp out in the woods and others were staying in the city of Tampa at the NYA building. I met and talked with many of them and we all were taken to various places for training. On weekends we went in several directions but mostly to the pool in Sulphur Springs and to Tampa just to walk around and enjoy the city. The pool was really a small natural lake with many crevices and rock formations and contained the clearest water I had ever seen. There was also a spa and a casino which I dared not enter. There were some pretty girls around the pool and I suppose I "noticed" them.

Gallups Island

I remember going into a bar for the first time in my young protected life. But my experience with alcohol had been limited to a taste of home brewed beer and the even more horrible tasting wildcat whiskey which had been illegally produced in the hills of Winston County, Alabama. This was the beginning of my education in the mores of socializing with people from varied backgrounds. I sat with the group and watched them indulge and occasionally allowed myself to taste the various drinks they seemed to be enjoying so much. But I had never acquired a taste for alcohol, nor did I require its stimulation in order to enjoy a social atmosphere. This fact, rather than any desire to be a loner, made it difficult for me to establish immediate close friendships with the other guys. I guess I also was afraid of losing control as I had seen others do.

At the end of the two weeks, I felt I had experienced my first real vacation and was eager to get on another train for the long ride to Boston. The two weeks had set a pattern for my time at Radio School. I was more of an observer than an active participant in the fun and games. However, I had been impressed with my glimpse of the Sunshine State I had heard so much about, and I thought it would be a good place to visit again. Distant future things like retirement never entered my mind, but if it had, I'm sure Florida would have been near the top of my desired destinations.

But all good things must come to an end, they say, and it was now time to get aboard another train and head north. Waiting to board the train, I noticed there was another group who had been housed at the NYA facility. These, along with my CCC camp colleagues, became what we later called our "southern group" of my future classmates. As I sat and observed the others who were talking and laughing and playing pranks, two who caught my interest were the Jacksonville pair—Bill Brewer and Art Sheddan. They were opposites in personality. Art was the older-looking of the two and he was a steady, serious type but with a shy grin which I liked.

Bill, on the other hand, was a young, boisterous kid who was full of talk and laughter, a schemer who seemed to be bugging Art with nicknames and good humored pranks. He spoke in a drawl that was even slower than mine and was always very comical with everyone.

I was later to learn to appreciate Bill as a serious person who went on to become very successful in his career with a Ford dealership. Bill has become my closest friend of all who survived World War II. We still communicate regularly.

Bill Ishee, who was from Mississippi, was on board, and I spent some time talking with him. He had been an alternate selection and only got in at the last moment, for which he was grateful. Apparently he had been in the NYA training for a short time while others were already getting amateur radio licenses. Bill was a very straightforward person and I always enjoyed talking with him. He eventually became one of the top students and after the war had a great career as an accountant. Bill has been retired for several years and now lives in New Iberia, Louisiana.

Our train left Tampa at around 3:00 p.m. on April 6, 1941 and we were so excited, and in my case apprehensive, about our future. But we were able to take our minds off the problems of fitting in as we learned more about each other. It seemed we had a lot of similar backgrounds and experiences. Just about everyone had finished high school within the last year and had to forego college for various reasons. All of the students in my class had been selected from the National Youth Administration (NYA) program. We later learned that the five classes which preceded us were drawn from the CCC program which was in some ways similar to the NYA. The main difference was that the CCC groups were stationed in rural areas of national forests or other similar areas while NYA units were mostly located in cities and towns. The school I had attended was located in an abandoned appliance factory in North Birmingham.

It was at about 7:00 p.m. when the train pulled into Jacksonville. We were surprised when Bill Brewer's family met the train. As we looked out the window they had a very emotional reunion with Bill who had only been gone for a couple of weeks. (A little over a year later I was able to meet this very nice family when my first ship made an emergency stop at Jacksonville. More about that later.)

Over the next day or so we began forming friendships that would last all our lives. However, now in 2004, only a few still survive.

Gallups Island

Leaving Jacksonville we rode north through Georgia, and some of us slept through the Carolinas. We slept in our seats while others talked and walked about on the train. I was tired and was able to get a few hours sleep before we saw daylight in southern Virginia, as I remember it. By late afternoon we arrived in our nation's capital. I guess that was the most thrilling sight I had seen up until then. Crossing the Potomac River, which I had read so much about, and then picking out the famous storied monuments and the Capitol gave me a feeling of pride akin to reverence. Everything was so well ordered and clean. I was not sure I had seen the White House, but I remember thinking, "What a beautiful city."

We then proceeded up through the great industrial cities between Washington and New York. People got aboard who spoke in different accents from ours, and they seemed to us a bit less friendly. I gazed out the window and read signs and marveled at all the activity, the heavy traffic and bustling people. As we passed through a medium-sized town in Pennsylvania I read a sign which I remember to this day. It read "WHAT CHESTER MAKES MAKES CHESTER." I wonder if that sign has survived as long as my memory of it has.

When it got dark I saw little and even less as we approached New York City. The train seemed to dive into a tunnel and not come out until we arrived at Pennsylvania Station in midtown Manhattan. We remained on the train and in a few minutes it was underground again and resurfaced north of the city, so I was unable to see much of that great city. The next time I would be in New York was about a year later as I went aboard my first ship.

We were able to glimpse many cities as we streaked on into the night. Then it was midnight and we arrived at our destination. Someone hollered, "WE ARE IN BOSTON!" and everyone cheered. Another commented, "We are a rebel army invading Yankee country." But I for one felt more apprehension than aggression.

We left the train without ceremony and scrambled onto a waiting bus. That vehicle wound in and out of mysterious-appearing streets and avenues until we arrived at a dark wharf. From the parked bus it was only a short walk along the wharf to a gangway that led up to a small ship with a sign which read "US COAST GUARD" and below that "USS *Yeaton.*" I later learned it was what is known as a Coast Guard cutter. Some crew member yelled from a port hole, "You'll be soorreee!" It was a tired and uncharacteristically subdued rebel band as the *Yeaton* plowed its way through the dark waters of Boston Harbor and arrived at our new home at about one o'clock in the morning.

A crew member directed us toward a rather large lighted building up the hill from the dock. It was too late for anything but sleep so we each selected a bunk and quickly went to sleep for about five hours. The brassy sound of a bugle playing a strange tune (which I later learned was reveille) would wake up the near-dead. And that is what I felt I was that first morning on "The Island."

Figure 5. Gallups Island

I understand that a Captain John Gallop, in 1630, got ownership of the 16-acre island which now bears his name. The spelling was changed to "Gallups Island" sometime in the 19th century. As the Union found need of campgrounds and training areas in the Civil War, Gallups Island was bought by the state and turned over to the federal government. Some 3,000 Union troops lived and trained there during that war. After the Civil War, a quarantine hospital was built and operated on the island until 1937. In 1940, the need for radio officers became acute, and the US Coast Guard established a radio school with students recruited from all over the country. This was a unit of what became known as the US Maritime Service. Other schools in New York and elsewhere would train officers and seamen for other positions on merchant ships.

When I got to Gallups Island the school routine was well under way with the first class only a couple of months from graduation. Some of the more advanced students who could pass the Federal Communications Commission (FCC) license tests were being shipped out early.

As I got dressed and made for the mess hall for breakfast on that first morning, I was able to get my first look at the facilities. Our barracks building was the largest on the island. The dozen or so buildings included a galley and mess hall, several classrooms, laboratories and an administration building. Supporting facilities included a post office, a power generating system, a sick bay, offices and a small canteen. So the island was not only insulated from the outside world but was to a large degree self-supporting. The facilities were originally designed and built to educate 400 students for a year, but later in the war I understand that it held 1,000 who were there for a shorter time. There were no women on the island.

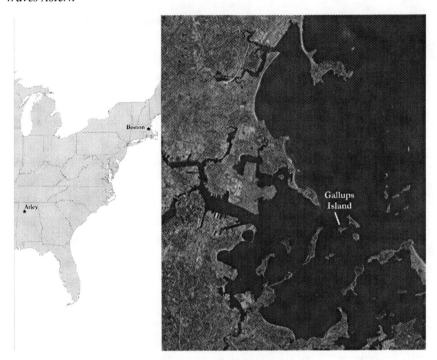

Figure 6. Boston Harbor

All of this, plus the strict military discipline, created an intense program of study with few distractions. The food was good, and we had daily exercises of calisthenics on the parade ground. I remember getting up and, with a team, racing other boats over to another island a mile away and back to a hearty breakfast.

One of the first things the school did was to issue each student a stack of clothes of approximately the right size. Later we did much trading with others so that eventually we were pretty well fitted. These included dress and informal blues, dungarees or work clothes, underwear or skivvies as they were called, and socks and shoes. Sailor caps were required, of course. A heavy pea coat was included but not needed in the summer. We were assigned a bed and given linen and covers. Each guy had to take care of laundering his clothes on weekends. We were trained in the way the Navy rolled clothes so they would not require ironing.

Over the years I often wondered how well I kept in contact with my aging parents by letter. Just recently my sister Gloria gave me a little note book in which my father kept certain financial records. It contained 17 dates and amounts of money that I had sent to him during that year. He called them "debts to Spurgeon," but I never allowed him to repay me. When I think of what a great man and father he was to me, I have good feelings about my ability to help at that critical time in all our lives.

Our class, which was designated as R6 platoon, included the southern unit and many others from other areas of the country. Sam Notaro, from New York, was named our platoon leader. He was a very good choice. Sam was firm and fair and unflappable. He was also a very good student.

At the beginning, R6 consisted of about 45 students but the number gradually decreased to about 30 who finished a year later. Some left for personal or family reasons, but most left because they couldn't make it with the heavy academic routines.

And heavy it was. Our days were filled with classes in radio theory, Morse code, mathematics, seamanship and shipboard life, including life saving techniques and just plain learning to cope. That first week was hectic, and it never seemed to let up. But I enjoyed it more than any studies I had ever experienced. I was learning from good teachers who were petty officers in the Coast Guard. Chief Summerfield, who taught radio theory, was the favorite of our class.

I thought, "This is not unlike a Sunday School class because we had to accept on faith things we can only visualize in the mind." But we could understand from their results in making a radio work that magnetic fields, electric currents, amplification and radio waves were there even if we couldn't see them. The chief told us that Ohm's law explained mathematically how voltage, current and resistance were interrelated in electronic circuitry. I mentally connected it to how trying to understand the Trinity had made my life more meaningful. This period was something of an epiphany in my young life.

Evenings were filled with talk and lots of study in the library. It also gave me a good time to observe and listen to the many regional accents from all over the US. The people from the Boston area seemed to be very proud of their long history of leadership in establishing and developing our democracy. One feature of their accent was their penchant for dropping the letter *r* from some words and inserting it at the end of others and their special way of pronouncing certain vowels. "Let's go to Bastin, pawk auh cah in Hahvawd Yawd, and try to pick up girls from Canadar or Cuber." And the guys from New York and New Jersey would refer to us as, "youse guys." It didn't take long for us southerners to translate the meaning of "y'all."

As if learning a new dialect, if not a language—plus the study of the inner workings of an atom—was not enough, we had another discipline to master. Our brains were battered for hours trying to translate intelligence from a constantly interrupted tone using crude tools. Dots and dashes plus spaces comprised the clues for each letter or other character as designed by a long-dead inventor named Samuel F.B. Morse. At that time, Morse code was still the only way ships could communicate at sea, far from land. In order to graduate and pass the FCC exam as a 2nd class operator, we should be able to translate these little dots and dashes at a speed of about four per second, and to become a full fledged 1st class operator, at just was over six per second. That would mean receiving a message at 25 words per minute. Sending at the same speed would require four wrist movements per second for graduation and six for the 1st class license. Some people failed to make it.

On Saturday morning we wore our dress uniforms when we stood at attention for inspection by the commanding officer and staff. If we had passed our tests and passed inspection, we were allowed to leave on the *Yeaton* for Boston.

Bill Brewer wrote in his memoirs that our favorite teacher and guardian of our morals, Mr. Summerfield, warned us against drinking that "panther piss" they served in Boston. He also wrote that we ignored his warning and hit a few bars on our first trip into the big city. I also remember strolling through the Boston Common and observing people walking around and sitting on benches. Bill and his friend, Leon Aboud, had friends living on Beacon Street which was a high-class area along the Charles River. On the other side of the river was Harvard University in Cambridge. I was not with them that day but did my strolling with Hubert Newton from North

Carolina. Hubert and I had things in common, like undeveloped skills in breaking the ice with members of the opposite sex. We did venture into the Scollay Square where we saw a vaudeville show at the Old Howard theatre. We spent the night at Sailor's Haven on Milk Street where we could stay for practically no money, as I remember it. On Sunday, it was back to the island for church services and getting prepared for another full week of the same.

Figure 7. Spud with Hubert Newton at Gallups Island

After some weeks of staying in the barracks on weekends, Bill asked me if I wanted to accompany some of the more socially active going into Boston and "trolling for female companionship." Bill complimented me by saying that they had decided that my appearance might be the "bait" they needed. Then he punctured my ego by saying, "Then after we meet them, our personalities will take over."

My close friends were Brewer and Sheddan from Florida, Rampy and Barber from Texas, Newton from North Carolina, Ishee from Mississippi and Breeland from Louisiana. Fred Digesu, from Alabama, was a friend also, but he had a very close call and was delayed into the following class after an accident. In seamanship class we were practicing firing a gun which was sometimes used for shooting a line from one ship to another. This cannon sent an 18 pound lead shot with a line attached to a distance of about a hundred yards. Since the gun was in a fixed position and fired in the same direction the lead shot always landed at a particular spot. After many previous firings the shot had dug a hole at one end of the parade ground. One day it seems Fred decided he would read his comic book in the little dugout place where he would not be seen. Then he fell asleep and missed the class. As luck would have it the shot glanced off his head. It cracked his skull and sent him to hospital for weeks. Fortunately he recovered and came back to Gallups. Digesu spent the war years at sea after which he came home, picked up an engineering degree at Auburn University and enjoyed a long and successful career with the Von Braun team in Huntsville. I have not seen him, but did talk with him on the phone once in recent years.

My ancient memory of details of events which happened more than 60 years ago has been augmented by a periodical called the *Gallups Islander*. This bulletin of the Gallups Island Radio Association, GIRA, was edited by Stan Jennings from class R58, vintage 1944. Stan worked in publishing for the National Geographic Society and formed his own publishing company in Washington. He also edited a beautiful GIRA book, *We Came from All Over, We Went Everywhere*. It contains a wealth of information about the history of Gallups Island, the radio school, and dozens of personal stories by graduates who traveled separately throughout the world and had experiences which were both varied and yet somewhat similar. Just about all had combat duty in every war zone of World War II. I have enjoyed rereading it as I try to remember things we did during the year of 1941.

Another aid to memory is Bill Brewer's book, *Trumpet in the Dust*, which gives a vividly beautiful picture of his life, augmented by pictures of people at Gallups.

The summer of 1941 was a busy transition time for me. The Gallups Island routine and study kept me from being too concerned with the European war which was beginning to look global. I

Figure 8. Mail from Home

spent spare hours on weekends in the library reading books and newspapers which contained little news from the southeast. However, I had frequent letters from my family, especially my sisters. Mary was the most prolific but she had already left for Chicago and her own career and marriage to Ralph Kelly. She was never to return south except for an occasional visit. Gloria was still in high school, and she kept me informed about how some of the boys were already volunteering for military service. My father and mother wrote regularly, and Mama would remind me I was ever in her prayers. She was a worrier, and I was more concerned about that than any danger I might face.

I always dreaded duties like KP and night watch. Washing dishes and working in a kitchen was not my cup of tea. With a gang of sisters, I never had to experience this at home. Night watch was a four hour shift of sitting in the duty officer's room for 45 minutes then doing a 15 minute tour around his 16-acre empire. Punch clocks were stationed at several outlying points to insure performance of the proper ritual. It was a lonely walk as I looked out over the water and heard the constant harbor noises like fog horns, buoy bells and a haunting blast from an occasional ship entering or departing that busy channel. History had always been a favorite interest, and I often thought of the events recorded about the Boston area and even the little island of Gallups. Occasionally my mind would venture to how the future of our country would involve me. But a diversion from my set course had never been considered. In that regard, I was just drifting with the tide.

Figure 9. Rowing Drill at Gallups Island (from left: Sullivan; Sewell; Brewer; Campbell; Digesu; Sheddan; Newton; Kornegay)

Summer blended into fall, which seemed like winter to one from the Deep South. At Thanksgiving some of us were invited to visit and feast with a family in a small town north of Boston. I was very grateful for their thoughtfulness and enjoyed the meal and social interchange. We talked about the common and different customs of New England and Southern peoples. The local family told us that they knew about southern hospitality, and they wanted to make us feel at home. The meal was outstanding and I felt lucky to be celebrating this holiday in a very traditional way with such a nice family and not far from where the first Thanksgiving took place.

I found the people in the small towns to be as easy to meet as any down home. But in the city of Boston they seemed more like I had imagined, or maybe had been told. Stan Jennings tells a story in his introduction to his book, *We Came from All Over, We Went Everywhere.*

It seems that cab sharing had become a useful exercise in wartime even in Boston. As Stan hopped into a cab already occupied by a proper Bostonian, he offered his hand and said, "My name is Jennings." The Bostonian replied, "Mine isn't" as he turned to read his newspaper.

It was a Boston Irishman who wrote:

> *And this is good old Boston,*
> *The home of the bean and the cod,*
> *Where the Cabots spoke only to the Lowells*
> *And the Lowells spoke only to God.*

But since my name was neither Lowell nor Cabot, I met few if any "proper Bostonians." However I did come in contact with a number of interesting people in the city on the weekends. That is, when I had a bit of cash left over from my monthly pay which had increased to $36 per month. A peek at Dad's record of his "debts" tells me that I sent $6 on November 5th and another $6 on the 25th. From this I deduce that I had $24 to buy toothpaste, shaving cream and other necessary personal items. So perhaps I had a ten spot to take into the city on a weekend. The calculations above also indict me by revealing that I had failed to tell him that my pay had been raised. Oh well, I'm sure he would have understood my memory lapse of our agreement that I would send half of my pay.

The island was a busy place as December arrived. The school routine never let up because the war in Europe still threatened and American ships were being attacked as they ventured into the war zone. An American destroyer was sunk by a submarine while protecting ships in the Atlantic. One of the first casualties was a young man from the little village of Houston, Alabama, some ten miles from my home. His name was Wade, and I think he was one of the two that my brother Julian and I scrapped with as we walked from Double Springs to Arley one Sunday in 1933. (Details of that adventure are recorded in my brother Julian's memoirs.)

On Gallups Island we talked little of the war as many of us were making plans for the break at Christmas. I was one of the few who would remain on the island because I had neglected to put away money for a train ticket to and from Alabama.

The day the war began for the US, no bugle awakened me because it was Sunday. I opened my eyes to see daylight and noted that most of the double decked bunks were empty because most students went to Boston on Saturday and returned Sunday night. As was my usual routine I had breakfast, wrote a couple of letters, then strolled over to the chapel for the services which were conducted by the chaplain from the Sailors Haven in Boston.

As I sat down in the library that afternoon, I picked up our copy of the *Boston Globe* and noted it was Sunday, December 7, less than three weeks until Christmas. The front page had items of the war in Europe which looked gloomy. Inside as I looked for the editorial and sports sections I noted that some Japanese diplomats were in Washington for talks about differences between our countries. Routine stuff about far away places I thought as I turned to the comics and read Little Orphan Annie, Andy Gump and Li'l Abner. Then I got down to my homework so that I could keep my grades above the 90 percent level. By this time it was just a routine for me but I still enjoyed learning about electronics and all the other required studies.

I walked back to the barracks to wash up for dinner in the mess hall, or snack as it usually was on Sunday evening. I noticed some of my classmates and some others at a table listening to a radio. As I approached them I heard words like planes, bombs, Japanese, and Pearl Harbor. Then President Roosevelt was talking, and we all realized this was war!

Gallups Island, along with the whole country, was stunned by the vicious attack on Pearl Harbor which killed hundreds, destroyed a major part of the US fleet and crippled the naval base. The Axis powers of Germany and Italy joined Japan and declared war on the US. But the President united the country with his famous speech, "December 7, 1941—a date which will live in infamy!" Congress quickly passed a law requiring all males over 18 to register for a military draft. All construction for building planes, tanks and ships was immediately expedited. The first of the famous Liberty Ships, aptly named the SS *Patrick Henry*, had been launched on September 27, 1941. When Roosevelt made his speech, he stated that 14 more were sliding into the water that day. During the war more than 2,700 of this design were built. The President called it an ugly duckling because of the simple, but practical, design. They carried the bulk of the war materiel to Europe and all war zones over the next four years. Naturally this put additional pressure on the radio school to get the radio officers ready.

All this made me even more remorseful about not planning to go home for Christmas. We were told we would go to sea immediately upon graduation and getting our FCC license. Graduation was set for March instead of April as originally planned. Not only was I spending Christmas a thousand miles away from home and among strangers, but I wondered when I would ever get to Alabama again.

I survived that Christmas by burying myself in reading. My interest was in electronics and our library had a wealth of books on the subject. Television had been invented and was experimentally operating in New York and other large cities. I studied the theories of how it worked in great detail. Although I understood the system, I wondered if all that circuitry could ever be perfected so that it would operate as planned. Since I had never seen it, I guess my faith was weak.

On Christmas day I attended church, reread my Christmas cards which all contained personal notes, and listened to the radio for news and Christmas music. That evening I was on watch duty, and as I walked alone around the darkened island, I wondered why one mad Austrian could begin his protest in the beer halls of Munich and spread it over the entire world so that it eventually affected the lives of almost everyone. As I write this account in 2003, I candidly confess that part of the previous statement is from my memory of that 1941 Christmas and part is from my experiences since then. The following Sunday was my 20th birthday and I celebrated at a party of one.

As 1942 began, our studies became even more urgent and intense. Most of my class had progressed in Morse code so that we could actually monitor the international distress band of 500 kHz. That is when I heard my first faint SOS. The dreaded three dots, three dashes and three dots, which meant a ship in distress, chilled me, and I tried to visualize what it was like sitting in a ship's radio room somewhere in the Atlantic. This distress message was followed by others. Some were weak and others stronger, and they always included coordinates of the ships' positions, so I was able to spot their location on a map. Many seemed to be along the US coastline within a few miles of the beach. At the time, I wondered why they were not being reported in the news. I later learned many dozens of cargo ships were sunk within several miles of the US coastline during the first year of the war.

Then came February and the cold rain and snow and constantly dark days on that little island gave me a claustrophobic depression. For the first time I had serious misgivings about my decision to pursue this course. Finally that short month, which always seems so long, was over. It was now March, the first month of spring. The weather began to improve and frantic activities of finals and some parties occupied our time and thoughts.

By the middle of March I had graduated from the Gallups Island and passed my FCC exams for a radio telegraph and a radio telephone license. Everyone was so busy that we had few goodbye parties. But I remember my feelings of a gnawing fear that I was seeing most of these friends, who had become like family, for the last time. And that was the case.

Within a week I was on a train bound for New York City. As I exited the big train station and entered a strange street, I stopped and looked around and up. How many emotions can one experience simultaneously? Awe, fear, exciting expectations, loneliness? I suppose I was just plain confused. But I finally managed to find the offices of the South Atlantic Steamship Company. There I signed some papers and listened to a few minutes of instructions about my new assignment as Radio Officer on the MV *Colin*. I took my bag with all my earthly belongings down to a waiting taxi which carried me through the canyons of buildings to a dock on the West Side of that great city.

Chapter 4
My First Ship

As I got my first look at my ship, I thought there must be some mistake. The stack was astern like a tanker, and it flew a Panamanian flag. But the name was plainly displayed as MV *Colin*. The crewman who was guarding the gangway answered some of my questions as he inspected my identification card and papers. The *Colin* was an Italian ship which happened to be in a US port at the war's beginning, so it was taken over by our government. A diesel engine powered this ship (called MV for motor vessel), whereas most were steamships which were designated SS. It had been given Panamanian registry because it did not meet US regulations for safety, and other reasons. I had no idea why the engine and stack were astern like an oil tanker and not amidships as on other freighters. The helpful guard directed me to my cabin and the radio room. My little cabin had barely enough space for a bunk, a small closet and a chair. But it offered privacy for the first time in a year, and I was satisfied with it.

I threw my bag on the bunk and proceeded to find the Captain's office. It was on the same deck and not far from my cabin. I tapped on the office door and heard a voice with a British accent invite me in. The Captain reviewed my papers and noted that I was going to sea for the first time. He seemed to be relieved when I told him I had graduated from Gallups Island. He asked about my knowledge of languages. I told him I spoke only English, "And with a southern accent." He smiled and said, "Well, prepare to be surprised when you see your radio room."

Captain Blank, as my hazy memory has renamed the pleasant man from London, had left a British ship for the extra pay he would receive by heading a motley crew of mixed nationals on this strange ship. It seemed that MV *Colin* was full of surprises. The Captain told me about the previous Italian crew, who had expressed their loyalty to Mussolini in his decision to join forces with Hitler by damaging the ship's engine. A heavy anvil had been winched above the engine room and released. Precise replacement parts were not available, and the maintenance crew was still trying to adapt and fashion pieces so that the diesel would start and perhaps even run with some dependability. I pondered our future.

My first look into my radio room caused me even more concern. Nothing was like the RCA and Mackay Radio receiving and transmitting hardware we had been trained to use at Gallups. Instead I saw the Italian nameplate "Marconi" on pieces of equipment which were configured to give few clues as to their purposes. I hastily reached up on a shelf for an instruction book and blinked. Not a word in a language I could read. It was Italian. As I opened a small door and saw the battery room, I thought, "Thank God no one could disguise a battery."

At this point I was so tired and disappointed I decided to go to my little cabin and rest. In the officers' mess that evening, I met several of the ship's officers and was in for another shock. Many were foreigners; all somewhat older. I saw no one with whom I could relate. I tossed and turned in my bunk that night wondering how I could refuse this assignment and try for another.

After getting some sleep, I went to the radio room to think and made the decision that has carried me through life: I would not give up on a difficult technical challenge. I went to work at trying to master the procedures for tuning the transmitter from my basic knowledge of radios and a few words of Italian instructions I had been able to understand.

The *Colin* was loaded with war materiel destined for the beleaguered British forces that were desperately resisting Wehrmacht General Erwin Rommel's rapid advance across Egypt. Since the Germans controlled the Mediterranean, it was necessary to circle South Africa and approach the coast of Egypt from the southeast. It sounded like a three-month voyage before we would return.

April Fools Day seemed appropriate for putting this odd-looking ship back into an ocean which was largely controlled by Nazi submarines. It took the engine crew an hour with a small "donkey" diesel engine to generate enough air pressure to start the main engine

My First Ship

which powered this strange ship. Sometimes it wouldn't start and the process would begin again. The day we sailed it took three hours, but finally I heard the loud bang indicating the engine was turning on its own. The engine slowly built up revolutions, and after a brief warm-up, the Captain ordered the deck crew to release the big hawser lines and we slowly began to move away from the dock.

As we passed the Statute of Liberty and the famous New York skyline, I had a great feeling of pride in our country. Then I saw our strange looking Panamanian flag flapping at the stern of this tub with its motley crew. I must have felt this was not my choice of a way to serve my country and maybe even begin a career.

But it was time to get to work, and I put a log sheet in the typewriter and began my first watch as the sole source of communications with the outside world. The Captain soon looked in and, using the universal nickname for the radio officer, asked, "How's it going, Sparks?" I told him everything was fine, there was not much activity on the band. Since the war began, ships' radios kept silent to conceal their position except in an emergency. Incoming information from shore stations was generally encoded. It was my job to decode it using a set of code books.

As we slowly moved along the New Jersey coast on my first day at sea, I began to see the partially sunken hulks of ships which had been torpedoed in the past four months. On the second day, I heard my first SOS from one not too far to our south. Later that day, for the first time, I saw a ship attacked. I heard the distress signal and a short message giving essential details. As the freighter began to settle into the water, its crew launched life boats. By visual Morse code signals using a blinker light we contacted the survivors who did not need our help but preferred to be rescued by a small patrol boat which had appeared within a short time.

Some hours later I heard our engines misfire and stop. We were dead in the water while the engine crew worked frantically to get that stubborn diesel up and running again. The crew routinely pumped air to start the engines, and in a couple of hours it finally started and we were moving again.

The engine stalled dozens of times over the next four days until we reached the entrance of the harbor of Jacksonville, Florida. We were stopped more than we were moving. Along the way, I witnessed a dozen ships being attacked or sinking. We thought it was a miracle our lagging ship hadn't been attacked. Someone suggested it may have been because of the Panamanian flag, but others flying Panama's colors were not spared. We finally settled on a theory that the Germans had learned that some ships were fitted with concealed heavy armament and served as decoys. They may have suspected our stalling and starting was a ploy. I began to wonder if it was my guardian angel up there looking out for me.

Figure 10. North American East Coast

Just outside the entrance to Jacksonville we saw a lifeboat carrying several people. They refused our offer of assistance, but did ask me to send out their SOS. I said I would, but the Captain

My First Ship

thought we should not break radio silence. So we simply reported to authorities as we entered the port of Jacksonville. I later learned that their radio officer was Art Sheddan from my class at Gallups; he had been able to visit his home in Florida unhurt so soon after going on his first ship.

Our ship put into Jacksonville to get some vital parts and supplies. We were there two days, and I took the opportunity to call the home of Bill Brewer, who had been one of my best friends at radio school. Bill's Mom and Pop, along with his brother Lefty and his sister Kate greeted me as a special friend of young Bill. They knew something of our Gallups experiences and never tired of anything I could relate about our shenanigans over the past year. Lefty was drafted before he was to have a tryout for baseball pitcher for a major league team. In his memoirs, Bill tells the sad story of how Lefty died at Normandy. War is such a waste of humanity. Upon leaving I felt almost like a member of this lively and emotional family. And the food reminded me of my Alabama home.

It took us another week of short runs and long stops to get into the US naval base at Guantanamo, Cuba where we remained for some days as they tinkered with the defective engine. As we put to sea again we saw fewer sinking ships, but the distress signals continued. I read that the US Merchant Marine lost 10 percent of our ships during this first six months of the war. But the Liberty ship construction was beginning to catch up with the losses. We sailed, and I wished we had literal sails, so that we could have made better time. Again as we headed across open water it was still stop and go, but mostly stop. As we reached a position about 500 miles from any land that pesky diesel died.

Captain Blank, after it was apparent that our crew would not be able to make repairs, came to me and asked, "Sparks, could you call for help?" I assured him, with as much bravado as I could muster, that I could. But I hoped he didn't detect the worry nor see the sweat beads on my face. I found books with listings of all shore radio stations and finally found one in Trinidad, British West Indies. Then I turned to the ancient Marconi transmitter which had not been used for months and I wished the Captain would find other duties elsewhere. But he stayed and watched, and I timidly turned on some switches and watched the big vacuum tubes light up. I quickly switched the high voltage on and then immediately off, as I observed how the several meters reacted. I was able to find the proper switch and selected the emergency band. (Fortunately, numbers are the same in all languages.) Then I turned on the power at minimum and again watched the meters. It was obvious that it was way out of tune, and I experimented with some knobs which I guessed to be for tuning. After some false starts, I finally was convinced that the rig was in resonance so I slowly increased power. Then I proudly turned to the Captain and asked, "What shall I tell them?" He gave some sentences, and I quickly encoded them and sent the message. Just as quickly I received an answer acknowledging the message was received. Phew! What a relief.

When the word got around the ship that I had been successful the crew showed a feeling of some hope, and I thought I even detected a small decrease in skepticism. But I had only a day to strut around the decks; on the following day everyone kept asking to be reassured that I got the message through. The Captain and crew were anxiously scanning the horizons, and by the end of the second day, their skepticism toward me turned to some very threatening stares.

The afternoon of the third day, I retreated to the relative safety of a locked radio room until I heard a commotion. I cautiously ventured out and heard someone say, "The lookout has spotted a small speck on the southeastern horizon." Hour by hour the speck became larger, until as last someone with binoculars shouted, "It's a small tug." As it came closer someone said, "It's *still* a small tug."

In a bit over a week of tugging, the little boat pulled us safely into the harbor of Trinidad. Was it the Germans' reluctance to attack the suspiciously unknown ship, my guardian angel or just plain luck?

During the next two months of hot, humid weather I had little to do except keep the emergency batteries charged. After I got bored with sleep and the ship, I decided to see the city. It was my first experience with a foreign culture. The population was mostly black, but some seemed to be of a mixed race. A few were white. It was a British colony, and the people spoke with a modified British accent.

My First Ship

There was fear of being caught in one of the frequent rainstorms and of tropical illnesses. I remember the workers' expressions as a storm cloud approached: "Feva comin' mon." Then they would immediately leave the job and head for cover.

Their calypso style of music and song had been brought from Africa and was heard everywhere in bars and clubs along with the ever popular song, "Drinking Rum and Coca Cola." Once in a while I tried one of those.

The Captain had been able to get to know the British governor and invited some of us to go with him for dinner at the Governor's Mansion. Along with the Captain, a US naval officer, and the purser, I rode out to a hillside residence which was surrounded by a high iron fence. I felt I was learning to act just a mite sophisticated as we sipped our gin and tonics after the Governor toasted the king. At dinner I sat next to one of the Governor's daughters, and we managed some conversation across a vast cultural abyss. I wondered if her interest in me was anything more than just being polite.

We got some mail for the first time, and I was interested especially in one letter from Julian. He had been accepted as an air cadet for flight training somewhere in the Southeast and was expecting to get home to Arley in the summer. I envied him on both accounts.

By late June the repair crews had made some progress in getting our engine to run. However, the Captain decided this ship was too slow and undependable to make the long journey around South Africa to Suez and back. So our cargo was transferred onto another ship, and we took on a cargo of bauxite ore. I suppose I was the one most thrilled to learn that our destination was Mobile, Alabama.

Mail from home came in again, and I had a big bundle to read as we began the trip to my home state. I had letters from my family in Alabama, my sister Mary in Chicago, and from my classmates all over. My sister Gloria wrote that Julian was home from Air Force cadet training somewhere in Alabama. Everyone was so glad to see him and so proud of his appearance in his handsome uniform. I was hoping he would still be there when I arrived. Then I remembered that I had many days of dangerous waters to cross and our arrival also depended upon the success of engine repairs.

But lady luck was with us, and we arrived at the entrance to Mobile harbor on the last day of June, 1942. I thought back about this ill-fated trip and mentally searched for some way it had been helpful in the war, which was still going poorly. The cargo destined for the war in Egypt was now on its way, having been delayed several months. Then I thought about the thousands of tons of bauxite in our cargo holds. Maybe it could be smelted into aluminum and fashioned into the skin of the plane on Julian's first flight overseas. These were crazy thoughts from one grasping for some purpose in all the past three months of cruel comedy.

We docked in Mobile, and my duties were completed. I took my pay, which had accumulated to over $500, a sum which exceeded my wildest dreams of a couple of years ago. With it, I was able to purchase some real leather luggage and a few items of clothing. The chore of getting together the right colors and styles was never an easy one for me and still isn't. But now in 2004, I am fortunate to be living with one I consider to be an expert. Funny how I can appreciate the end result of matched colors, but have no clue of how to find it.

Mobile in 1942 was known as a good port, a somewhat smaller and less well-known version of New Orleans. With their early history of French settlers, they celebrate Mardi Gras, but on a smaller scale than the "Big Easy." But I was glad to say goodbye to the *Colin* and the crew.

The train ride to Birmingham was only a few hours, and I was met by my sister Evelyn and her husband, Arvel Waldrep, along with Betty who was now a very pretty toddler. The next day I took a bus for the short ride to Jasper where I was met by Julian and my younger sisters, Gloria, Joyce and Doris. It was hugs for the sisters, and a respectful hand shake with the guy in the sharp uniform of an Air Force cadet.

As we traveled the 20 miles to what was then our home at Arley, Julian and I had plenty of experiences to relate. It had been more than two years of interesting activities and changes for Julian and 15 months for me. Our young sisters were willing to listen for the time being. Julian filled me in on some details of his year in Los

Angeles and the frustrating way he was drafted into the Army after being accepted as an aviation cadet. But now he was pleased with being well established in flight training. I summarized some of my experiences at Boston and a few of the events on my first voyage to Trinidad. But the most horrible details of the war I kept to myself.

As we arrived at the little farmhouse which had been built while I was away, Mama hugged Julian and then me, as usual, which I understood. Papa gave me a knowing grin as he firmly shook my hand. Somehow I always felt I had a clear channel of communications with my father.

During the next few days we enjoyed many hours of conversation, good food and sleeping in the new house, which had magically appeared while we were away. Our oldest brother Calvin had taken over the farm with its large fields and old house some 500 yards up the road. We both found time to scout around the community for old friends. Paul Davis was still home and I talked with him about his plans. He was still undecided but leaned toward just waiting for the draft. Most of the guys were already away. So our little village was somehow a strange place to me.

As Julian filled me in on his Air Cadet training and his anxious anticipation of flying in combat, I thought of how glamorous it would be compared with my recent experiences. I wondered if I should pursue some similar service activity. It was after he had left and I was spending some time in Birmingham that I followed through on my urge. I went to the Navy recruiting station and made inquiries. The upshot was an interview, a day-long written test and a physical examination. Soon I was notified that I had been accepted as a Naval Aviation Cadet. But after much soul searching and worry, I decided not to sign the papers. Another year of training was not my desire at that time. Instead, I traveled by train to New Orleans to sign up for a new ship. I bought a newspaper in Birmingham and read it on the train. An item about a convoy to Murmansk, Russia caught my eye. That was the ill-fated Convoy PQ17, largely destroyed by a combination of planes, submarines and surface ships which came from bases in occupied Norway. There were some two dozen ships lost out of about 33 which began the trip. I vowed to avoid that area if possible, and I didn't mention it to my family for obvious reasons.

"The Big Easy" was interesting and enticing. The French Quarter was bustling with laughter, and pretty girls made passes at me. I remember a long bar with a poker game in progress near the entrance. As I stood and watched the bluffing and calling, I was tempted to accept the invitation to join in, but I prudently refused. Being prudent was probably the right course because these guys looked tough.

Within a few days I was assigned to a ship that was being built in Brunswick, Georgia. I took the train back to Birmingham to spend some time with Evelyn, Arvel and young Betty. Then it was back up to Arley and some more time with my aging parents.

Papa explained how he had decided to sell the farm to Calvin, who was making annual payments at the end of crop years. We had long talks about his health and financial problems. Then in a shaky voice he gave me his thanks for the help I had been able to send from Boston. At this time, Julian and I decided to send an allowance each month as soon as we were able to do so. I silently vowed to repay the many benefits I had received from this man who had done so much for so many.

My interest in the war was always keen, and I read of it in the *Birmingham News*. In the Pacific, the Japanese were still overtaking many small islands and seemed to be a threat to Australia. In the European theater, Hitler had occupied most of Europe and even some of North Africa.

Some news indicated we might at last be at the beginning of an offensive. But mostly it was bad news. One item said our forces were moving into Morocco and some Mediterranean countries such as Algeria and Tunisia. The war in the Atlantic was still tense. German submarines were traveling in wolf packs and were attacking convoys, merchant ships traveling in a formation of about 30, surrounded by naval destroyers and other military escort vessels. It seemed Hitler had responded to the convoy system with his own plan of multiple submarine attackers. All this gave me plenty to be concerned about as I awaited my next adventure.

Chapter 5
Sea Duty

In the winter of 1942, I went to Brunswick, Georgia, to board the newly commissioned Liberty ship, SS *Felipe de Neve*. It was one of the hundreds which had been launched since the start of the war, each being given the name of a famous or not so famous American. This routine of traveling to a strange city and going aboard a strange ship was to become a routine. This time I met my new captain who was a large man with the Danish name of Bjerregaard, another foreigner who seemed very nice. I told him of my recent experience on the *Colin* and he was sympathetic and said he was sure this ship would be better—and it was.

Everything was better. The crew included some younger people and also had a small Navy gun crew for manning the anti-aircraft cannon and a couple of larger guns for combination air or surface use. The small detachment was commanded by a Navy lieutenant who became a good friend. Several of us soon formed a card-playing bunch of buddies.

My cabin was larger and included the essential bunk, a closet, washbasin with mirror, a small desk and a bench-style settee. Everything was new and clean. And best of all, the radio room was outfitted with new American transmitters and receivers. Things were just like I had trained with during my year at Gallups Island. My morale was now improved and I was eager to set out to sea on another voyage.

After making a couple of test runs out of the harbor, we began the trip up the coast to New York City for loading our cargo. The trip up the East Coast brought back many unpleasant memories. Things were tense for the three days it took, which was much less than the week it had taken for the MV *Colin* to travel that far in the opposite direction. We saw no hostile action and I only heard three distress messages. The ship performed well under the capable captain and the crew, which was more to my liking.

While the cargo of munitions, which I later learned was mostly explosives, was being loaded I had my first chance to really see the big city. Everyone of the crew seemed busy so I decided to explore New York City alone. After putting on my most comfortable walking shoes, I left the dock and saw a street leading to the east away from the waterfront. I wanted to be as inconspicuous as possible so I walked briskly and avoided looking up at the tall buildings. (I had been told that this was a dead giveaway of a tourist.) When I found my first subway station entrance I entered and bought a ticket. A study of a wall chart told me that most things of interest were to the north. As I boarded a BMT car I quickly observed that making eye contact was not the way to appear to be a native so this I avoided. But I did learn to observe people using peripheral vision. Most were talking or reading or just looking out the window at blank walls and an occasional station with signs to read. Trying to classify their profession, social status or place of birth or even country of origin was difficult for me at that time. But I began to develop a set of signs concerning conversational style and accent, mode of dress and other outward physical clues. Future visits to the city helped me to develop this instinct.

I just had to exit when I saw the Times Square Station sign. This, however, was not what I was looking for, but it did show a variety of humanity, shops and general atmosphere. I turned east onto 42nd Street and soon was seeing the upscale shops of Fifth Avenue. A couple of blocks on that was enough so I again turned east on 44th to Madison Avenue with its hundreds of offices. Hollywood had taught me what supposedly went on up there and on Park Avenue which was the next avenue over. Then I backtracked westward to Fifth and turned north to Central Park and gasped, "What a contrast!" It looked like, as someone said, "How God would have landscaped nature if he had had the money." An exaggeration, but walking through the pleasant park made me wonder if it was not the best place for the natives to occasionally come and escape the daily bedlam. And maybe avoid or at least delay a nervous breakdown.

Sea Duty

It was about a mile of pleasant walking to the other side of the park where I took the subway south to Battery Park. From here I viewed Long Island, New Jersey and way over to where the ferry landed at Staten Island. The Statue of Liberty was visible in between. Of course I arrived back at my ship very tired and took a nap before dinner.

In early December 1942 we were loaded and ready for delivering some vital supplies to Great Britain. It was my first experience with traveling in convoy. This method had been developed because of the many German submarines which were actively tracking single ships in the Atlantic. Before we departed the Captain and I attended a convoy conference, which included others from each merchant ship and also the naval escort ships. Each ship was assigned a rank and file position and there were many operations which had to be coordinated. Orders of communications procedure and codes were discussed and planned. It was always important for the Captain and the radio officer to work closely as a team, especially in a combat situation. We set sail into a very active war zone almost exactly one year after America's entry into World War II.

The speed of this convoy was set at 10 knots, which was just under the top speed of the slowest ship. As a tactic we would zigzag at intervals in order to confuse any tracking enemy ship or submarine. This meant that our trip to Britain would take about 10 days. As the only radio officer, I worked an 8 hour day shift and set the automatic alarm to monitor the distress and calling band during off time. I would often copy news which was transmitted by news services in Morse code in those days. This meant that we could keep up with the major events of the war and other news. However, I was also copying the "traffic list" every four hours around the clock. When we had a message I would stay around until it came through, so I never had a full night of sleep while at sea. Sometimes during the middle of the night as my alarm woke me, I would still be half asleep while copying the traffic list. The following morning I would look at the log to make sure that I did it, even though I couldn't remember being up.

It was smooth sailing on calm waters for a couple of days out of New York. Then the weather worsened, as is usually the case off the Grand Banks along the Newfoundland coast. It was then that I learned that a Liberty ship can be very uncomfortable in rough weather. Rolling and pitching makes for difficulty in walking or almost any other activity. Sleeping was difficult because of the rolling. Some people got seasick but usually I just got tired. By this time I had made friends with some of the younger officers and we passed our spare time playing cards or just conversing in the saloon, the name used for the officers' mess. But the weather made these games uncomfortable and we gave them up at those times.

Distress messages from ships being attacked were fewer. This fact I attributed to the convoys and also because in convoy it was not always necessary to send an SOS as the escort crews saw the attack.

Our weather had improved on the fifth day out of New York. As we sat down to eat our dinner at 6:30 p.m., or 1830 in ship's time, everyone was in a better mood. The table edge guards, which kept plates from sliding in rough water, had been lowered and the waiter gave us white linen table cloths. Then, as we viewed the menu we heard and felt a loud blast from our starboard side.

We rushed out to the main deck and saw a huge plume of fire that hung a hundred feet high above where the tanker had been. Someone said, "They carried aviation fuel." The ship's alarm broke the deathly silence as we watched the flames settle into a lot of debris. I ran up the two flights of stairs, which we called ladders, and I could see a destroyer rushing to the scene while dropping depth charges. But there was no sign of a submarine.

Everything was normal on the emergency band. I heard no SOS and the automatic alarm had not been activated. A quick trip to the bridge showed the Captain was calm as he told us that it was definitely a torpedo from a sub and that he hoped it was over.

We saw the destroyer searching for survivors, but as far as we could tell they found none. After a few minutes we silently made our way back inside while we took out our handkerchief or picked up a napkin and wiped our eyes and some blew their noses. No one spoke as the waiter brought coffee which had not been ordered. After several sips the second mate ventured, "I'm not very hungry." Then guarded conversation began on subjects unrelated to what we had just seen.

I went back to the radio room to assure myself that everything was working. I turned off the auto alarm and monitored the distress band. And as I sat at my radio desk, I heard the explosion of a torpedo hitting the second ship in our convoy. This time I saw out my porthole a freighter across the convoy. Although it sank slowly, there was no SOS on the distress band.

Over the next five hours, we lost ten ships at approximately thirty-minute intervals. Ships were lost at various places in the large convoy, so it became obvious that we were under siege by a submarine wolf pack. One ship, which was carrying explosives, blew up with no survivors, as had been the case of the tanker.

At around 2300 the Captain suggested that some of us should go down and have our delayed dinner. Nothing else needed to be said, so I made my way down to the saloon. A silent foursome of off-duty officers sat staring at the table. The second mate said he wasn't hungry anymore but the waiter served more unordered coffee to all. With nothing to do, we sipped the tasteless stimulant and someone suggested a game of pinochle but got no response. The purser mentioned our cargo which he said "contained enough TNT to level Stuttgart." Someone offered a comment that we might be sitting in a dangerous spot. Sometimes an understatement can be amusing. Then the oldest member of the engine crew, the third assistant engineer, suggested that maybe we should be wearing our life jackets. I, as the one who often tried to act the comic, but had absolutely no sense of timing, said, "Don't you think a parachute would be more appropriate." As usual my little quip fell flat.

At about 0100, when all had been quiet for two hours, I went up to my room, said thanks be to God and a prayer to my unnamed guardian angel and went to bed—and tried to sleep.

The next five days were uneventful except for several submarine alarms, which fortunately turned out to be false. But the recent experience did put us on edge, and for me it was another item to be stored in my memory under *forgettable*.

Liverpool was the first big foreign port for me. It appeared to be a busy industrial area and a very important unloading port for supplies to US and Allied forces. The Navy lieutenant, the purser and I decided this would be a great time to visit London. So we took a train across the Midlands and the big industrial cities of Birmingham and Coventry. The latter was the first city to be bombed as the "Battle of Britain" began a couple of years before. We expected to see damage but what we saw was depressing. Hundreds of factories and other buildings were destroyed and none had been rebuilt. We quickly learned that food was scarce and people might have been desperate except for the courageous leadership of Winston Churchill. We were able to get into the gallery of the House of Commons and to witness the Prime Minister in action. This one man who is arguably the greatest of the modern era was largely responsible for his country being able to hold off Hitler until our country was drawn into the war.

London was also in shambles and we soon were able to experience an air raid and some time in a shelter with the Londoners. These people exhibited that well known quality of proud stubbornness and keeping a stiff upper lip. To witness their sheer physical and intellectual toughness gave me a clue of how so few on such a small portion of the world's land mass could have such a major effect on civilization. We saw the city, met the people and absorbed a bit of history and culture. I read the *Times*, the *Manchester Guardian,* and other great newspapers and caught up on the progress and, in most cases lack of progress, of the Allied forces around the world. The beginning of the offensive in North Africa was a hopeful sign. Our bombers were beginning to pound the enemy around the clock. The British had the night shift and the Americans were taking up the day shift. I wondered how Julian was doing in his flight training.

Arriving back on the ship we were told that, instead of returning to the States, we would load more war materiel and head for Casablanca. That sounded like another adventure because the movie with Humphrey Bogart and Ingrid Bergman had just been released.

As a matter of fact it was showing in London while we were there, but we had no time for such with so much else to see and do. But we did find out enough about it in the papers to give us a feeling of anticipation about the intrigue of that French/Arabic city.

As we left Liverpool and headed south, we steered clear of the French coast because that country had been occupied by Germany. So we were on a lookout for submarines and even planes and surface ships which were based in France. We saw some planes, but they were not able to penetrate our protective escort. I remember one submarine which surfaced in the middle of our convoy. Many guns were firing at it, but I was never sure if it was hit. Christmas Day came at about this time, but it is one I am unable to remember. Must not have been a big celebration.

The convoy proceeded south and into the warmer waters off France and Portugal. I sometimes operated the radio direction finder which was located in the chart room. There the Captain and the second mate navigated our course. I studied the geography of the area and talked with the older men about what to expect in Casablanca. I learned that the Arabic country of Morocco had been a French colony for a century and still was. After the fall of France and the German occupation of most of that country, the Nazis had put pressure on the Vichy government to keep the Allies out of Africa. But Churchill had other plans. He had met with Roosevelt in Casablanca to map out Churchill's "soft underbelly strategy" of occupying Africa and gaining control of the western Mediterranean. First the Allies would build bases in Morocco and Algeria to support further invasions. They expected to fight the Italians and Germans in Sicily and the other islands to gain bases for eventually attacking Italy and Southern France. We knew little of this plan at the time, but I was learning geography while living history.

Casablanca was different from any place I had seen. The port was busy with both Navy and merchant ships, some anchored and others at dockside. The workers were mostly Arabic and dressed the part. But the officials were French and I was intrigued with the chatter in languages unfamiliar to me. The French were very animated in contrast with the more impassive English. The purser and I ventured into town and walked through the narrow streets with markets selling a variety of interesting merchandise. I bought a large hassock which was made of embroidered leather. However the stuffing was not in it so it was light and folded to a size I could carry in a bag. We wandered the streets and ended in a bar with a restaurant which was full of people of many nations, including American and British soldiers. I wished to be able to understand the babble of conversation but I understood little.

The year 1943 arrived and we loaded again with materiel destined for Oran, Algeria, another French possession. We headed north for a day when we entered the Straits of Gibraltar. Within an hour we saw the famous rock which I had always identified with the Prudential insurance company. This British possession was a gathering point for convoys entering the Mediterranean, which was still submarine-infested. We spent a couple of days touring the city and the area. Of course we had to observe the antics of the hundreds of monkeys who lived in crevices of the big rock. We also were able to buy a few duty- free items which were made in England.

The Captain and I attended the convoy conference which planned our course and other details, and we departed for Oran. One ship was sunk by a sub which surfaced in the middle of our convoy. The escort vessels quickly destroyed this interloper and also picked up survivors of the freighter. The next day we sailed into Oran as an air raid was in progress. But we were able to move to the dock and I breathed a sigh of relief.

Oran was somewhat like Casablanca but not as well publicized in the movies. I had read that the French fleet had gathered in Oran after the Germans had overrun Algeria in 1940. The British had attempted to sink the fleet by air attacks, with little success. I saw some of the remains of that navy still in Oran.

We did the usual walk around the city and ended in a café for dinner. Good French food was served while we talked with some American and British soldiers. It was obvious that there was a buildup for moving into some of the islands of the Mediterranean. But we were always careful about talking of plans in such an environment because of the unknown loyalty of surrounding audiences. Generally we felt safe and there was no terrorist activity at that time. Later we tried a bar and I had my usual one drink and the others had their limit.

We remained there for several weeks and the routine became boring, so I spent time just reading and sleeping. I often got and answered mail from home. In those days we were restricted from saying anything of our activities and all outgoing mail was censored. So my letters were often short and probably uninteresting. But my mail from my parents and sisters was great. They kept me informed of what had happened and who had gone where in our little village. Once in a while I heard from my brother Julian. He had been promoted to first lieutenant and was training in Florida to fly the B-26 bomber. I wondered if he would be coming over to that part of the war zone. Of course he never mentioned such details as to where he would be stationed overseas.

We shuttled among various North African cities during that spring and when June arrived we were in Algiers loading troops and equipment for some destination unknown to us. While there I spent time enjoying this beautiful city. The Aletti Hotel was a hangout for meeting interesting people and we did. This first class hotel of that time was a center of social activity and overlooked the harbor, so it was very convenient for the crew to drop by for an evening drink and maybe a new acquaintance. Algiers was my favorite port in the Mediterranean.

When July 4 arrived we had one last visit to the Aletti and celebrated our Independence Day. I had a couple of Buds. The next day we loaded some GIs and many vehicles and headed east with a whole slew of ships. This was obviously part of an invading force. As we pulled into the little fishing port of Gila, Sicily, we knew that this was our destination. Aircraft were already bombing the beach area beyond. (I later learned that Julian was involved in this action and that he had been stationed near the cities of Oran and Algiers when I was there. But our paths never crossed.)

Many other ships from other ports arrived, and it was the largest fleet of freighters and naval ships that I had ever seen. We anchored and waited. Then we witnessed one of the great tragedies of the war.

Many planes carrying paratroopers flew over us and some ship's gunner began firing, thinking they were the enemy. This triggered guns from other ships and several hundred Americans died under friendly fire. This bothered us as I'm sure it did the gunners. But it seems this was not so unusual in wartime.

Other than that, the operation was a success and the island of Sicily was secured in a few weeks. Italy was the next target. We returned to Algiers to await orders. It came and I heard someone shout, "We're going home!"

We were tied up to a dock, and cargo destined for New York was being loaded. My young friend Jim, one of the Navy gunners, came to me with a proposal. He said he had been able to "liberate" some beer cases from a nearby ship which had recently arrived from the States. Although there was a regulation against having this commodity on a ship, it was never strictly enforced. But this guy lived in quarters with several others without private storage so he wanted to know if he could put it in my closet. Something was mentioned about having one at the end of the day on the homeward journey. So I said, "OK." I was a bit startled when he stacked them to the top of the closet.

It was the day before departure to the good old USA and I had just returned from the convoy conference with Captain Bjerregaard, when Jim came to me. He said he had a tub of ice up on the bow and wondered if he could pick up one case. I said O.K., and he left. After dinner I decided to go to Jim's little party and have a brew. What a beautiful scene: A full moon, no air raid, and four guys having a cold beer while discussing home after all the months of war. So I sat down on the steel deck as he handed me a bottle which was cold and wet. I noticed the Budweiser label was coming unglued and could be slipped off. I stuck it on the side of the gun mount and commented that this would mark this special day.

The next morning was the day of our departure and I awoke with my worst headache ever. I struggled to open my eyes to see my walls were redecorated with dozens of Budweiser labels. The glue had dried and adhered. My floor was covered with bottles, some broken, and the fumes! It all was indescribable! I struggled to my wash basin and doused a distorted face. Then I turned and saw an empty closet. A hazy memory and present evidence told me that the party had grown and relocated—and grown again while my absolute limit of two beers had been exceeded.

Captain Bjerregaard looked in, frowned and told me he was sorry he had felt he should decline our invitation to him to join our party as he came on board the night before. Then with an understanding grin he said, "Just clean it up Sparks." And that was punishment enough.

By the time we passed through the Straits of Gibraltar the following day I had recovered to become more aware of the dangers we faced once again. Then we saw the open water of the Atlantic and I felt chills as I remembered our last crossing. What seemed years was just seven months ago. I thought of my home and family in Arley and how my life had changed and maybe changed me, but in what direction? I pondered my future as this war seemed to be only beginning. This mood continued for the ten days before we saw land again. In New York, I said goodbye to all my temporary friends and took my pay and left.

But where to go? As I walked away from the dock I suddenly decided to visit the Seaman's Hospital at Staten Island. It seems I just needed to talk to someone, maybe a doctor. I boarded the ferry and sat and closed my eyes to the entire harbor scene until we approached the island. The taxi only took a few minutes and I walked into the white building and approached the receptionist. She looked up from her typing, and I said, "I need a doctor." She gave me a quizzical look, picked up a phone and dialed and talked. "Go to room 108 and sign in," she said and added, "And check back here before leaving."

I sat and waited in a room with a half dozen other guys. Without resorting to eye contact but with my excellent peripheral vision, I saw that they were a good mix as to age and dress. I wondered if they had felt some of the same problems of dealing with the reality of this war.

The doctor's greeting gave me an impression of genuine interest as he shook my hand and said, "Tell me what it's like out there in the Atlantic, son." He was older than I expected and had an intelligent twinkle in his eyes. I said that it was pretty horrible for my first trip and on the way over to Europe but we had no problem on the way home. So maybe the subs are moving away. Obviously he had heard many stories and he said, "Yes, that's what I gather." Then he got down to business by asking me to relate my early memories. I began by telling about my childhood on the farm and my parents and large family. He asked about my faith, and I gave my history of growing up in a Southern Baptist Church. Then he carefully probed into my sense of ethics and beliefs and asked many other questions which I don't remember clearly.

At the end of our discussion he told me that he had many cases of guys who had combat problems not unlike mine. I mentioned my habit of trying to forget the worst experiences. He said that was O.K. but not to overdo it. Then he got on the subject of my fundamentalist moral code. He said his early training in the Jewish faith had been as strict and he still held to these standards. But out in the real world he had been able to adjust his thinking enough to be comfortable in our modern society. He said that my feelings of guilt about things which mattered little could be improved if I followed his example. This was a very professional psychologist and I only repeat what I remember of our session. I'm sure that my memory isn't complete and may be wrong, but this is what I got from that session.

As I left I stopped by the front desk. The young lady handed me a note which said. "Call me at home"—and there was a telephone number. I made eye contact with a couple of very Irish eyes and said I would, and left. On the ferry back to Manhattan I thought about what I had heard over the past hour. Maybe he was right, but I still had a long way to go before feeling comfortable with myself and my thoughts. Then my thoughts drifted to those Irish eyes and I wondered if it was time to think more seriously about female relationships. It had been years since I had more than casual contact with one of the opposite sex. And everyone knows that high school connections are fleeting and soon forgotten. At least that had been my experience.

In the small hotel where I registered, I undressed and slept for hours. When I awoke it was already dark and I was hungry. I picked up the note from the bedside table and dialed the number. She answered and I introduced myself as the guy you gave a note today. She gave her name, Pat White, and said she detected that I was troubled and wanted to know more about me. I gave her the basics of name and where I was from and a little information of my recent experiences. After a few more exchanges of facts I asked if she had eaten dinner. The upshot was that I got in a taxi and sped to Greenwich Village and rang the bell of a modest looking apartment. She looked dressed to go out so I asked if she knew of a good place to eat. She did and we walked a block and soon were sitting at a table of a little Italian restaurant. I wanted to listen and not talk, so I asked her to tell about herself. She was from Boston and had lived in New York for a year and worked as a receptionist at the hospital while trying to break into modeling. She had a few small jobs which paid too little to support her. I mentioned my year in Boston Harbor at Gallups Island. She said, "I've heard of it." We talked and it was a good time but soon I got tired and we left. After walking her home I caught a subway and returned to my hotel and slept long and hard.

I was just plain shaky and had feelings of doubts of being able to cope. But I did spend some time shopping for a few items of clothing while I wondered if I should go home to Alabama. That evening I called Pat again and she suggested some show that she knew about. We ate and went to something that I cannot remember enough about to relate at this time. Actually I found Pat very nice and was attracted to her physically, but frankly I just didn't have the energy and enough feeling of stability to pursue such thoughts. Pat seemed to detect my problem and she said, "Spud, I'm going home to Boston this weekend. Why don't you come with me and meet my family and you and I can see Boston again?" I promised to think about it as we said goodnight.

I sat in my little room in the midtown New York City hotel and considered my future. It was early August and I knew that going up to Boston would be more comfortable as to weather and I did have fond memories of the city. And Pat was a very pleasant person to talk with. Julian was away at war and most of my friends in Alabama were in the service or away at defense jobs.

My radio was on and I heard some war news and then Frank Sinatra was singing,

"Pardon me boy, .. Is that the Chattanooga Choo Choo,
Track twenty nine . . Boy you can give a shine.

You leave the Pennsylvania Station at a quarter to four,
You read a magazine and you're in Baltimore.

Dinner in a diner .. Nothing could be finer,
Than to have your ham and eggs in Carolina.

When you hear the whistle blowing eight to the bar,
Then you know that Tennessee is not very far ….

Or something like that. I wish I could write as well as he could croon.

I thought of my home in Arley, my parents and my whole family. Something tugged at me to keep my feet on the ground and to return to my roots. Could it have been my guardian angel?

So the following day found me on a train heading south. The night before I had an abbreviated conversation with Pat. I thanked her for all the talks which seemed to be calming, and I wished her a good trip home and we said goodbye. (I hope she has been as happy as I have since. Bea wonders why I remember all these details, and I guess I really didn't until I started reliving my past life.)

Waiting for me at the Birmingham station was, as usual, Evelyn with her pretty three-year-old daughter Betty. On the street car to West End we talked about some of my experiences and Evelyn gave the latest family news. Gloria, who had one more year in high school, had a job in Birmingham for the summer. Julian was still overseas but wrote often. He seemed to be enjoying his tour in the Mediterranean.

I was eager to get up to Arley and the family but decided to stay a day or so in Birmingham. Bill, one of my older brothers, had married Kathleen Hamner and they were now living in the same end of town as Evelyn. I wanted to spend a night with them and to meet their new baby, Jimmy.

Evelyn needed groceries so I walked up the three blocks with her. The Hill's Grocery Company store on Tuscaloosa Avenue was the best in that part of town. I was interested to see what was still available in our stores after seeing the scarcity of such things in England and North Africa. The store seemed to be as full as I had remembered it. Evelyn picked several items in a basket and I carried them to the checkout counter. As we waited in line I noticed the pretty young blonde who was operating the cash register. What I found especially attractive was the pleasant smile she gave to everyone. She seemed to be interested in each customer. I thought that might be just part of her job.

Evelyn had talked with this girl as if she knew her and as we left and walked down toward Woodland Avenue, I somehow felt that "the smile" had implanted itself indelibly in my mind. I asked Evelyn who she was, and she said she thought she was from Double Springs. Our sister-in-law Kathleen had been one of her teachers at Winston County High School.

I went over to Bill and Kathleen's house and saw my new nephew for the first time. I hadn't seen Bill since he came back from California and was married, so we had some catching up to do. Maybe I ate a lot because Kathleen suddenly also needed groceries. I suggested that I would be glad to drive her over the several blocks to the store. To my delight, she accepted the offer. As we entered the Hill's store I glanced at the checkout counter and yes, she was there.

As we went through checkout, I finally got my introduction to the girl with the smile. Her name was Obera McCullar and she preferred to be called Bea. I thought of it as short for beautiful. She did offer a smile to me but reserved a greater one for little Jimmy. This was the first time she had seen Kathleen's baby. But I was already planning to be back the next day at lunch break.

So I came back and Bea was able to get a break and we settled into the little café across the street for a Coke and a sandwich. She told me about her family who now had moved from Double Springs to North Birmingham. Her father and mother were much younger than mine. Her sister Nell was two years older than Bea and brother

Don two years younger. She knew some of my older siblings and explained that her reticence to warm up to me was because she just assumed that I was married. The ice was broken and we talked of our somewhat parallel backgrounds in Winston County. This is what is known as the "Free State of Winston" because it had tried to secede from the Confederacy during the Civil War. It was the home of the beautiful Bankhead National Forest and other scenic areas. I told her a bit about my recent travels but not the bad parts. Mostly because I just didn't want to think about it. As we walked back to her job, I suggested a movie and promised to call that evening.

I called and she had picked the musical, *Hello Frisco Hello* with Alice Faye and John Payne. So I borrowed Bill's car and picked her up at her home and we drove to downtown Birmingham. I don't remember anything from the movie but the talk with Bea made war seem so far away and all was well with me. This cheerful young woman had affected more cure than all of New York City.

Finally it was time to visit my dear parents and try to explain my delay. I think they understood, but Mom was fearful that I might be growing up too rapidly. I assured her that I was 21 and had been forced into maturity in the past two years. Dad, as was his habit, just gave some encouraging words of wisdom. My younger sisters had grown into young beauties. Gloria was spending the summer in Birmingham and working. The two young high school students, Joyce and Doris, were rapidly growing up and still helping around the house.

Then I returned to Birmingham. It was a Sunday and Bea had arranged for me to meet her family. She had often talked of them and I'm sure she had given them some information about me, so it was a good visit. Bea's mother had fixed a meal and it was delicious. She appeared to be a very gracious lady with multiple talents. Bea and I were together almost daily for the next week. Then I got the call that ordered me to go to Norfolk to take a new ship to sea. It was tough to leave but duty called. So we said goodbye with the understanding that we would write often. I left with a good feeling about having a girlfriend for the first time since high school.

Sea Duty

Although it was not brand new, the SS *Howell Jackson* was a fine Liberty Ship. It was almost identical to my last one, but the complement of crew was a bit different. Two young cadets were on board and lived in the cabin next to mine. One was in training to become a third mate and the other for becoming a third assistant engineer. I had been assigned two Navy radio operators so that we could man the shifts around the clock. It was a strange arrangement. They worked under me but reported to a Navy officer who was in charge of the naval gun crew. This could only work if the Navy lieutenant and I could be compatible. Fortunately that became the case.

I can remember many of the crew's names. Probably, that was because we remained together for more than a year. The names I remember are Captain Allen from Massachusetts, Lieutenant Burt from Michigan, Purser Mulvey from Connecticut, Cadet Graham from New Orleans, and Radioman Hale from Tennessee.

Captain Allen was a relatively young man, not much older than me, and Lt. Burt was in his thirties and had been a soap salesman until the war came. These two sometimes clashed but I was able to be friends with both.

In September of 1943 we were loaded and sailed for England once again. Before we left I mailed the letter to Bea I had been composing daily since I left Birmingham. I was feeling pretty good but wondered if my old depression would return as we set sail again.

The Navy had been able to gain control of the Atlantic, and we had few signs of action on the trip to Newcastle. The most dangerous part was as we circled north of Scotland and down the eastern coast by Edinburgh and on to Newcastle. The Germans controlled Norway and had many bases along its coast, not far from our route. We made it with only a few alerts. But my feeling of anxiety was creeping back.

At Newcastle we had mail, and I read Bea's several letters first and then the rest. The letter I had been composing daily, I finished with some words of answers to her many questions. But since we were restricted from talking about our journey and its destination, I was not able to give much information.

We remained in port for three weeks, and during that time some of us toured up to Edinburgh. We learned something about the history of the many battles among the Scottish clans and with the English. I was able to meet some of the many Campbells in that lovely country, learning that mine is their most common name. Edinburgh is a very beautiful and fascinating city. As a proud descendant of Scotland, I had my picture made wearing a kilt made of material in the Campbell Tartan.

We loaded military materiel and headed back around Scotland and south to the Mediterranean again. Our first stop was Algiers, where more mail had been forwarded, and then on to Naples, Italy. While there, between air raids we visited the resort Isle of Capri and the ancient ruins of Pompeii. While in the harbor of Naples we saw Churchill again as he sped by on a PT boat, reviewing the fleet. I always thought that he enjoyed all the many activities he was able to dominate with his personality, and I certainly admired him for what he accomplished. At this time the Italians had surrendered to the Allies but German troops were still in the northern part and heavy fighting was going on at Anzio beachhead.

From Naples we made a call to Sardinia and picked up several hundred Italian soldiers who had surrendered and were being returned to their home. They were only on board overnight, sleeping on the deck in the open air. I heard that Julian was stationed there at this time but had no chance to find him during the short time I was there.

We returned to Oran and prepared to sail for home. By this time I had become close friends with some of the officers. Lt. Burt was always ready for a party and sometimes I participated. The night before departure some of us went with him ashore to celebrate a happy goodbye to foreign lands. Remembering our last party on the *Filipe de Neve*, I hesitated but felt I could observe my limit of two drinks so I went with them.

Our first stop was a well known bar where I sipped and finished half my limit while some others did better—or was it worse. The talk was of plans upon arrival back home when we all would depart in many directions, while my thoughts were of a certain smile. Then the lieutenant exhibited his leadership training by pointing us in the direction of the famous casbah district. This was off limits to troops but our converted soap salesman seemed to feel that he was exempt from this silly regulation. He charged out front with his favorite words on such an occasion, "We're on the loose for moose or goose." And I knew that little rhyme meant something other than duck hunting. In that strange district, which included the worst of a mixture of Arabic and French cultures, he found a bar. The stage show, which would have been X rated in Las Vegas, we watched as the group indulged themselves and I observed. I peripherally saw that the young engine cadet seemed duly shocked but the deck cadet Lewis Graham, who was from New Orleans, was not.

As we looked around we spotted a table of field grade American officers enjoying the atmosphere. Lt. Burt commented that he had no fear that they would report his breaking the military off-limits rule. Suddenly the lieutenant stood up and said, "Let's go." Outside he seemed to spot the "Moose" he was looking for. He boldly walked up to an American jeep with a private sitting in the driver's seat. The lieutenant, who suddenly had mentally been promoted to captain, took the front seat and "ordered" us to get into the back. Then he turned to the poor private and said, "I'm commandeering this vehicle for a secret mission." In a shaky voice the youngster said, "But, sir, I'm waiting for my commanding officer to come out and go back to the base." Burt looked him in the eye and said, "Private, this is a command," as he pointed to the gold braid on his sleeve.

Then the terrified young man drove us, as the lieutenant directed, 50 miles south of Oran to the town of Sidi-bel-Abbes. Burt explained to his secret mission accomplices on the way that we would be able to visit the headquarters of the famous French Foreign Legion when we got there. Well we got there late at night and drove up to a heavily walled compound with an armed guard at the iron gate. Yes, it was such a place but no we could not go in! So we had to be satisfied to view, through bars, some buildings which no doubt housed many sleeping mercenaries. On the long trip back to Oran I wondered, and still do, what happened with the young private? I hope his commanding officer let it go unreported or if he didn't, I hope the indiscretion by the group of senior officers was also recorded. And here I am recording my part although I was not in the military and that place was not "off limits" for me—although I suppose it should have been.

Another ten days in convoy back to New York. A quick call to Bea and as she talked I thought, "Even her voice smiles." Our crew said their goodbyes without a celebration as most of us were returning for another voyage on the *Jackson*. Reloading was to take two weeks, and I hastily arranged to take the express train, the Southerner, for the overnight trip to Birmingham, where I was met and hugged with a smile.

During the next few days we went to Arley where Bea met, and was approved by, my parents and other members of my large extended family. Then we returned to Birmingham to spend some time with hers. We had time to talk a bit about my experiences and her new job at the Women's Missionary Union headquarters in Birmingham. Then the exciting time was over as I boarded the Southerner for the return trip to New York. It was a cold February day and Bea asked me how long I would be gone. I said it depends on the war but probably about six months. As we kissed goodbye I tasted salt from a tear of one or both of us.

Captain Allen told me that about all of the same crew would be with us on our next trip, although the two cadets had finished their training and would soon sail as officers on some ship. He said our next destination would be Cardiff, Wales and Bristol, England. And, yes, we would probably go back to the Mediterranean. I asked if Lt. Burt had returned and he said, "I'm afraid so."

Soon after we got out of port I once again experienced how rough the North Atlantic can be in winter. It seemed that the entire voyage was composed of rolling and pitching so that sleep was scarce and eating difficult. Sea sickness seemed to be epidemic. But it did take my mind off the never-ending war and separation from loved ones.

Copying news from press wireless, I learned that Hitler was still in command of Europe and still threatened to reach Moscow. Stalin had demanded a western front to take some pressure off the Nazi siege. The small successes in the Mediterranean had not satisfied him. I had a feeling the war would take many more years.

Cardiff, Wales was our first stop, and this was my first time to hear Welch spoken. They all spoke English, but we had trouble understanding some words. Then we went on to Bristol, England. It seemed to be just another British city, but Lt. Burt insisted upon going out to see the sights. I feared he only wanted to get the view of the inside of some pubs, but I agreed to go with him.

Captain Allen had invited us to come by his hotel room for a drink. Although Scotch was scarce even in bars, our captain had used influence to get a bottle. After our first drink, he let us know that he was going out with his friends from other ships. We took the hint and bade them goodnight and went our way. Our way was to the first pub we found. They were in the process of closing because they had run out of product. We found another and had one drink before they closed for the same reason. This aggravated the lieutenant and he finally said, "Sparks, I have an idea."

And as Dave Barry says, "I swear I'm not making this up," even though I wish I were. Although I had had only two drinks, I went along with Burt as he returned to the hotel and up to our captain's room, coerced a maid into letting him in and took the half empty bottle. Burt took some swigs as we walked back to the ship. As he reached the top of the gangway, he tripped and dropped it on the metal deck and broke it. It made for a very embarrassing scene.

The next day the Captain called us to his office. As we sat down the air was tense. Then I saw Captain Allen almost smile as he said, "You bastards" and we all laughed. But I still apologized to my friend and boss.

It was the spring of 1944 and we had been at war over three years and still no end in sight. I read about the island to island struggle by our Navy and Marines in the Pacific. My mail from home spoke of rationing of gasoline and a few other items. And over here in England just about everything was scarce. The purser, Mulvey, and I decided to take a train to London while our ship was being loaded with materials for the Mediterranean campaign. Somehow we avoided inviting Lt. Burt. We just wanted to have a sober look at the people I had come to admire so much.

The country was full of American troops and everyone seemed so busy. London was still being bombed but these hardy people had learned to live with it. I read about how the Russian people were under such a siege and that they were suffering even more. There was much sympathy among Allies to give them relief by starting a second front in Western Europe. I remembered when I was in high school and Stalin was considered evil because he had signed a pact with Hitler, and my feelings now were confused. Stalin was now an ally, and I guess all our memories were short.

Back on the *Jackson* new mail came in, and I had the thrill of reading about things in Alabama. It seemed so far away as we prepared to go in another direction with no plans to go home again. In May we made the familiar trip down to Gibraltar, where we left some cargo before proceeding to Algiers. A few days in that city and then to other ports and back again. All was routine until we arrived in Ajaccio, Corsica in early June. This was new territory, and I was glad to be able to see the original home of Napoleon who had once made waves somewhat like Hitler.

We listened to the news on the BBC and learned that the Germans were now bombarding London with a new weapon. It turned out to be the first news of the rocket V-1 which had been developed by a German scientific team headed by Werner Von Braun. What we didn't know was that the BBC was also broadcasting some musical signals to the French underground movement.

On the sixth of June, we got the news of the greatest sea-launched invasion in history. It was the day that now is celebrated as D-Day. Over the next several weeks a bitter battle began, bringing some hope as Eisenhower's forces retook a section of France. Then it was August, and we were loading tanks and trucks and even troops. There were rumors that our destination was southern France and we wondered. That part of France had been semi-occupied by the Germans, with nominal control by the Vichy government. On August 14, we stood by some 20 miles south of the Riviera beaches along with what seemed a hundred other merchant and navy vessels.

Sea Duty

That night was eerie as we sat out on deck and watched and heard the 16-inch shells scream overhead and hit targets on land, coming from Allied battle ships a few miles behind us. Some were tracers which gave a visual picture of their trajectory overhead. We heard Army Air Force bombers as they flew over and dropped their destructive loads.

We began moving in toward the coast and by daylight we were within sight of the city of St. Raphael, about 50 miles east of Toulon. There began the frantic operation of unloading vehicles and troops on small landing craft which carried them to the beach. With binoculars we could see and hear gunfire at the beach, but mostly it appeared the tanks and trucks just disappeared into the town. Some of us offered to help with loading, and our assistance was accepted by the soldiers.

On the second day, Purser Mulvey and I decided to ride the landing craft to the beach. It was better than the boredom of sitting on the ship with nothing much to do. We must have harbored some scheme because we put on our US Maritime officers' uniforms instead of the work clothes we usually wore on the ship. Our ranking of ensign was just a formality we wore as a shield from being accused of being a slacker in the States or other countries. I had taken the test and was promoted to first class radio officer but never bothered to apply for an official promotion in rank. Since it had nothing to do with pay scale and my status on the ship would not be changed, I just didn't think it worth the effort and cost of a new dress uniform. I wonder what regulation we violated that day as we walked ashore dressed as military officers but without any official status.

The beach was just a place for unloading equipment from a barge to US Army trucks. We talked with a driver and I believe it was Mulvey who asked if we could ride with him. The driver said he was heading to a new base being established about 50 miles inland and he would return that same day, so we hopped into the cab and rode away to another great adventure. The towns appeared deserted and we saw no action, although we often heard machine gun fire and an occasional bomb blast in some undetermined direction. I kept thinking that we should stop and catch a ride in the homeward direction, but Mulvey wanted to continue. He said he always wanted to see this country and that he would like to find the Chanel perfume factory. What a dreamer he was and what foolish youngsters we were. After we had traveled about 30 miles the driver stopped as we saw a bridge had been blown out.

The driver radioed for instructions and we wandered down to the small stream and saw a little cottage on the other side. We were able to scramble across on some rubble left from the bridge so we went to the cottage door and knocked. My French was limited to a few trite expressions like *Oo la la* and *c'est la guerre,* although I had no idea how they were spelled. Mulvey's high school French gave him only a slight advantage over me and he did manage by some sounds and body English to convince the harried looking Frenchman that we were Americans. The cottage owner invited us in with many excited motions and some words to his wife in the little adjoining kitchen. We sat down in the small sitting room but hastily stood up as a young girl shyly peeked around a door.

Her father spoke sternly to her and she came in, did a little curtsy and held out her hand. I had a mental picture that came from some movie of bending down to kiss that hand but didn't have the nerve to do it. So proper introductions were over and we rather clumsily sat and tried to communicate. The mother came in holding a tray with tea and some sweet-tasting pastry. It was surprising how much intelligence we were able to pick up in the half hour of Mulvey's talk and our interpretation of the Frenchman's attempt to tell a story. It was obvious that he welcomed the Americans and also that he hated the Germans. By the gesture of a finger across the throat he gave us the impression that the French were taking care of the Germans who had long been there to control the population.

I got the impression that he was relieved as he saw us to the door and nervously glanced at his young daughter. We said goodbye and attempted to repeat his *au revoir* and headed back to the stream. Alas, our truck was gone! Nothing in our limited experience told us what to do but instinct led us back across the stream and we began backtracking on foot.

We walked for miles along a deserted road, by grape vineyards and farm buildings, until we came to a small village. We entered a little square with houses all around, but no sign of life. We then saw a door open a bit, and after some time it opened wider and three German soldiers in uniform walked in our direction with their hands held high as a gesture of surrender. One was an officer who handed me his Lugar pistol and began talking in fairly good English. They wanted to be captured by the Americans who were taking prisoners, while it appeared that the avenging French were not. I surmised that they, like me, just wanted to go home. Finally an American Army truck rumbled up and we flagged it down.

To make a long story a bit shorter, we were happy to arrive back on our ship later that night where we tried to convince our friends of how we were able to "capture" three armed enemy soldiers, take their weapon and get them a ride to the beach headquarters as prisoners. Fortunately we had the non-smoking gun as evidence and I felt that some believed us.

By early September we were ready to return to the good old USA. Someone suggested a party and I declined with thanks. The trip back was uneventful and I was very glad to see the Statue of Liberty during that first week in October. After all the formalities of signing off, I said goodbye to some good friends, and as was the case so often during that war, I have not heard from any of them again to this day. But all the memories, mostly good, have remained with me.

Chapter 6
Henry Bacon

Julian and another brother, Tommy, met me at the Birmingham station on an October day in 1944. Julian had driven up from Lake Charles Air Base in Louisiana where he was training new bomber pilots in the new model A-26. It had been 10 months since he finished his combat missions in the Mediterranean. Tommy and his wife, Frances, along with their children, Butch and Sandra, had recently moved from California to Birmingham. We had a lot of catching up on news and our activities. We all found their lives more interesting than mine.

At Tommy's house I thought, "I really don't know these strangers from California." Tommy had left home before I started school and had not returned but once in the next 18 years. He had married and begun his family while away, and this was my first meeting with Frances. She seemed to be fond of Julian, who had lived with them in California. We discussed the family reunion which was planned for the following day at Arley. As they talked, my mind wandered to another house in Birmingham, and I got up and asked, "Frances, where is your telephone?"

I was thrilled as Bea answered, and I told her that I would be right over. I borrowed the "stranger's" car and drove over to Sixth Street where we held a mini-reunion. So much to talk about and learn about with Bea. We went for a ride and parked and smooched and talked of our time apart and somehow the subject came up of our becoming a more exclusive couple. It hadn't been a problem with me, but I could see that Bea had some question as to my future intentions. I said let's talk about it next week, and I left thinking of this long war and the dark horizon of my future.

In October, 1944, the Campbells—father, mother and 12 siblings—were united for the first and only time. What a strange but close family we were and are. Some say it was like two family groups. To me, the younger half are my siblings, and the others—Lecie, Evelyn, Calvin, Bert and Bill—are like aunts and uncles, while Tommy might be a distant cousin. But on that day, fate had allowed us to travel from distant parts to celebrate with food, talk, love and pictures for posterity. It was the first of many reunions; unfortunately none ever again included all 14, but grew to include many of the descendents of George and Martha Campbell. (The history of what has now become a living institution has been well illustrated and documented in a volume which Bill Fuller, Doris's husband, has so generously presented to us all.)

Figure 11. The First Reunion, 1944

The next day, Sunday, I returned to Birmingham for some important discussions. Bea and I visited some good restaurants, saw a few movies and spent an evening in a local night club. I had a strong feeling that we were made for each other. But we could visualize no end to the war, and I was both legally and by my own will, committed to its finish.

On a beautiful October evening we sat on a bench at Red Mountain park under the half clad statue of Vulcan, Birmingham's "god of fire." I asked and Bea answered with a positive phrase. We were "engaged." We drove home and silently listened as Bing sang the Irving Berlin classic, *Always*. The next day we visited a jeweler friend who helped us select a diamond ring. I asked him why the price and size sometimes didn't track. He picked up his loupe and viewed a ring and said, "This one is less because it contains flaws which are only visible through this lens." I then picked one with a similar price and was smaller but perfect to his eye. I put it on Bea's finger and thought, "How appropriate."

The next night as we sat around the table with Bea's family, she slyly gestured with her left hand until someone noticed; we all laughed as her father proposed a toast. But we knew that our future happiness was in the hands of the gods of war. Only a couple of days were left in my leave time, so we spent most of it with my big family.

After sad goodbyes I answered the bid to go to Boston and sign on to another Liberty ship. Boston was a familiar city, and as the taxi left me at the dock, I thought I saw the old Coast Guard Cutter *Yeaton* at its same mooring place. It was good to relive the memories of two and a half years ago at Gallups Island and all the adventures and problems in the meantime. As I approached my ship, I thought there was something different from the other Liberty ships I had seen. In addition to its weather beaten look it had extra reinforcing metal plates welded on its side. I looked up and read the name, SS *Henry Bacon*.

As I walked up to the bridge deck I noticed the light on in the Captain's office. I threw my bag on the bunk and walked back across and tapped on his opened door.

A slightly built older man introduced himself as Alfred Carini. He gave me a quizzical look. He was wiry with a somewhat intense and stern-looking face with a small trim mustache. He asked my age and experience and seemed relieved as he reviewed my documents: a first class radio telegraph license signed as satisfactory by three captains, and a diploma from Gallups Island in 1942. I said I was 22, and he mumbled something about looking 17. He said he had already interviewed Bill Hermann, an older man, who had come directly from the radio school at Sheepshead Bay, Long Island, NY.

Although he had no experience and only a few months' training with only temporary documentation, the Captain said Hermann could be helpful in covering the radio bands. We had a good conversation, and in the process, we seemed to bond with a respect which was to serve us well over the next months. I learned this captain expected every officer and man to do a job in keeping with his idea of old-fashioned discipline and teamwork.

I asked about the steel plates that had been welded on the sides of the *Bacon*. He looked serious and said, "That and the extra heaters have been installed here in Boston and should give a hint of our destination." I thought of the cold and rough water on the dreaded Murmansk run. We had heard of the many convoys battered by weather and attacked by German submarines, aircraft, and sometimes even battleships, as they sailed near the coast of Norway. For five years, the Nazis had occupied Norway, which served as a base for attacking convoys vital in the Russians' defense of their country. The Germans made every effort to stop these ships from getting to Murmansk. My survival instincts told me to get off this beat-up ship while I could. However, I was still young enough to have a flicker of desire for great adventure. I had often wondered what the Russians were like. I made a little gesture of a salute and left the Captain's office.

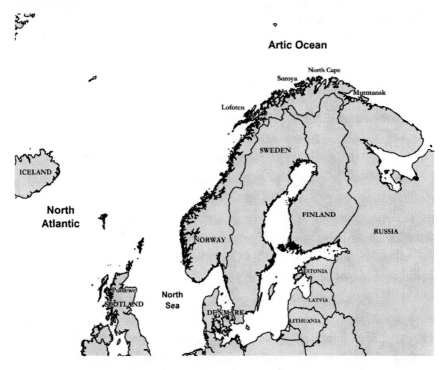

Figure 12. North Atlantic

My cabin was the same as I had known except for the larger radiator. I hung my clothes in a closet that reminded me of Algiers when I made the mistake of allowing beer to be stored there. As I started down the short hall to the radio room I saw my new assistant, Bill Hermann, standing in the adjoining room. We introduced ourselves, and I asked him to come with me to see the radio equipment.

Originally from Ohio, Bill had been in New York for several years. He was a musician and entertainer with an impressive background with big name bands and in musical shows like "Best Foot Forward" and "By Jupiter." He was also a music arranger with Ben Bernie's band. He had a great personality. Although he was ten years my senior, he confessed that he was still a novice in the technical field of radio communications. His three months training at Sheepshead Bay had allowed him to start with a Temporary Limited License and to go on a ship in a capacity similar to the interns on my last ship. After that he would return to school for more training before being fully qualified. He was married to Judy, a singer with the band, who anxiously awaited his return to New York. I mentioned some of my experiences and of course included the fact that I was engaged to my sweetheart in Alabama. We immediately became friends, and I assured him that I would help him to learn about our job. I don't remember if we discussed our destination.

At dinner in the saloon, I met many of the officers I would live with on this voyage. There was the 60-year-old chief mate, Colchester, who appeared to be too old for this duty. Donald Havilland was a gray haired 49-year-old Chief Engineer with a winning smile and a firm handshake. Others included the Purser, Bob Hunt, a slender young North Carolinian who was destined to become my best friend on the ship. John Sippola, the Navy officer who would command the gun crew, was a light haired Finnish descendent from Minnesota. Each talked about his previous experiences around the world, which sometimes paralleled mine. Bill Hermann was the only one with no previous experience. It appeared to be a very capable group with the possible exception of the Chief Mate who seemed a bit shaky.

I went ashore and toured the familiar city with Bob Hunt. He and I were the only officers from the South, and we were naturally drawn together. We strolled through the Boston Common Park and had a beer at the Silver Dollar Bar. The last time I was there I didn't have the cash for such a treat. I called Bea and was thrilled to learn that she and her sister, Nell, had decided to come to New York while our ship was there for loading. I told her we would arrive there about November 23; I would reserve a room for them at the Pennsylvania Hotel, a short walk from the train station. I had stayed there and it was first class. We closed the conversation with audible kisses.

We moved from the dock and anchored out in the bay. I could see old Gallups Island clearly with binoculars. What memories that little place brought back. I got down to work as the Captain ordered us to a drill that I had never before performed. We put a lifeboat in the water with a small crew including myself with the little emergency transmitter. It was a job normally done by the second operator, but Bill admitted he had no experience; the Captain ordered me to do it while Bill stood by in the radio room to monitor the signals. It was not difficult in the calm water to erect the two-section, 25-foot mast with an antenna wire connected to the little rig. I pushed the buttons to activate the battery operated transmitter and sent some test signals. I later wondered if our captain had some premonition when he ordered the drill.

Back aboard, I reported to Carini that the drill seemed to be a success. He frowned as he told me he had been in the radio room and Bill had trouble copying the simple test signals in Morse code. I told him I should have sent them slower, and I would give him some practice as we had time. I could tell the Captain was still skeptical about Bill's ability.

The ship was empty and tossed a bit in the wind as we left Boston harbor just before Thanksgiving in 1944. We soon entered the calmer waters of the Cape Cod Canal but encountered rough seas again between there and Long Island Sound. It took two days to get to a dock on the East River. As soon as we were berthed, I went ashore and took a taxi to the Pennsylvania Hotel. Bea had been there a day, and I was late getting to New York. It was a happy reunion as we had time to talk, take long walks around the city and enjoy some good New York dining. The next day we shopped for clothes for me and Christmas gift purchases. I took her to a new experience in eating—a giant food dispensing system. Bea was fascinated by the Automat where we selected individual food items, put in coins that opened the small doors and loaded our trays with the dishes; not unlike vending machines of today but on a much grander scale.

On the final evening together in New York we, with Nell, went out to dinner and watched a floor show. Later, when we were alone, we talked of our plan to be married when the war ended. When we said goodbye, I had a feeling it would not be long before we were together again.

Bea went back to Birmingham, and our ship was being loaded; it was food stuff in one hold, ammunition in another, with trucks and tanks amidships. One hold seemed to be filled with bags of wheat. There were many other items; some were plainly labeled "Murmansk, USSR." The decks were used to take four locomotives. Our hunches about our destination were confirmed.

We were headed for "the most dangerous waters in the world," Captain Carini told me as we returned from the convoy conference. These conferences were routine to me by this time; I had attended a dozen it seemed. There would be another before our final leg to the north began. In the little launch which carried us back to the ship, I showed the Captain the copy of the *New York Times* I had grabbed as we left the taxi and headed to the dock. The paper included items about the bombing of German cities by the RAF by night and the US B-24s and B-17s by day. One quoted a group of American manufacturing executives reporting from Europe that the war was far from over. The Captain and I exchanged thoughts about our families and our futures. He wanted the war to end so he could have some time to spend with his family. I thought, "Me too," and the word "family" had an added dimension.

Back on the *Bacon* I went about the routine of checking equipment and going over chores and instructions with Bill. We arranged a schedule so we each covered 12 hours per day. At times we both would be there until he became accustomed to the job. When there was no alert we could turn on the automatic alarm equipment to monitor the distress and calling band of 500 kHz. However it was always essential that we monitor the "BAMS" (broadcast to Allied merchant ships) schedule every four hours. At that time we listened for the traffic list and if our ship was included we would wait and copy the message. Then we would take the code books and decipher the words. Bill understood all this, but I was always concerned about his ability to copy at the speed it was being sent.

I liked Bill, and we had many discussions of our very different backgrounds and personalities. He was entertaining and sometimes played his clarinet for groups. It was a lively crew. My closest friend quickly became Bob Hunt, who was nearer my age and was also a southerner. He told me about losing his previous Liberty ship, the SS *James Oglethorpe*. Bob also informed me that our deck crew included two brothers from Mobile, Holcomb and Allan Lammon. I sought them out but they lived and worked in a different part of the ship, and our paths rarely crossed on the busy ship.

I remember a comical but somehow sad event that happened in the middle of the night. My cabin door was next to another door which opened to a space then another exit door to an outside deck. The space between served as a "light lock" so the first door would be closed before the other opened. Any light might give away our presence to the enemy. The door to my cabin faced my closet door in a somewhat similar layout. One night I was awakened to the noise of someone bumping around in my closet. I turned on my bedside light to see our old Chief Mate, Colchester, had taken the wrong door. He was strange looking with my shirts draped over his head. I helped the old guy to regain his bearings and never mentioned the incident to anyone before now.

As winter approached again, I was in the North Atlantic. I was becoming allergic to both. Fortunately the weather was calmer and enemy action limited to only a few alerts. Sometimes quiet suspense can be more wearing on the nerves than action. A couple of incidents broke our calm. The old chief mate "lost it" one night, causing us to lose our convoy position. He was relieved of his duties and later paid off in Glasgow. Once the crew became upset with the amount of hot spices the cook served in our food. Some thought it was to cater to our captain's affinity for Italian food, but this was not a serious problem.

We arrived in Glasgow a few days before Christmas of 1944. Some of the crew went ashore to see the big seaport town. Bob Hunt, Lt. Sippola and I spent a few hours walking around town; it was uneventful as this gunnery officer was a very serious and sober guy. Hunt and I were just a couple of Southerners in the country of our ancestors. I mailed some letters to Bea and my family. Given my apprehension about our northbound voyage and the problem of censorship, it was difficult to write; I could only hope the letters were interesting without much detail.

Some of the crew hoped we might unload and return to the US, but instead we were issued winter clothing: parkas, heavy sweaters, wool socks, felt boots with rubber soles, and blankets. This squelched any hope of going back to the states immediately. It was another lonely Christmas Day as we headed north toward Loch Ewe. On the way we saw scenic islands with many hills and lochs. Loch Ewe was a convoy assembly point for the northern Russia convoys. It had steep mountains on one side with a forested park on the other, with some small islands in the bay.

We anchored in the bay with about 30 other merchant ships which were to be with us on the voyage north. Captain Carini and I were the only ones allowed to take the little launch and go ashore and only to attend the convoy conference in the village of Poolewe. It was a somber session as we discussed all possibilities of enemy attacks. We were reminded this was the most dangerous mission that merchant ships had experienced during the war. The Germans were expending all their remaining naval forces in this area. We could expect submarine attacks, and aircraft were stationed along the Norwegian coast. Surface ship attacks also were a possibility. The convoy commander wished us good luck and said he hoped to see us safely into Murmansk in a couple of weeks.

I hardly thought of my 23rd birthday on December 28 as we exited the harbor and headed due north. We were escorted by two aircraft carriers, a cruiser and several British and Canadian destroyers. This was the strongest escort force of any convoy I had experienced.

It was only a couple of days before the escort was dropping depth charges as sonar indicated there were submarines in the area. Soon the weather became cold and bleak. We had sleet and snow and fog for most of the trip north; the seas were breaking over our bow, and we rolled and pitched for days at a time. It was a tiring and depressing time with little time for anything except for work and sleep.

Once when the Captain observed Bill having trouble copying messages, he awakened me to check it out. I helped him, and for the remaining time I never was able to get as much as four consecutive hours of sleep. I had to make all the message schedules (BAMS) in addition to my 12-hour shift. Bill was trying so hard and wanted to do it alone, but he still had difficulties. It was just too important; I had to be there.

On one occasion the *Bacon*'s gunners sighted a submarine surfaced inside the convoy and fired at it along with other ships in the convoy. Carini thought this was dangerous to the merchant ships and told Lt. Sippola, but the gunnery officer said his orders were to fire on sight. This is the only case I saw of a conflict of this sort.

One pleasant experience was seeing the brilliant display by the Northern Lights. Streams of multi-colored lights played across the sky in a show that not even Hollywood could surpass. The beautiful sky broke the drudgery and long work shifts. The weather improved as we circled around North Cape, and we arrived safely in Murmansk on January 8, 1945. It appeared the worst of our danger was over because the much-needed cargo was safely at its destination. Surely the Germans would not waste precious forces on empty ships returning south.

The Russians supplied an interpreter for our ship, and I was able to get to know him. He gave us hints as to how we should conduct ourselves ashore in Murmansk. I was eager to see this enigmatic country I had heard so much about. A small group of the ship's officers walked through the small town. There was a city hall, a post office where I mailed a letter to Bea, and a service club where we could meet people. However we found very few who would attempt to communicate with us. They either distrusted us or were not permitted to fraternize with foreigners.

Each officer was given 500 rubles, and crew members were given 300. The so-called exchange rate was one ruble for one dollar, but since there was no way to convert one to the other the rate was only academic. We were told we could buy anything we wished, but there was precious little to purchase. We were required to return any unused currency before departing. The only major item I got was a set of skis—only because it was available. Lt. Sippola had skied often in his home state of Minnesota. He tried, with little success, to teach me this art. Perhaps it was because the slopes were icy with very little soft snow. So I gave up snow skiing as a hobby.

I did pick up the game of chess. My job required very little time in port, and I had caught up on lost sleep. I spent the days with the interpreter. (I don't remember his name, so I will call him Boris.) He was a man in his sixties who had traveled the world in his younger days and spoke good English. Boris liked to play chess as did many people in his country. I was interested so he taught me the basics. In our first match he won in four moves with the "fools mate." I watched his strategy which was always bold and aggressive. He impressed upon me, as I learned more of the game, that one should avoid any defensive move but try to find one that advanced one's position in a forward direction in a way that would put pressure on the opponent. He said, "In a tight match one lost move means you lose and a defensive move is a lost move." My good friend Bob Hunt often sat in on these matches and learned the game. He and I planned to spend our spare time improving our technique in chess on the way home.

Boris was interested in news from the "outside world," and I offered him my copy of the *New York Times*. He seemed to want to read every word. I said, "Boris, you may take it home with you." He looked at me in a strange way and said, "Oh no, that is not allowed here." He laid the paper down and told me his story.

Boris was not Russian but came from the little country of Latvia. When the Soviets overran his homeland, he left and worked in England and other countries. As he returned some years later, he was shocked to see what had happened. The people were sad and some were hungry. The Communist system, good in theory, had not worked because it gave no incentive to the working people to produce. I said I thought it gave equality to every person, and he explained that only the top Communists lived well and that was a miniscule number of people. The military strictly controlled every move and even the thinking of the people. Most were deliberately kept ignorant of what it was like in foreign lands.

As he continued, I thought of what such a life would be like. I remembered when I was young and felt isolated from the world on the farm. I had been so happy to see the daily paper, and when we got the radio I so eagerly grasped for every word. During our long voyages, I felt so hungry for information. This gave me some idea what it would be to live in such isolation.

Every day as Boris and I sat and played chess he told me more. The workers up here in the frozen north were actually slave laborers. Most were women as the men were fighting the Nazis. Boris had also been forced into his job because of his knowledge of English. He slyly said, "But I am in heaven here compared with being home." That, obviously, was because of his contact with people from the outside.

Boris went on, "If you only knew what this government thinks of you as you bring them this help, you would be furious." He said the first thing they do is remove all labels or other indications of the origin of the equipment so the people will not know they are being supported by foreigners. I got a vivid picture of what he said, but found it hard to believe. He said, "And furthermore don't be surprised if you lose a ship as you leave port. This happens often, and they tow the crippled vessel back in where they repair it and take it as salvage." I wondered, "Why would the Nazis wait until we unloaded these ships to attack?" What a lot of weighty material for a young naive mind to process.

I made one last trip ashore and saw the people with a different eye. What I felt was a deep sympathy for these people. They were trapped into a life so grim and hopeless. The system was designed so they were not even aware of another way. For their leaders, my feelings were somewhat different.

We had been in Murmansk for about a month and unloading was completed. As we moved away from the dock and anchored in the bay, I felt I had learned some more about another culture. Basically they were not too different from my friends in Arley. But they were the first I had encountered that reminded me of prisoners. We soon had a dramatic demonstration to support my thesis.

Someone reported to Captain Carini they had seen two girls whose heads popped up from an empty cargo hold. Perhaps he was of the old school which held that women on a ship meant bad luck. The Captain dispatched his 1st mate, Lynn Palmer, who had been promoted from 2nd mate in Glasgow, to investigate. Palmer returned with two shabbily dressed and very nervous girls who appeared to be in their mid twenties. It was obvious they had been helped to stow away on board. There was a crude living arrangement in the unheated cargo hold. The old interpreter was no longer on board so Carini sent for Lt. Sippola, who could speak some Russian.

The women had been trying to find a way to escape from this frozen Hades and would do anything to get to some other place. It didn't seem to be too important where. They would not implicate anyone from the crew, although someone had to be helping them and getting them food. They cried and pleaded for the Captain not to call the local police. They claimed, and I believe, they would be killed if sent back. But Captain Carini was a stickler for regulation, and he called ashore to report the stowaways.

A police boat arrived quickly, and two burly men came aboard and without ceremony grabbed the girls. They resisted by kicking and screaming. One broke away and jumped into the icy water. It was obvious she preferred that to what was in store for her future. She was pulled back on the police boat and as they sped away, I gazed, wet eyed, along with our Mess man Chuck Reed and Purser Bob Hunt, as they disappeared beyond our sight. I now know that their fate was no doubt sealed even if they had been allowed to stay on board.

As our convoy got ready to form and leave the harbor, we became a participant in one of the most dramatic and intriguing events of World War II. We saw four British destroyers moving from merchant ship to merchant ship transferring people on board. One came alongside the *Bacon,* and we saw 19 women, children and a few older men come aboard.

The 19 were from a group of 500 Norwegians who had been picked up from the island of Sørøya, in the Norwegian region of Finnmark. Theirs is a remarkable story:

The German occupation forces which held Norway had established sea and air bases all along the coast. As the Russians were beginning to advance into Finnmark, the Germans became even more aggressive toward the Norwegians. Towns and cities such as Hammerfest were given "scorched earth" treatment as the Germans were forced to retreat. The island of Sørøya was seized, and the people forced from their homes. Some escaped to the mainland and others lived in caves when their homes were taken. Some died of exposure, and others probably took their own lives. The winter of 1944-45 was severe, and the plight and struggle of these people has been told in books and documentaries in several languages. Their story is still not generally known in the US.

King Haakon and Crown Prince Olaf had been exiled to England. Through the underground radio, word came to them concerning the desperate situation on Sørøya Island. Norwegian Lt. Per Danielsen was serving with the British Admiralty and was a prime participant in one of the most dramatic rescues of this or any war. Danielsen and another Norwegian exile, Dr. Gunnar Johnson, were put ashore to organize the people's escape, and the Admiralty planned for some destroyers to leave a convoy and go in under cover of night to pick them up. From there they were rushed to Murmansk. The Russians were asked to help but refused, so these 500 desperate and homeless refugees were transferred directly to merchant ships destined for Scotland. The *Bacon* was assigned 19.

(A very comprehensive and detailed description of this and the following adventures can be found in the book. *The Last Voyage of the SS* Henry Bacon, by Dr. Bob Alotta and Donald Foxvog, published by Paragon House.)

Bits and pieces of the story of how these people came to be deposited on our ship became known by the *Henry Bacon*'s crew, although we had no idea of the winter of horrors they had already survived. We welcomed them aboard and made room to give them as much comfort as possible. There were: Henrik and Ellen Pedersen, with their children Sophie, 2, and Inger, 4; Johan and Emilie (who was pregnant) Pedersen with their children Elbjorg, 6, Monrad, 7; Simon and Berit Mortensen with their children Bjarne, 4, Eldor, 6, Sigvart, 7, and Nils, 8. Others were: Ragna Pedersen, 40; Ansel Pedersen; Karen Pedersen; Ane Jakobsen, 67; and August Larsen, 16. They were 11 adults who had suffered so much for so long and eight children, some who had lived in a cave for much of their lives.

The *Bacon* was not built for passengers, but some larger rooms were emptied of crewmen to house our new guests. Bill Hermann, who lived in a room with four bunks, moved out and gave his quarters to a family.

These people had lived without toilet facilities for months, and a bathroom was assigned where they could cleanse themselves of lice and other problems of sanitation. Our kitchen staff began preparing large quantities of soup and food and delivered it to their quarters. It was easy to understand across the language barrier how grateful they were for this major upgrade in their living arrangement. Our attitude of being stunned gradually changed to understanding and friendship. The *Henry Bacon* and the entire convoy set out with a precious cargo of 500 happy souls.

On February 17, 1945, as our convoy left through Kola inlet, we lost one Liberty ship, the SS *Thomas Scott,* and two escort sloops, the HMS *Lark* and HMS *Bluebell,* to a submarine attack. I thought of what "Boris" had told me and just could not make myself accuse the Russians. (I later read it was a German sub from a wolf pack that waited in Kola Bay. I still have questions why the Nazis would allow the convoy in and use scarce naval units to attack some ships returning empty.)

The crew and passengers of the *Scott* were all rescued, but the *Bluebell*, which was very near the *Bacon*, exploded leaving only one survivor. It was a daytime scene reminiscent of my first convoy experience in 1942.

With its cargo of humanity, Convoy RA 64 proceeded northwesterly around North Cape, giving the Norwegian coast a wide berth. I later learned that on one ship a baby boy was born. (In 1995, I met ferry boat Captain Lebaron Russel Briggs, who had been named for the ship on which he was born some 50 years earlier.) With German reconnaissance planes sighted almost daily, we wondered when the enemy might strike again. Soon, the Germans began air attacks, and the escort carriers launched fighters. There was an air battle directly over the convoy with ship's gunners firing; I feared we would see losses by friendly fire as I remembered from the invasion of Sicily in July of 1943.

As we neared the arctic Bear Island a new enemy appeared. A southerly wind which soon reached gale force began to toss the ship about so that enemy aircraft and submarines became a secondary problem. By Monday, February 19, the wind reached Force 10 and the convoy had to slow down. By nightfall, swells reached 40 feet and waves swept across our decks. As the ship pitched and rolled the

Waves Astern

screw would sometimes rise above the water and the engine would race, causing severe vibrations. A problem of a broken oil line caused Chief Engineer Havilland to order the engine stopped for repairs. During this time the ship rolled so severely that it approached the critical angle of 45 degrees. With superhuman effort, and maybe luck, the engineers made emergency repairs and some control of the rudder was returned.

I had been on duty in the radio room so long I forgot about sleep, and eating was difficult. The next day winds dropped to Force 8 and I tried to get a few hours sleep. I was awakened by another air attack which lasted three hours. Like everyone, I was too tired to eat or sleep except for catnaps in my chair. On Thursday morning the barometer began dropping rapidly, measuring winds of Force 11. We lost rudder control again and could no longer hold position in the convoy. By 1600, a barogram recorded by a British escort dropped off scale—below 28 inches of mercury, a record low for this area during World War II. After winds reached Force 12, the Captain changed our heading to give some control against rolling over. But that put more distance between us and the escorted convoy. The following day was February 23, 1945.

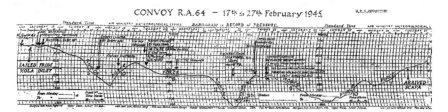

Figure 13. Barograph for Convoy RA 64, February 17-27, 1945

The morning started with a rapid rise in the barometric pressure and a decrease to Force 8 gale winds. I tried to sleep, but the ship still rolled and tossed so that staying in bed was a full time chore. Bill and I were so tired we were almost in a daze from lack of sleep and the constant severe

Beaufort Wind Scale		
Force	*Knots*	*MPH*
8 (gale):	34-40	39-46
9 (severe gale)	41-47	47-54
10 (storm)	48-55	55-63
11 (violent storm)	56-63	64-72
12 (hurricane)	64-71	73-83

motion of the ship. There were very few people moving about the ship; everyone was attending to his duties. My friend and waiter, Chuck Reed, told us he had made a survey of the ship and had found two lifeboats so severely damaged that they could not be used or even launched. This left only two which could be used if needed. Life rafts had been torn loose from their moorings, and the ship's ballast had shifted, causing a list to port. Some damage had been done to the ship's superstructure by the giant waves of the past days. Damage to our steering was severe and seemed beyond repair. The anemometer on the bridge had peaked at 112 mph. We all felt that without the Captain Carini's skill and determination, we would not be still afloat. Bill Herrmann commented that he wondered if he was walking on the floor or a bulkhead. At 1000 I received a message that torpedo bombers were headed for the convoy. I reported this information to Captain Carini, and the tired old man only commented that maybe the escort planes and ships would be able to take care of them. He ordered everyone to stand by at battle stations. He told me we were about 50 miles behind the convoy and just north of the Arctic Circle. I heard someone shout, "Here they come!"

Someone counted 23 H-111Ks and JU-88s torpedo bombers, and I wondered why so many were needed to attack one crippled Liberty ship with a cargo of old men, women and children. As I said a prayer, a thought flashed of home and Bea, Dad and Mom, and our families. I quickly returned to the radio room and told Bill that we could expect a hit at any time. I heard our five-inch and three-inch guns, and the 20mm cannon were firing intermittently.

Gunnery Officer Sippola was a cool and controlled person. He carefully held fire until the lead plane was coming into the range of his shells and then ordered "Fire." This took out the leader and confused the others. As they regrouped, he repeated the technique until he had brought down at least four and some said five of the 23 planes.

Captain Carini handed me a hastily written note, and I returned to the radio room to send the message, "Under attack by enemy planes." I added our position and our identifying call letters. I knew that the escort ship's radiomen were monitoring this emergency frequency, and I received an answer from a Scottish shore station. I went to the bridge and reported this to the Captain. I saw more planes as they turned and began approaching from two directions. I went back and told my friend that our gunners had some success but, "It seems to be only a matter of time before we are hit."

Time seemed to stand still. As we sat in silence, I said a prayer for the safety of the ship and crew and passengers. I thought maybe I still had a guardian angel looking out for me. I glanced over at Bill and saw that he was whispering while fingering his rosary beads. We waited for what seemed hours but were actually only a few minutes. We felt a dull thud which shook the ship and almost immediately the stern dropped. I knew the hit was in the aft cargo hold. It was only a few rapid steps to the bridge where the wizened old master was already writing out the SOS message. He said, "Sparks, send this out and then bring the emergency transmitter."

People have often asked me if I was scared in that precarious situation, and I always say, "I have been scared many times in wartime attacks, and yes I was until the moment we were hit and the ship obviously was doomed. My feeling at that moment can only be described as a sudden release of tension." Once when I was very tired in football practice and once when climbing a mountain, I reached what is called "second wind," and suddenly I felt exuberant and strong. My breathing, which had been labored, was even and regular. That was how I felt as I went about my duties in a very calm and measured way as I had been taught. I believe that all the years of waiting for something like this had created a subconsciously tense state which was released when the expected hit actually happened. This is hard to explain, and I'm sure it is hard to understand, but it is a fact.

I sent the SOS and it was answered from Scotland; I knew the convoy's escort ships had the information. I talked with Bill a few moments, then I took the lifeboat transmitter as the Captain had ordered and reported to him.

Captain Carini had already put the Norwegians in a lifeboat. Then he selected six of the youngest seamen to get in to handle the oars and control the lifeboat. He turned to me and said, "Sparks, I'm putting you in with the Norwegians because I feel you are the most experienced to make sure the signals get out so that these people will be saved." He indicated he didn't expect the *Bacon* to remain afloat for long. He seemed to have a first priority of saving the passengers with second priority being the youngest crewmen, then came the ones who would most likely have the skills to handle the chores in the lifeboat. Obviously he put himself last in line to be saved. As I said goodbye I felt I was lucky to have known such a brave man.

The lifeboat was successfully launched, and we pushed away immediately because the waves were still 30 or 40 feet deep, threatening to crush us against the side of the ship. Our young crew with their oars and a rudder were able to head the boat at a 90 degree angle to the waves so it would not be swamped by the seas. My task was difficult in such rough water. I had to unleash and erect a two-section mast with an antenna wire across the top and clamp the mast into place at the base. As the boat was overloaded with people, the task was difficult. By the time I finished I was sweating even in that extreme cold. All this and the rapid pitching and rolling of the boat made me sick, and I hung my head over the side and vomited. Then I connected the antenna to the transmitter and with the proper tuning sent the signals that gave a rescue vessel a beam to home in on.

Only then was I able to look up and see that another lifeboat was being lowered into the water. I could see the Captain and some men were still on the *Bacon* since we only had two boats left after losing two in the storm. The extra 19 passengers complicated it even more. I saw some of the crew jumping into the water or already swimming around looking for debris to hang on to. I had a feeling of guilt but realized the Captain was right as I remembered our drill in Boston Harbor. The guilt I felt was for all my friends who were left without a place in a lifeboat. That applied especially to my young friend, Bob Hunt, who was not a strong person, and I feared he would not survive for long in the Arctic sea.

Figure 14. Drawing of Henry Bacon by Monrad Pedersen

We drifted away from the mortally damaged ship and could no longer see people in the water. In about 15 minutes I saw the *Henry Bacon* for the last time as the bow rose and slid quickly into the water. Then one lone German plane flew low over our lifeboat. I was relieved that he only looked and didn't strafe us. I sat and thought of what it must have been like on the ship after I left. I knew there was only one remaining usable lifeboat and the life rafts had been released too soon by a crewman. There were about 90 people including the Norwegians on board. Our lifeboat held 26 and the second could take that number. That would leave about 38 with no place in a lifeboat. I wondered if any of those would survive much time in the cold water. It was certain no one could live overnight.

My duty was to try to help save them by keeping the radio signals operating. The small battery would only power the transmitter for about 30 minutes. I operated for a minute and waited 10 minutes then did it again. I was pleased to see that all indicators showed it was sending the signal effectively.

The Norwegians had acted bravely and with discipline under the command of the leadership of one of the fathers. Some were helpful to me as I struggled to erect the antenna mast. Then they sat quietly as our boat crew kept us headed properly into the seas.

Later someone began to sing, and they all seemed to join in with a Norwegian song. I later learned it was from their church hymnal.

No aircraft from the convoy was sighted, and the first good news we had was about three hours after the sinking when we suddenly saw the British destroyer, HMS *Opportune*, appear on the dim horizon. We all gave a loud yell because it was getting quite dark at that latitude in late afternoon. As the beautiful ship turned and put us on her leeward side, we began what was another very difficult operation. The seas were about 30 feet, and one instant we would be level with their deck and then suddenly 30 feet below. Each time we reached the peak level we would quickly hand a child or mother to a waiting *Opportune* crewman. This routine continued until all except for our crew and a few of the more able-bodied Norwegians were left. Then we all scrambled onto to deck of the *Opportune*. Finally, all were aboard uninjured.

My memory is blank until the next day when I became conscious and found myself in a bunk with about two feet of space above. The quarters were small, with maybe a dozen bunks stacked four high. All the occupants were British, and they were talking about my condition. I guess I was a mess and smelled of vomit. One defended me by using a common oath and commenting that I had nothing to help me get cleaned up. No change of clothes, no towel or wash cloth, no tooth brush or razor. Nothing but the filthy clothes I had slept in. And that sleep was for 12 hours. Someone gave me a towel, soap and a tooth brush. I struggled up and went to the small toilet and began trying to get clean. There was no shower; I stripped and washed with one end of the towel and brushed my teeth without tooth paste. I washed my clothes by using the wet end of the towel until most of the smell was gone.

I was taken to a mess table where I discovered how these hardy people had been surviving on the very basics of sustenance. I drank some of the generous daily ration of rum as was traditional on British ships. I asked what had happened with all our crew and was told that another lifeboat load had been picked up by another destroyer and an unknown number from the water was still alive, although some seemed to be in bad shape. No names were known.

After a couple of days of living in this condition and trying to sleep with the noise of the forward part of the ship rising out of the water and pounding back down all day and night, I gained even more respect for these people and the way they had lived, fought and survived the war conditions.

I asked someone to take me to the ship's radio room where I talked with one of their radio operators. He told me how they had heard my SOS from the *Henry Bacon* and later the weak signals from the lifeboat. With their direction finder the *Opportune* had been able to home in on the beam and find us. Otherwise he doubted if we would have been rescued in time. The escort vessels could not stay around all night; they were required to protect the whole convoy which was traveling south away from the scene. I was glad to know I had performed my duties.

The week we spent traveling on HMS *Opportune*, while trying, was a definite improvement over the last week on the SS *Henry Bacon*. I am forever grateful to the crew of the *Opportune* for saving the Norwegians, some of our crew and especially my own life. To the British nation I salute you for what you did in World War II. I am forever an Anglophile.

As we arrived in Scotland, the Norwegians were put ashore first. We all said goodbye and parted as friends who had melded into family during these last two weeks—a fortnight that had seemed more like months.

The surviving Merchant Marine crew was housed in a small hotel which had been used as a seaman's club. We had a glorious reunion with the men who were picked up on the other three British destroyers. I was so happy and relieved to see Bill Herrmann looking so well and ready to help us celebrate with music. There stood my good friend Chuck Reed, Third Mate Joe Scott and Dick Burbine with his trimmed mustache. I hesitantly asked if Bob Hunt was there and someone said, "Bob was in the water alive, but he couldn't stand

Henry Bacon

the cold, and I saw him slump forward and die with his life jacket still supporting his dead body." They talked of his bravery and expertise in giving medical assistance to the ones who were injured. There were many stories of the heroism of others like Captain Carini and Chief Engineer Haviland who died so needlessly it seemed. Then I had a talk with Bill and he seemed to understand why I was selected by Captain Carini to go in the lifeboat with the survivors. This was the saddest happy reunion imaginable.

So I left the group, went to my room and prayed for the souls, and the families of my forever lost shipmates, who were:

Alfred Carini, 62 - Our captain from Brooklyn, N.Y.
Lynn Palmer, 37 - Chief Mate from New York.
Robert Hunt, 20 - Purser and my best friend from North Carolina.
Holcomb Lammon, 23 - Bosun from Mobile, Alabama.
Robert Cramer, 18 - Able Seaman from Ohio.
Fredrick Funken, 24 - Able Seaman from Kentucky.
Donald Schiesher, 23 - Seaman from Illinois.
Donald Haviland, 49 - Chief Engineer from Massachusetts.
Edgar Snyder, 37 – 1st Asst. Engineer from Illinois.
Joseph Provencal, 41 - 2nd Asst. Engineer from Massachusetts.
John Mastracci, 40 - Chief Cook from Massachusetts.
Cornelius Kearns, 39 - 2nd Cook from New Jersey.
Carl Fubel, 22 - 2nd Mate from Massachusetts.
James Martin, 25 - Night Cook from New York
George Shipka, 18 - Mess man from New Jersey.
John Sippola, 26 - US Navy Lt. Gunnery commander from Minnesota.
Steve Allard - US Navy Signalman.
Mason Burr - US Navy Gunner.
Charles Harlacher - US Navy Gunner.
Cyril La Fountain - US Navy Gunner.
Donald Mayden - US Navy Gunner.
William Moore - US Navy Gunner.

Kermit Price - US Navy Gunner.
Raymond Reid - US Navy Gunner.
Earl Rubley - US Navy Gunner.
Louis Walker - US Navy Gunner.

From somewhere we were given basic items of clothing and we shopped for more. We ate some good Scottish food and I drank a beer. Then the mail arrived! Bea's letters were my first priority, and I read them rapidly. She was working routinely, and was still in love! I read the ones from my Mom and Dad and many sisters. Julian was still training pilots in Louisiana and enjoying being home. All seemed to wonder why they had not heard from me in some time. I mailed the letters I had been writing without going into any detail about our recent adventure. I told Bea that I would be home in a month and wanted to talk about our wedding.

I learned from the Glasgow newspapers that the war was going well. Budapest had fallen to the Russians, and on the western front, the Allies were well into Germany. Turkey and several South American countries had declared war on the Axis countries. A small item told of the sinking of the *Henry Bacon*.

On our third day in the club, a volunteer worker pointed to another and said. "That lassie over there says if you don't ask her out, she will ask you." So I did and we went for a walk and a snack as we talked. Later, the same volunteer told me the girl's complaint now is that all you wanted to talk about was some girl in Alabama. I said, "She's right and Bea is in Alabama, and she is SOME girl."

In mid March we were put aboard the liner formerly known as the SS *Manhattan* which had been converted to a troop ship. We made a relatively speedy trip home to New York City. I called Bea immediately and asked, "What do you think about getting married soon?" She answered, "Uhhhh." Then she said of course we will.

That evening I met Bill Herrmann's wife, Judy, and we went out to dinner. They were thrilled about my upcoming marriage and wished us to be as happy as they were. Later we went by the NBC radio studios where Bill introduced me to Fred Waring and many of his band members. We said goodbye for the last time as Bill mentioned he would be going back to school for further training. (Bill died at 87 in 1999, and Judy lived for two more years.)

One month after that fateful day in the Arctic I left New York on an Eastern Airlines DC-3 for Birmingham, after stops at three cities. As I hugged my future bride, the cold water and the horrors of war were only vague memories.

Bea and her family were busy with planning and arranging for the wedding, so I visited my family in Birmingham and then went to Arley to see my parents. Everyone was thrilled I had gotten home safely and all congratulated me on my engagement. I thought of what Bea and I could do to get away on our honeymoon. I talked with my brother Calvin, and he agreed to let me use his car for a couple of weeks. Gas was scarce and each car was only allowed a few gallons per week, but he had extra rations for his farm equipment which he offered me. We could go to Florida, a state I remembered from 1941. As I drove alone back to Birmingham I thought of what a very lucky guy I was.

Chapter 7
Marriage

Bea and I were married in the chapel of the North Birmingham Baptist Church in Birmingham, Alabama on Saturday March 29, 1945, with some family members in attendance. The Reverend A.M. Tate conducted the service, after which the wedding party went to Bea's parents' house for refreshments.

After the reception we said goodbye, got into my brother's car and drove to the Redmont Hotel in Birmingham. I carried my bride over the "threshold" and our honeymoon began. The next morning Bea ordered breakfast to be brought to our room, and we ate as we looked at a map and planned our drive south.

By noon we had passed through the original Confederate capital of Montgomery. Farther south in Dothan, we stopped at a military base and had coffee with my high school classmate, Barney Hamner, who was stationed there. I had not seen Barney since high school days. Then we went to a grocery store and picked up some items. These included bread and cheese and fruit and a bottle of wine. From there we drove on down to the Gulf coast and scouted around for a room.

We found a little beach-side cabin that was a part of a cluster; most of the cabins were empty because it was March and wartime. We had just what we were looking for. It was getting late, and we quickly donned our swim suits and hit the water. It was chilly, but I felt no cold. Bea was more sensitive and didn't care to venture too far out. We ran on the sand and fell and hugged and got up and ran some more. At dark we returned to the little honeymoon cabin, Bea fixed our simple meal and it was just right for the occasion.

After a few days we decided to explore. I computed that we had enough gas ration coupons to go southward for one more tank full, and we would have enough coupons left for the two fill-ups needed for our return. We drove along the two lane road and enjoyed the view of the Gulf and its white sand beach. We passed Mexico Beach, Beacon Hill and Oak Grove. As we approached the fishing town of Apalachicola we saw the island of St. Vincent which is noted for its bird sanctuary. We walked along the bay and saw many fishing boats. It was lunch time and we ate some great seafood, just another happy couple enjoying the coast and being together.

Figure 15. Honeymooning in Florida

Our gasoline allotment dictated that we stop at some small town in North Central Florida. I thought I would like to get down to Tampa and Silver Springs where I spent time just before the war, but we had reached our southbound limit. We settled in and spent some days exploring the towns of the area. The days flew by and it was time to begin our return to Birmingham. After two days of leisurely driving through Florida, Georgia and Alabama, and two tanks of gasoline, we were back at Bea's parents' house.

We walked in to see that they had a visitor. Bea's mother said, "Spud and Bea, I'd like you to meet Mrs. Alma Hunt." The very gentle lady was the mother of my friend Bob from the *Henry Bacon*. She had come down from North Carolina after being informed that Bob was "missing in action." She had been able to locate me because Bob mentioned in a letter that I lived in Birmingham. She looked at me with hope that I could give her some assurance that her son was alive somewhere. How do you tell a mother that her son was frozen dead in that far north water and that he had no place in the lifeboat while I did? I could only try. It was the hardest thing I had ever had to do. Mrs. Hunt was a most gracious lady, and she handled it with as much control and poise as possible, much better than I did.

This experience brought back the chilling reality of war into my conscious mind, and I had to go out for a walk. I thought of the last four years and wondered if I could face the next one. In Europe the Russians were overrunning the small countries of Poland, Czechoslovakia, Hungary and others in a ruthless way. I wondered if the Russians would ever let them be free again. The Western Allies were advancing toward Munich in the south and Berlin in the north of Germany. We were retaking many of the small islands in the Pacific. I just wanted to find a place to live in peace where I could forget the last four years completely. There was an item in the *Birmingham News* about the sinking of the *Henry Bacon*. The mention of my being lost was, as Mark Twain once was quoted as saying, "greatly exaggerated." As I was home at the time, no one was alarmed by the *News* item. It had been a mistake; my name was listed instead of Mobile native Holcomb Lammon.

We said goodbye to Mrs. Hunt and soon we were visiting my family in Birmingham and then up to Bea's home town, Double Springs, where my brother Bert and his wife, Madge, lived with their young son, Bill. There, I was able to meet many of Bea's relatives

Marriage

and friends. Time up on the fruit farm of her grandmother and her uncle Wilbur Bearden was good. Then we went back to Arley to return the car to Calvin with our sincere thanks for his generosity. As we traveled through the little community of Houston where Julian and I had the slingshot fight with the Wade boys some dozen years ago, we heard on the radio that President Roosevelt had died.

This strong leader who, from his wheelchair, had led our country out of the great Depression and during our biggest war, was no longer with us. He was replaced by Harry Truman, who had played the political machine game in Kansas City to reach the level of Vice President. We wondered how well he would perform in this exalted position. Little did we know.

Just before the end of April, we had another bittersweet goodbye, and I flew back to New York to board another Liberty ship, the SS *Thomas Wolfe*. I was interested in the plaque which stated that he was known for his books such as *Look Homeward Angel* and *You Can't Go Home Again.* I mused…. On that day, April 30, 1945, in Berlin a ruthless dictator and murderer realized that his life was hopeless so he ended it with a bullet fired into his temple. And the lives of millions of unsuspecting people began to improve.

Captain Thompson said our trip would take us south through the Panama Canal and down to Chile. I was relieved that it was not to Europe again, but under the circumstances, it held little appeal. For me it seemed that the war was ending, and I still had to stay in the sometimes depressing isolation of shipboard life. I sat down and wrote Bea what I could of our trip and tried to make it sound positive. I went ashore and bought a stack of books on electronics and engineering. My thoughts were beginning to project into some postwar time which I hoped would be soon.

Our course along the same waters as my first ship was peaceful this time. U-boat captains no longer viewed us through periscopes, and we sailed alone with confidence. My subconscious tension was replaced with a desire to plant my feet on terra firma. I read and studied my books as we slowly made our way south. The weather gradually warmed and became hot as we arrived at the first lock of the Panama Canal. It was fascinating to see the process in which a series of nature-powered elevators effortlessly raised our 10,000-ton ship 85 feet to the level of Lake Gatun. From there we traversed many turns and through deep canyons some 40 miles to another series of locks which dropped us an equal amount to the sea level of the Pacific.

The need and feasibility of a canal, which would save many thousands of miles for ships making the trip from ocean to ocean, was noted as early as the 16th century. But it required many centuries of studies and political negotiations for the rights to build a canal. In the later years of the 19th century an international consortium controlled by France did a study and decided that it could build a sea-level canal. But the group was never successful in solving the financing and engineering problems which were complicated by the prevalence of yellow fever in that tropical climate. In the early 20th century, the United States Congress passed a law creating a group to study the problem. In 1908, President Theodore Roosevelt turned the project over to the Corps of Engineers of the US Army. The plan was revised to a simpler and less costly one by using locks and the natural lakes. An Army doctor, Walter Reed, and others were able to solve the problem of exterminating mosquitoes to control yellow fever. The ten-year project was completed, and the first ocean steamer passed through on August 3, 1914.

We docked in the port city of Balboa in the US controlled "Canal Zone." The Republic of Panama capital of Panama City was close by, and we did a short tour of that large city, which is one of the oldest European settlements in the Western Hemisphere. I mailed some letters to family back home and quickly returned to the ship. We proceeded through the Gulf of Panama and on into the Pacific Ocean. Our next stop was Callao, the port of the capital city of Lima, Peru. There we had a look at another historic Spanish settlement.

In Lima, people were celebrating VE day. The Western Allies met the Russians in Berlin and Germany surrendered. After the initial euphoria, there seemed to be confusion as to who would occupy what part of Europe.

In retrospect we know world leaders were playing a serious game with history. In Prague, the people were longing for General

Marriage

Patton to advance into Czechoslovakia; General Eisenhower was restraining the eager general and being the diplomat; Churchill was urging the Western Allies to cautiously move into Prague and Berlin; in Washington, the new president, Harry Truman, was uncharacteristically timid; de Gaulle was overplaying his hand; and in Moscow, Stalin was ever the crafty chess player as he made aggressive demands for more control of Europe. On the 10th of May, the Red Army took Prague and the Cold War positions were beginning to be set.

In the Pacific war, the American invasion and occupation of Okinawa was concluding, and there was talk of big battles ahead as Japan was to be invaded next.

In early June we arrived at our destination of Antofagasta, Chile, where we unloaded and took on our return cargo of the mineral, sodium nitrate. The chemical, also known as saltpeter, is used in fertilizer and explosives, and Chile has about the only mines where it is found. The country is unique—a narrow strip of land that stretches 2,260 miles along the Pacific coast of South America, from sea level on the west to 22,000 feet at the peak of the Andes. The mountain range makes a naturally protected border with Bolivia and Argentina on the east. Chile's semi-vertical landscape, to a great extent, can be observed from a ship plying the coastline. The water of the southern Pacific was clear, and we could watch giant squid as they searched for prey. They are carnivorous and cannibalistic. If one squid is injured and bleeds, it is quickly attacked and devoured by others. These sea monsters were large enough to be a hazard to us. No one went swimming.

We learned, to my dismay, that our next destination would be the west coast of the US. During the long northward trip from Chile to the West Coast I had time for some reading and study. I had planned to be ready to take the exam for my 1st class radio telephone license sometime soon. I knew this might be helpful in getting a job in the radio broadcasting industry after the war. But I had time to copy press wireless and keep up with the progress of the war with Japan.

Our final destination was Seattle, but as we traveled along the California coast, we received orders to put into Long Beach Harbor.

While some unloading was going on I went ashore and called Bea. We talked about our plans, and I told her I would be free for a month. We decided she should come out and meet me at my brother's house in San Diego. (Tommy and Frances had settled back in California.) Bea said she would immediately begin planning to come out. Within a week we were docked in Seattle, and I was free to leave the ship. Since I had time, I decided to take a Greyhound bus down the coast to San Diego. I guess I didn't realize that it would take three days and nights to get there. When I finally arrived, Bea was already there. Tommy and Frances, with their children Shirley, Butch and Sandra, gave us a great welcome.

Tommy had bought a service station and was busy all day. Frances showed us around San Diego, which was a very busy city. We saw thousands of US Navy sailors and marines from the nearby base. The talk was of the war in the Pacific, and the marines were expecting to leave for the big invasion of Japan. Everyone expected our losses to be great because the Japanese had been such stubborn fighters, willing to commit suicide for their country rather than suffer the disgrace of capture.

Bea and I talked about our postwar plans. We considered staying in the west as my brother had done early in his life. At some point we discussed San Francisco as our choice of where to settle. Neither of us had been there, but Bea had met some girls on the train coming out who were going there for work. I knew it would be a place I could sign up for another ship if the war continued. I hoped that would not be necessary, but I knew if the war lasted more than another month, it would be necessary.

In the middle of July, 1945 we made our way up through Los Angeles and into beautiful San Francisco, Herb Caen's "Baghdad by the Bay." We found a room at a downtown hotel and enjoyed seeing the city. We walked the shopping areas around Market Street and rode the cable car up to the Mark Hopkins hotel and had lunch at the famous "Top of the Mark." The Golden Gate Park was a good place to walk and talk. As we walked along Stanyon Street we noticed a sign "Apartment for Rent." We stopped and talked with the lady who owned the two-level house in a row of bungalows. We looked

Marriage

at the little efficiency apartment which, along with the garage, was the first floor of the house. The lady told us the cost and we left to talk about it.

My brother Julian was stationed at Hamilton Field Air Base, located some miles north of San Francisco. He was back from a flight to the Far East and invited us to come out to his base. We swam at the Officers Club and ate and talked. I was impressed with his many exploits and successes in the service. He seemed so satisfied that I thought he would continue in an Air Force career after the war.

Julian was off on another flight to the Far East, and Bea and I returned to San Francisco. On August 6, 1945, we heard a radio bulletin with breaking news. People listened in awe as the announcer told about a B-29 raid on Hiroshima, Japan: "The whole city was destroyed." Later I read for the first time in the *San Francisco Chronicle* about the Manhattan Project which produced the bomb that killed and maimed so many Japanese but saved the lives of countless Americans by stopping the greatest and most destructive war in history. It's ironic the decision to use the most destructive weapon ever devised was made by the haberdasher who knew nothing of it until he became president the previous April. He soon grasped the horrible necessity of making the decision to use this weapon.

Truman then showed his impatience by ordering another and even bigger one to level Nagasaki three days later. The message was heard loud and clear, and the Japanese leaders offered to surrender on August 14, 1945. The celebration in San Francisco began. Bea and I were in the midst of it, and she was kissed by what seemed the whole Pacific Fleet before we could make our way back to the hotel. Sadly, things got out of hand and several people were hurt and a few killed as people got drunk and out of control. But it was something to celebrate. The next day, VJ day plus one, I got my assignment to go to Vancouver, B.C., and a new Victory ship. I had a week to get there.

Bea and I rented the apartment at 187 Stanyon St. and were able to see some of San Francisco as she looked for a job. The landlady suggested the Federal Reserve Bank. Fortunately a position was open, and I was happy that she would be busy with something interesting while I was away.

On the flight to Vancouver from San Francisco, I reflected. The war was over, and I felt that I had served my country from before it started to the end. My decision of that April day in 1941 had brought me many thrills and chills; also many lonely hours and days and months. But I had never allowed the word "regret" to control my thinking.

Now I was needed to help bring home some of the 16 million conquering heroes. The GI Bill of Rights, which would generously ease the shock of so many into civilian life, excluded the Merchant Marines, a relatively small group with no political influence. Even the President made the case that the Merchant Marine had delivered the goods of war while their chance of death or harm was greater than any branch of armed service.

I began to think about my future, how to leave sea duty and get some roots; find a career which would support us while I continued my education. But before I could move into the future, I had to complete the job at hand.

The Victory ship I took out of Vancouver was a successor to and improvement over the obsolete Liberty ship. The Victory's engine was more modern than the Liberty's, which was designed in the 19th century. The Victory was faster, larger and more efficient. I was sure our trip back through the canal and to England would be more comfortable, but I was not too enthusiastic about going back to Europe.

Marriage

Figure 16. Spud at the Empress Hotel

At our first stop, the purser and I toured the beautiful city of Victoria where we saw the Empress Hotel and beautiful parks.

As we traveled down the west coast of North America and through the Panama Canal, I studied for my first class telephone license to prepare for possible employment in the broadcast industry. I also listened to radio broadcasts of the British Broadcasting Corporation and other stations as nations jockeyed for control of territory. Germany was being divided into four occupation zones which were controlled by the US, the Soviet Union, Britain and France. Berlin also was divided into zones. Stalin used his craftiness to gain control of a large portion of Germany which surrounded the capital of Berlin. It was soon obvious this was a serious mistake by western powers. In addition, Stalin was in control of virtually all the Eastern European countries. The groundwork was laid for the Cold War which continued for 45 years.

The Soviet power play to gain some control of Japan was not successful. Some think the quick finish of the Asian war brought to a close by the atomic bomb may have been a deciding factor in the US gaining almost complete control of the occupation of Japan. However, Stalin was able to gain influence upon the future of China. Soon the major countries of the world would become divided into two power zones, one influenced by the western democracies, and the other by the Soviet Union.

The war was responsible for the loss of more than 15 million lives with the Allied nations losing two thirds of that number. The Soviet Union's losses were by far the greatest, with China second and Japan third. US losses were less than 300,000. However, the dollar cost was greatest for the US

We arrived at Liverpool, and while the postwar cargo of mostly food and manufactured goods was being unloaded for our friends, the long suffering British, I made another trip to London. Although the war damage was extensive, some reconstruction had begun. The people seemed so happy the long war was finally over.

My letters from Bea were cheerful. She also was thinking of how and where we would settle; she enjoyed California, but I could detect a longing to see her family in Alabama. I wrote back and told her I would return sometime in December.

As the Victory ship, *Cape Palmas*, sailed into New York harbor, I was as happy as any newly arriving immigrant to see that symbol—the Statue of Liberty. I was free to live my life in a great and generous country without fear. With freedom came responsibility of competing for the good life.

Bea met the big Douglas DC-6 that brought me to the San Francisco airport; we were reunited again and it was good. She was still working at the Federal Reserve Bank, and I spent my days preparing for the Federal Communications Commission exam scheduled for the next month.

I also spent time looking for a car and visited a new car dealer. There wasn't a car in the display room, but a salesman was taking orders for the long waiting list. He gave me a form and in the space for branch of service I wrote *none*. When he read that he gave me a somewhat accusing look and said, "I suggest you visit our used car lot." I found a few aged heaps and all were definitely "veterans," but their stickers had new car prices. The salesman explained that new cars had price control stickers while the used cars price was based on supply and demand. The postwar period of scarcity was obvious.

That Christmas in San Francisco was the first time since 1940 I spent the holiday with "family." The family of Bea and Spud exchanged gifts, went to church and sang carols. The war was over and we thanked God; I thought of some guardian angel smiling down on us. We decided to go down to San Diego for a few days after Christmas; I was there for my 24th birthday, December 28, 1945. Bea called her parents in Alabama, and they wondered when we would be coming home. She said, "Probably sometime in the spring." We returned to San Francisco, and I went to the Federal Communications Commission office and sat for my exam. A quick grading by an official assured me that I had passed and would hear from them soon. With this knowledge, I visited some radio stations and inquired about work. Each time I was given application forms, and each time I had to write *none* in the "branch of service" line.

In February, Bea resigned her job, and we discussed leaving for Alabama. She was experiencing some pains, and I took her to a doctor. She came out and said, "I've some good news and some bad news." I asked her to tell me the bad news first. She said, "I'll have to have an appendectomy tomorrow." I was so disturbed I almost forgot about the good news promise, but after some pause, I asked, "And what may I ask is good after that?" She smiled and said, "You're going to be a father."

The doctor said Bea should go immediately to the hospital. We took a taxi to one in Oakland; the surgery was performed that same day. Since the attack of appendicitis was acute, the doctor was concerned that her pregnancy might be interrupted. Fortunately, Bea's recovery was normal, and she was able to recuperate at home.

We talked with our landlady and she agreed we could be released from our rental contract by March 1st. We had many arrangements to take care of in the next ten days. Most things could be done locally, but the big problem was finding and buying a suitable car. I found nothing in San Francisco, and someone suggested that in Burlingame I might find what I needed. I got some cash and took a bus south to that town. After searching and trying various older cars, I finally decided on a 1942 Plymouth. The car looked good, but it had been repainted and I thought I detected it was olive drab underneath. I still think it had been a military vehicle. At least *it* was a veteran. If I had been one and had the time to wait, I could have bought a new one for what I paid for the old one.

Bea felt good enough to travel, and on the first of March, we headed south. We were sorry to leave while Julian was away on a trip, but we thought we had no choice under the circumstances.

On our first day we made it to my brother Tommy's house in San Diego. I had the brakes checked, and it was necessary to reline them there. That gave us a couple of days to visit with them. It was good we had that rest because the following day we drove straight through to El Paso, Texas. Bea felt fine and we decided to take the opportunity to visit Carlsbad Caverns in New Mexico. As we walked down the many steps we were enthralled by the beauty of the stalagmites and the stalactites. When we were half way down, I noticed Bea was pale and unsteady on her feet, and then it happened: she fainted! As I picked her up the guide was already there with ammonia from his first aid kit. Then she felt well enough to continue, and we rode an elevator back to the surface.

It was late at night when we finally arrived at Bea's parents' house in Birmingham.

Chapter 8
Post War Adjustments

Bea's family greeted us as returning heroes. She had never been away for more than a week or so, and now was home with the promise of presenting her parents with their first grandchild. I was glad to be back and had a great feeling of relief that we made it so quickly and without major incident.

Soon we were able to visit all of my large extended family and catch up on their changes. My father and mother still lived in Arley, and Julian was in the Air Force in California. Younger sister Gloria had been working in Birmingham while Joyce and Doris were still at home in Arley. I had a slew of new nephews and nieces that had been born to my older siblings during the war years. It was great to see them all.

I soon learned that my mother in law, Clara McCullar, was one of the world's best people. She was so versatile and talented, and one of the most caring people I have known. Seeing these qualities had been passed onto my wife's genes only reinforced my devotion to her. Bea and I took over the duplex her parents had rented in Birmingham after they decided to return to their home in Double Springs. We bought a few items of furniture and Bea, helped by her mother, made it very livable. I set out to look for work.

Our country was in a state of flux. Millions of returning veterans were rearranging their lives as we were, and more millions were changing from wartime jobs to new careers. Universities and colleges were filled with new students. My skills were not needed, and the only thing left for me at such a time was a job selling women's shoes. Burt's Shoes was one of the low priced lines and required less salesmanship than speed in measuring and selecting size, color and style. Since pay was based upon numbers of sales, I went home with an average of $50 per week, I could have computed my thousands of moves around the store by making a few assumptions of percentages and my efficiency. I had no time for such nonsense and reflected that I was using this experience to help suppress the most horrible events of war into my deep subconscious.

Bea kept busy with her household chores and making visits to Doctors Harris and Fields, two good specialists in gynecology and obstetrics. The delivery was to be in September. For spiritual reawakening we found time to attend the First Baptist Church to hear the sermons of Dr. John Slaughter.

We met and socialized with other young couples like the Colliers, the MacDonalds and our next door neighbors, the Ketchams. I met Arnold and Jackie Sartain. Jackie was Bea's friend from high school, and Arnold was employed at a radio station. Arnold and I were licensed radio amateurs, and we had many common interests, so we soon became close friends. Arnold arranged for me to fill in as an engineer operator at one of the local radio stations. I was happy to end my career in the shoe business. It was good to get back into the technical field, even if only temporarily.

Bea's labor pains began and increased in frequency on the morning of the 26th of September, 1946. After much pain for her and anguish for me, she delivered Lynda Gail Campbell at 7 pm that evening. What a beautiful baby girl and what proud parents we were. Lynda developed rapidly and was soon trying to communicate. She seemed to understand much that we said and was impatient for us to understand her. We remember when she first began to try to sit. She was making a noise like "chuss chuss," and we couldn't understand what she was trying to tell us. Bea noticed the distant sound of a train whistle. Lynda was gleeful that we finally understood she was saying "Choo Choo." From that time on she added more and more words to her vocabulary. Early on we were aware we had a very bright youngster.

Post War Adjustments

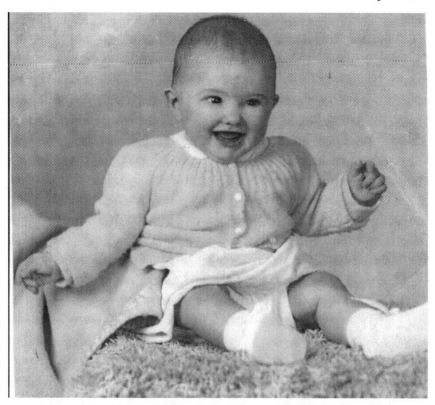

Figure 17. Lynda in 1947

Soon I was able to get into a regular "permanent" job with radio station WBRC, the NBC outlet. That is, it was permanent until the next year when an ex-employee returned from a defense job and the union insisted, with agreement by management, that he be given the job held by the employee with least seniority—me. It was a shock, but I was hired by the local ABC network station WSGN, owned by the Birmingham News Company. There I worked with my friend Arnold Sartain.

The old Plymouth was becoming unreliable, so I got on the waiting list for a new one, and it came with the introduction of the 1948 model. Monthly car payments complicated our already tight budget, but we enjoyed our trips to visit Bea's parents and others on weekends. Bea drove the new car with her parents, her brother, Don, and baby Lynda, to Colorado Springs, Colorado for a visit with her sister, Nell, who had married Robert Stewart. Bob had served in the Air Force and was attending college in that scenic area.

During this time Harry Truman had become a surprisingly strong president while filling out the late president's term and was elected to a full term. His greatest problem was dealing with the Soviet Union as they tightened their control of all the countries of Eastern Europe and a portion of Germany. General Lucius Clay, who was the commander of the American sector of Germany, was seeing some of the beginnings of the Cold War. Stalin found it necessary to fence off his sector of Berlin because his economic system could not compete with the free enterprise in the western controlled parts of the city. Despite the fence (and the wall built in 1961), thousands fled the Communist zone, and many were killed in the attempt.

Churchill described the philosophical and political "Iron Curtain" that separated the borders of Soviet control. In 1947, Secretary of State George Marshall in a speech at Harvard proposed an economic recovery plan to support the countries most devastated by the war. It would include the Soviet Union, but when it was passed by Congress, Stalin considered it an imperialistic plot and refused the offer. This was the beginning of the "Marshall Plan" for the recovery of Europe. Also during 1947, Congress created the Central Intelligence Agency.

In my part of the world in 1947, my three sisters, Gloria, Joyce and Doris all were married. That left brother Julian as the only one still single, and he was engaged to Marie Hamner from Arley.

I was enrolled in evening classes at the University of Alabama, Birmingham Center. I attended for two years until it got to be too much of a strain on our budget and my time with family. I gave it up and silently vowed that my offspring would be given as much education as they wanted. At about this time Bea became pregnant again. I was giving serious thought to getting a bigger house in a new neighborhood. We drove around and found a lot in a new development on Shades Mountain at Bluff Park. We bought a half acre on Park Avenue for $900. Our budget would only allow $150 down; the developer agreed to payments of $15 a month on

Post War Adjustments

the balance. We could only dream of being able to build what we wanted, but dreams are important too.

In June 1948, Stalin tested President Truman by blockading Berlin. This power play was intended to force the western powers to leave the capital. But the US and Britain countered with their own gambit. An intensive airlift was launched, and eventually the USSR agreed to reopen road and rail communications into the beleaguered city as the Cold War threatened to become hot. Radio broadcasts were used to give news of the west to the people of Eastern Germany. The broadcasts became institutionalized and were called RIAS (Radio in the American Sector). The occupational governor, General Clay, suggested a larger program of radio to be beamed to the eastern European countries.

On December 29, 1948 in Birmingham, Alabama, a bouncing baby boy, Stephen Gary Campbell, was welcomed into the family by Spud, Bea and Lynda. This was the family we wanted, and we decided to have no more; Dr. Fields had informed us we had a combination of blood types which increased the risk of having a "blue baby." Lynda and Steve were our contribution to the baby boom of post World War II.

Steve was also a good looking and healthy kid, until he developed pneumonia at two and half months. A quick call to our pediatrician, Dr. Royal, brought him to our house with his little bag. (Yes, they made house calls in those days.) One shot of the new drug penicillin cleared up the illness. A few years earlier it could have been fatal at such a young age. Steve developed quickly, and his motor skills were especially good. He walked at nine months and climbed to daring heights very soon. His interests in learning from pictures and exploration kept him and us busy. He, like his sister, was fun to have around.

During the summer of 1949 we were visited by my sister Mary and her husband, Ralph Kelly, along with their two boys Dick and Pat. They were a very lively and enjoyable family, and we always treasured time with them. One evening, on the spur of the moment, we decided to drive down to West Palm Beach, Florida to visit my oldest sister, Lecie, and her husband, Lee Dickerson. The four adults and four kids piled into the Plymouth and headed south. The sedan was full and it had no air conditioning, and with several babies and toddlers occasionally needing changes of linen, we kept the windows rolled down. But it was fun and Ralph kept us laughing with his Irish wit. We drove all night and some slept but Lynda stood all night and looked out the front to "see the ocean." When she saw it she was happy to go to sleep with the rest.

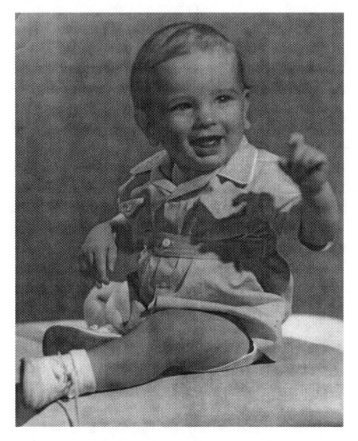

Figure 18. Steve in 1949

We had many stops for sandwiches and drinks, and bathroom breaks. Steve was only six months old, and Bea would only allow distilled water for him. After several stops and inquiries for this scarce purified product, Ralph and I went into a bar and ordered whisky and water and hold the whisky. That poor thirsty boy attacked the glass like a dropout from AA. It was quite a time before Ralph

Post War Adjustments

and I were brave enough to let Bea in on our secret. We drove on straight through the thousand miles to West Palm Beach.

It was a happy reunion with Lee and Lecie and their five children. Lee's well-to-do friend, who also was originally from Arley, invited us to go deep sea fishing. Ralph wanted to bring some beer along but the friend said he would supply the "drinks." As we reached the fishing area Ralph wanted a drink; he opened the cooler and exclaimed, "Pop!" But we did have luck and brought home a fresh fish dinner. Ralph had his with a Bud; he blamed me for the alcohol-free excursion because the friend thought I was a teetotaler. All because my father was a Baptist minister.

Figure 19. Fishing in Florida (from left: Ralph Kelly; boat owner; Harrell Dickerson; Spud; Lee Dickerson)

On April 25, 1950, I was at work at the radio station when Bea called with the news that my mom had died in a tragic fire, trying to save animals from a burning barn. We were devastated that this God fearing lady, who had spent a life caring for 12 children and helping her minister husband in winning souls to the Christian faith, had her life ended so tragically. I found a place to be alone to pray for her soul and for my dear father as he faced the future alone.

As my life changed, so did the world. On July 4, 1950, Radio Free Europe began broadcasting to the Eastern European countries of Poland, Czechoslovakia, Hungary, Romania and Bulgaria. It was organized as a people-to-people effort and was to be supported by donations from Americans.

Around this time, our thoughts moved to plans for building our "dream home." We were not eligible for the low-interest loans made available to veterans by the GI Bill of Rights. We took our plans for a three-bedroom, ranch-style house to the Seale Lumber Company and talked with an expert. He suggested we hire a contractor and apply for a Federal Housing Administration loan which was available to anyone who could show economic responsibility and ownership of a lot. We did and soon discovered that in addition to the lot we would need about $2,000 cash. We had nothing saved and were living from paycheck to paycheck.

Then I had a thought: that $2,000 is about the profit the contractor would make on the building project. I talked with my cousin, Cortez Burns, who had built some houses; he agreed to work for weekly wages with me being my own contractor. I visited the person to whom we still were paying $15 per month for our lot. He saw my problem and quickly agreed to give us a clear title deed, and we would continue our payments on a verbal contract as a personal loan. I don't know the legal implications of this arrangement, but it was now possible to get a construction loan from the lumber company and apply for an FHA loan to pay off the cost of the building at completion.

Little did we know the toil and trouble the next four-month time limit on the construction loan would bring us. First we moved to a basement apartment on Shades Mountain in the home of the Miltons. Charles Milton was to become a great friend, and his paving company did some work for us at a good price.

Steve was one and a half years old when he gave us a scare. He climbed into our Plymouth and found the key in the ignition. It was interesting to turn the key like Daddy and find that it made the car move. I caught him just in time to stop the car as it crept toward an embankment. Afterwards we were more careful about taking the key when we parked.

Post War Adjustments

Our days were full as we started the construction project. After an early shift at the radio station, I began by finding a subcontractor for the foundation. Then it was order materials and supervise the digging and masonry work until dark. Each day it was the same with new details. As we began the construction program, I was helped by some of my coworkers; radio engineers became carpenter helpers and electricians. For what seemed years but was only months, Bea and I spent half of every day doing low skilled jobs and making small changes as the need was noticed. From time to time we called upon our neighbor and friend Buddy Bailey, himself a contractor, to give us advice and help. Buddy and his wife, Nina, were great friends from then on.

Lynda and Steve spent much time in the house with us. Lynda, ever the little lady, sat and read or just observed, and Steve was our chief inspector, inventorying parts which he removed from various boxes. Sometimes he might lose a screw or door knob from the stack of supplies which was awaiting installation. Fortunately he was just as efficient at relocating them. We had fun, but after about three months it got tiring as we both had lost some weight and maybe a bit of our enthusiasm.

But we had to keep going; we had only one month do the finish work and painting. Then we must pass the FHA inspection before the construction loan period would end, or we would have to pay off the $9,000 construction loan mortgage with cash we didn't have, or lose our house and lot. Because of the limit in time and money, we did some jobs which were beyond our skills. We lost more weight and added more grey hairs. Then time was up and we ordered the inspection.

Bad news! The wizened old FHA inspector was a retired contractor and quickly analyzed our plight and told me that a novice should never take on such a project. The not so bad news was that he was also human and wrote up only a few items which could be redone by skilled workmen. We thanked him and called Buddy Bailey. This great friend brought his crew and redid our (un)handy work; we paid a small fee and reordered the inspector back out just in time to prevent foreclosure. In the end, we had a house with a 25-

year FHA mortgage for $9,100 and with a bank account at the same level it was when we started four months earlier—zero. What we had was a livable house for our family. What we didn't have was a house full of furniture!

We moved in with the bare necessities, and after some rest from the building process, I started doing TV repairs in my spare time so we could begin furnishing our new home. Lynda had seen the new broadcasting medium, television, at a neighbor's house and wondered why we had no such luxury in ours. We bought a small Crosley model and we all acted as if "the medium was the message." We often had neighbors over to watch comedies like "Broadway Open House" and Milton Berle. But Lynda soon tired of this and returned to her picture books.

Around this time, NBC news reported rumors at the very secret agency, Atomic Energy Commission that the US had countered the Soviets' testing of their atomic bomb with the development of a "super bomb" some 200 times the strength of the ones used at Hiroshima and Nagasaki. This hydrogen bomb was tested at Bikini Atoll in the Pacific with awesome results. Meanwhile, the United Nations was discussing the Korean border dispute, and Julian had graduated from Howard College where he had attended under the GI Bill. He had married Marie Hamner in 1948, and in 1949 they were proud parents of Teresa. In 1950, Julian was called back into the Air Force and they were living in Memphis.

In 1951, the Birmingham News Company, my employer bought TV station Channel 13, and I was transferred there. It was interesting work, but somehow I felt television was not my calling. I still worked many hours repairing TV sets after eight hours at the station. We were able to complete the furnishing of our house, but I wondered if I would ever be able to meet the needs of my family on one salary. I looked at our two bright children and thought of their future and my silent vow to give them a complete education. In retrospect I can see that we were caught up in trying to keep up with our friends by having the latest model automobile, burdening us with a perpetual car payment.

Post War Adjustments

Our social needs were being served by backyard barbeques with many close neighbors like the Liddles, the Cooks and the Maxwells, and our spiritual life by membership in the new Shades Crest Baptist Church. Lynda and Steve had their neighborhood and school friends, and we had settled into the suburban lifestyle of the post war years. But I was too concerned with work to enjoy my family and the peaceful community as I should have.

I once was working in my basement TV repair shop while babysitting three-year-old Steve. I was concentrating, trying to figure out what had failed in a TV set, when I looked up to see my toddler come in with two peanut butter and jelly sandwiches, one for me and one for himself. Our kids were always self sufficient, and I admired that in them.

In September 1952, Lynda was enrolled in the first grade class of Mrs. McDaniel at Bluff Park Elementary School. She was excited; she had spent many days in the care of her grandmother, the librarian, at the Winston County Library at Double Springs. She was already in love with books and still is. Her teacher sold us a set of World Book Encyclopedia which was very useful in the education of our two children over the next 12 years. The combination of text and pictures made them ideal for young children.

It was a very stressful time for me. I was busy working two jobs in order to support my family, and at the same time, I could see the need to spend quality and quantity time with my wife and two children. I decided to cut back on the TV repair job and renew my energy for the other activities.

I first tried my hand at carpentry and built a chest of drawers for Lynda's bedroom. When finished and painted, with decals on the front, it still looked amateurish. I decided carpentry was not my forte. Steve had a toy riding car with pedal power. I adapted it to battery power with a gear-shift lever for forward and reverse. A foot pedal acted as a simulated gas feed. Braking was accomplished by the inertia of the electric motor as the driver's foot lifted off the "go" pedal. Steve and Lynda worked out a time-sharing plan. I did the maintenance and sometimes minor body repair as they had minor crashes. Bea stood by for first aid. She and I enjoyed watching as much as they did driving.

In August 1953, US military strategists were startled by a claim by Soviet Premier Georgi Malenkov that the USSR had tested a hydrogen bomb, an event confirmed by the new AEC Chairman, Admiral Strauss. It was just a few years after the US tested its first super bomb; our adversary was not far behind us. Ironically, it was about this time that convicted atomic spies Julius and Ethel Rosenberg became the first US citizens to suffer the death penalty for espionage. Needless to say, civilian defense was a major item in our government and in the thoughts of many Americans. Building bomb shelters became a new industry.

The next year brought a major financial crisis in the Spud and Bea Campbell family. Some difficult decisions had to be made.

Chapter 9
Changes

The new year of 1955 opened with some optimism in the family of Spud and Bea Campbell. Lynda was excelling in her third year at Bluff Park Elementary and Steve was eager to begin school. He was delayed a year because his birthday came after the beginning of school. He had turned six on December 29, 1954 and was spending much time poring over the pictures and trying to read captions in the new World Books.

The worldwide economy was hopeful; Europe was rebuilding and the new agency, Atomic Energy Commission, had predicted a boom in new power generation using atomic energy. It was projected this industry would be especially helpful in under developed countries and where other cheap sources of power were scarce.

At the TV station, I had been assigned to do a survey of the channel 13 coverage in all of North Alabama and to work with local service personnel in terms of improving the reception. In this interesting assignment I worked directly with the station manager, Henry P. Johnston. Things looked good for my future in this position, but then disaster struck.

Wage and conditions negotiations, which were under way with the local union, broke down and a bitter strike began. I had very good friends on both sides of an issue which I was certain would continue indefinitely. My position looked untenable. After talking with Bea we decided that our best solution would be relocation and a change of careers. I called my brother Tommy in California, and he agreed to help me get a start in his retail furniture business with a goal of maybe opening a second store. We listed our house for sale, and I got into my Oldsmobile and headed west to investigate the possibilities.

Julian had been stationed at a college in Wilburton, Oklahoma, where he was teaching in the ROTC program. I visited with him and

Marie along with their two daughters. It was nice to be with them for a few days as they entertained me with things such as a prisoners' rodeo. Being inside a prison was a new experience for me.

In Buena Park, California, I found Tommy had a very thriving little business. He was a natural salesman and had managed to build his store sales to a point that he had a great life. They were building a large house in nearby Anaheim and seemed to be able to travel extensively. I decided I might remold myself enough to survive in this totally strange lifestyle. After all, I saw very few other options at the time. After a few weeks of working in the various phases of the business, I decided to bring my family to California.

As I drove the 2,000 miles back to Alabama alone, I had plenty of time to reflect. I was thankful for my family and especially the way Bea was able to keep things moving in a positive direction. She had managed to sell the house and much of our furniture and was preparing to make this major move with all the problems it brought. We tried to think of it as a new adventure. We hoped the interruption of a school year would be a new educational experience for the children. Fortunately, Lynda and Steve seemed to see it that way.

Back in Birmingham, we made a quick round of goodbyes and loaded up a rental trailer for the few items of furniture we could take along with our personal belongings and headed west. It was a long trip, but in some ways exciting as we observed the many variations in terrain, climate and people across our great country. We arrived safely and unloaded into the small apartment I had rented. After adding a few items from the furniture store, we had a rather livable place but it was a comedown from our "dream house" in Bluff Park.

I returned to work in the store as Bea took the two children for registration in a new school system. God knows what an adjustment they had to make with everything and everyone so new and different. Steve was in his second school in two months. They both seemed to be doing well, but after a few months I was notified by the principal to come in to talk.

Figure 20. Spud and Tommy in the Furniture Business

He opened by stating that he was always interested to have students come in from various parts of the country, a common occurrence in California at the time. Lynda and Steve were the first he had from Alabama, and he indicated he always considered that state was behind in education. "But your two have surprised me," he said. "Their teachers report that they are well grounded, and I think Lynda has the best basic background of any student I have experienced." He told me that in the Stanford Benet test, she had scored a record for the school. I said I was proud of them and the good school they had attended back in Bluff Park. I indicated that I hoped they would do as well in this school, and he said he would try to see that that they did. This anecdote is not intended as a comparison of school systems or a judgment of students, but as an illustration of the many influences on educational performance.

We enjoyed many things about Southern California. Disneyland was nearby, and we visited there many times with our two children. The snow capped mountains were within a short distance. We drove there and rode the chair lift to the top of Mt. Baldy. In our home town of Buena Park we could tour Knotts Berry Farm.

On the downside was the heavy traffic, especially on weekends, which made the Sunday afternoon drives unpleasant. People from all parts of the US and the world came and settled in California. It is interesting from that standpoint. But while we appreciated having my brother and his family nearby, we still missed the many others from both our families.

My plan to open a furniture store by the beginning of 1956 continued as I was busy working with Tommy in his store. However, I began to have doubts that this would be something I could do. I was neither inclined nor trained to do sales work. Bea and I discussed our options. I had seen an ad for technical help by the Los Angeles engineering firm, Holmes and Narver, Inc. I went downtown and talked with them. They were looking for communications and television specialists for overseas work. The company was a prime contractor for the Atomic Energy Commission in the Marshall Islands of the South Pacific. I completed the application form and was immediately given an interview. I would have to sign a two year contract and stay in the isolated area for that time with one month home in the middle of the contract. The most attractive thing the job offered was pay that would be roughly twice as much as I could make at home. In addition, if I completed the contract my pay would be free of federal taxes. I went home to consider it.

Bea and I agreed the plan to invest our life savings into the startup of a retail furniture business was risky. I felt it would not work out, especially as I was not enthusiastic about working in the furniture sales business. It was obvious to me that Bea and the children were not completely satisfied with being so far from their friends and relatives, although Bea would support whichever decision I made. After weighing the advantage of working toward financial gain against the disadvantage of a temporary separation, I decided to go to the option which matched my training and to accept the Holmes and Narver offer.

The company gave me a month to settle my affairs by returning my family to Alabama. We said goodbye to Tommy and his family and our friends in Buena Park, loaded the trailer and headed east. Moving back was simpler than the last move because we had no real estate to sell. I detected that my family was relieved to get back to familiar surroundings. Although I felt that I had failed in a venture for the first time, I was glad to move toward being financially more secure. I was able to suppress my feelings about being separated from my loved ones. I prayed that it was the right decision.

Back in Bluff Park we rented a garage apartment from Mr. and Mrs. Srygley who lived on Park Avenue near the school and our church. It was good that Bea, Lynda and Steve could be with old friends while I was away. They seemed to understand this separation was necessary.

It was a fast goodbye at the airport on May Day in 1956 because I was not able to do a long one under those conditions. I got a seat and buried my face in a newspaper. I read: Soviet Premier Zhukov, at the annual May Day military parade, said they could deliver atomic weapons to any point on earth. US Defense Secretary Charles Wilson confirmed the Soviets' claim. A new series of tests of A-bombs and H-bombs were to begin in the summer of 1956. I turned my thoughts to a great adventure.

Chapter 10
Eniwetok

My flight from Birmingham made a stop in Dallas. As we sat waiting for takeoff the man on my left, who had just boarded, seemed to want to talk. He said he was going to Los Angeles and then began questioning me about my home and my destination. I answered him and I continued reading. I noticed as we soared above the plains of western Texas that his questions were getting more personal about my life and work. Then I became suspicious. I remembered my neighbor in Birmingham had told me someone was at his house asking questions about me. Holmes and Narver had informed me that my new assignment would require a "Q" clearance, which was about the most stringent at the time. The AEC was sensitive about recent security breaches which may have given away valuable secret information to an adversary. I just looked up, made eye contact, and turned back to my paper. For whatever reason, he suddenly left the plane at Phoenix.

At the Holmes and Narver offices in Los Angeles, I was given a briefing and was told that I would leave the next day for the AEC atomic test facilities at Eniwetok. They said my background check was proceeding satisfactorily and if approved, my clearance would follow soon. If not, I would be brought back. By this I assumed that I was needed and they were fairly certain of my approval by the security powers.

The long flight from California to Hawaii was on a military Air Transport Command plane. I stayed overnight in that beautiful state then proceeded via Johnston Island, which was only big enough for a runway, to Kwajalein and on to Eniwetok. The latter two and Bikini are atolls in the "Trust Territory of the Pacific," and are administered by the US. An atoll is usually formed by a circle of small coral reef islands.

It was a warm day in May 1956 when I saw the atoll of Eniwetok for the first time. We landed on the runway of the main island where the military base was located. The island was also called Eniwetok, and we had a short launch ride over to Parry Island where the AEC offices and the support company, Holmes and Narver, were located. That little island, which was a bit larger than Gallups Island, was to be my home for the next 19 months. The atoll also contained several more islands in a circle about 20 miles in diameter. The next island to the north was Japtan, still intact with its natural vegetation of beautiful tropical trees and other flora, and therefore a recreation and exploration destination. There I saw giant lizards which were interesting and harmless even though they were as large as alligators. The other islands in the circle seemed to be barren and were being used as test sites for A-bombs of the size that were used in World War II on Hiroshima and Nagasaki. The large H-bombs were tested at Bikini Atoll which was some 200 miles to our north east and was uninhabited.

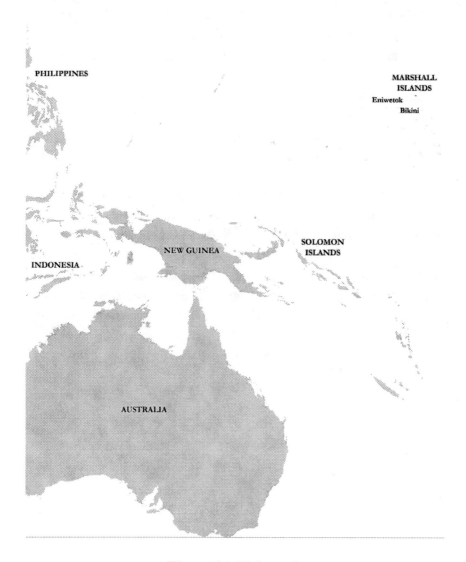

Figure 21. Eniwetok

Upon arrival at Parry Island, I was processed through the administration office and briefed. I would be assigned to the electronics building which housed the communications equipment, TV broadcast operations and associated shops and labs. My boss was Sid Lathlean, a man of my age from California.

But first I was taken to my quarters for settling in and rest from the long trip. My "quarters" were a cot and locker in a corner of a tent which housed a dozen men. My space was about 75 square feet with a small closet for clothing. My wardrobe became mainly a few pairs of shorts with a few shirts for "formal" occasions. Usually there was no necessity for a shirt. Footwear was sandals; shoes and socks were hardly ever necessary. No one had coats or hats, it seemed. Toilet facilities and showers were located in a nearby small metal building. In fact, it was about as close to nature as one can imagine. Swim wear was optional on the many good beaches with the crystal clear water and tropical seascapes. Many people had goggles and some had snorkels for diving into the mystic depths to view nature. There were no females within a hundred miles.

It was mind boggling to see this busy island with people of every imaginable technical skill and scientific knowledge living in such primitive conditions. My reaction was a feeling of being disconnected from anything rational. How did I get myself into such a life changing situation? This seemed more primitive than my early years at Arley, more confusing than Gallups Island, more lonely feeling than my first ship, and in a manner, as scary as the *Henry Bacon*. I lay on my bunk and wondered, "Where are you, Bea, my guardian angel?"

The next morning I awakened feeling better and more optimistic. It's good what a night's sleep will do for one's outlook. My first thought was to avoid the negative feelings of the night before; I knew where I was and why I was there. It was to eventually bring my family back together again and to have a better future for us all. So I began to enjoy the technical challenges I would be facing over the next months and the people with whom I worked.

The island contained the usual necessities of any small base or community of men. There were some large metal buildings for machine and scientific assembly of "devices" to be tested. We all ate in a big mess hall with dozens of tables and a cafeteria style food dispensary. The food was almost always good. There were also office buildings, storage facilities a small canteen for personal items, and a medical office and clinic. We had a little "A-frame" chapel where we could attend Sunday services, conducted by a chaplain from the military base, or just go and meditate or pray. Recreation and exercise facilities were available as were pavilions with picnic tables and a snack bar. In the evenings the bar was open for a few hours. We could play tennis or bowl or see a movie at intervals. There was a pretty good library with a variety of books to check out or read in a lounge. Some watched the films and newscasts which our little Armed Forces TV station presented.

    My work shift was 12 hours a day, six days per week sometimes with overtime. We had very little spare time for getting bored or drunk. One thing I soon suggested was to set up an amateur radio station to handle phone calls and other traffic back to families in the States. No phone lines were available for this purpose and the need was obvious. Soon permission was granted, and I was appointed "custodian" of the operation because I had the required "ham" license. Pretty soon I made my first call through the ham station of my friend, Arnold Sartain, back in Birmingham. I was able to talk with Bea, Lynda and Steve. We set up a schedule and made the call once a week for most weeks I was there. I have always appreciated what Arnold was willing to do to make this possible. Other ham operators in other parts of the country also made schedules, and we handled much traffic from that little radio shack out on the end of that lonely island. Operation of this service was extra curricular to our regular shift work, and I was happy to have several other volunteers. Our call was KH6BQ and it was a very popular contact for amateurs in the states and overseas. We avoided answering calls from certain areas. Certainly we were monitored by the security people. But as far as I know we never transmitted any classified information.

Eniwetok

Figure 22. Spud and Jim Wehrle

Speaking of security—as one can imagine, it was severe in those days. Each employee had to pass the strictest of standards, and one false move or indulgence would mean immediate travel back east. My self-imposed limit of two drinks was just right for their daily standard. The only exception I can remember was the guy who had to go in to disable a "shot" after an aborted firing. His nerves had to be steely as he reached into a device to disconnect a circuit without making an improper touch. He stayed cold sober but was allowed to celebrate a successful effort. Would it be any worse being completely disintegrated by a 20 megaton bomb, than by a bullet or small plastic bomb? I can't say. (And there's the one about the government study of this question that was cancelled when a sharp eyed GS-16 bureaucrat pointed out the difficulty of finding a survivor of both forms of death to interview.)

Sid Lathlean was happy to know I had a variety of experience in communications and TV broadcasting. My first assignment was to get the TV transmitter operating and to start the programming for the residents of the atoll. Our equipment was a package deal with the Armed Forces Radio and TV Network. The programming was local with kinescoped filming of some of the US network programs along with movies from time to time. Video recording had not come along at that time. Locally it was just the newscasts and some announcements by the AEC and military administrations of Eniwetok. It was a one man operation along with an announcer from time to time. To me it was a simplified version of the local Birmingham stations.

The communications task was transmitting and receiving data of tests and other information between Bikini and Eniwetok atolls. The problem was that the amount of information involved was too much for any existing system. There were no undersea cable links in that part of the Pacific. Short wave radio was too limited in bandwidth for the job. Our system, which was being developed by the Lincoln Labs unit of MIT, was experimental and state of the art. In order to handle the volume of information, we required a wide band system which meant moving up to the VHF (Very High Frequency) band that was assigned to this service and television. Unlike high frequency radio, this transmission would not deflect off the ionosphere and curve around the earth. And "line of sight" transmission was limited to less than a hundred miles because of the curvature of the earth. That is until some clever engineer discovered that by increasing the transmitter power and using a highly directive antenna, the beam would be "scattered" in the troposphere just above the earth and a minute amount would arrive at a distance of some 200 miles away. These wavelengths of radio energy acted somewhat like light rays; we can see it is scattered in fog and other particles in the atmosphere.

I was thrilled to be involved in the development of a new technique. The equipment was installed and working except for one big problem. The signal would fade severely at intervals due to random cancellation, caused by phase changes associated with scattering of the beam. We found that by using a duplicate circuit with space separation these fades would not occur simultaneously and we always had one with good strength. Then came the problem

Eniwetok

of automatically switching to the stronger signal. Our Los Angeles engineering lab had sent us components and circuits of a switcher they had designed. My next big assignment was to put it together and test it.

The bomb test program was rapidly approaching, and people were looking over my shoulder to get the communications system finished in time. The switcher worked as designed, and I installed it in our circuit, but we saw a new and serious problem. The vacuum tube circuit was far too slow to respond to the fast fading we encountered. Solid state devices on the island were limited to silicon diodes. The new transistors, which were developed by Bell labs a few years earlier, were limited to use in a few products. Bell had not been too eager to dispense the secret and patented theories they valued so much. I was completely unaware of the possibilities of this technique. So we reported back to Los Angeles, and I spent hours pouring over the dilemma at hand.

This was just the kind of problem that intrigues me so much I can get lost in it for days. That isolated island was just the right place for getting lost in a project. I was so deep in concentration, I worked right through mealtime. A hunger pang brought me back to reality, and I looked up and thought it would be good to see Steve here with two peanut butter and jelly sandwiches. But he was 6,000 miles away.

I experimented with several different ideas, and then by chance I was trying something I had previously wondered about. That is: what would happen if I tied two silicon diodes together so that it had three instead of two terminals? Eureka! I knew in a flash what I wanted to try. I fed voltages indicating the two fading signals into each anode and found that the common base would represent only the stronger of the two. I found a way to substitute this little solid state devise for the vacuum tubes of the switcher, and it worked like a charm. We had our system ready for the test program which was imminent. Everyone was happy except for the Los Angeles office engineers who never understood quite completely what I had done and neither did I. My only hope is that I had not infringed upon the Bell Labs patent on their solid state device of which I had no knowledge. Anyhow, that is my defense, along with the statute of limitations.

My mail from Bea was regular and certainly welcomed. I answered as often as I could find time with news that could be told. We were keeping up to date on goings on in our weekly contacts by ham radio phone patch. Lynda and Steve had settled back into their Bluff Park School, and both had excellent scholastic records despite the interruption of half the school year in California. I thought this spoke well for both school systems, our two good students and Bea's managing of their lives as I had more or less deserted them. My guilt feelings were suppressed by constant activity in my work, and operating the ham station arranging calls to loved ones of others in my predicament.

Our first test was an A-bomb of the size which destroyed Hiroshima. These were considered small and were set off on an island across Eniwetok Atoll about 20 miles from Parry Island. Some of us gathered at the picnic area awaiting the blast. We wore goggles so dense one could only see the sun. Even so, we were told to put our hands over our eyes and face away from the blast. I was curious so I turned toward the blast and saw the bones of my hands as seen in an x-ray photo. The intense light was followed by the boom and then the shock wave which felt like an earthquake. Although I witnessed many similar tests, I never faced the blast again.

We were required to wear a film badge constantly. This was a system to record the total accumulated radiation absorbed by our flesh. If we reached a level considered to be the maximum a human could safely take, we were sent home. The badge was to be kept within a few feet of the person at all times. The safe level was set arbitrarily by medical experts. Since knowledge of the area has increased over the years, the safe level may be different now.

My routine duties were often interrupted by an emergency equipment breakdown. Because of my training and experience, Sid Lathlean designated me to be the main trouble shooter in these cases. At times I worked with the physicists in the setup and testing of various sensors and radio transmitting equipment involved in the tests of explosions. However, I was only given information of details of "devices" on a need to know basis. But I was always eager to discuss the general laws and details of physics in order to understand better the field of atomic energy.

That year, 1956, was not good for the US in the Cold War. Our space program was behind the Soviet Union's. We heard the Russians were testing giant rockets which were much more powerful than any we had. And the Cold War was heating up with both sides testing these horrible bombs and building more in a race toward what seemed to be the real Armageddon. I visited our little chapel alone and asked for protection for my family and all others.

By mid summer of 1956 we had done a series of tests of the A-bombs at Eniwetok. Now it was time for the big show at Bikini. I was a bit disappointed when my friend Ed Garrigan had been assigned to fly to Bikini for the set up routine. Sid told me I might be needed at Parry Island for trouble shooting in the event of a breakdown. I still wanted to see the famous place for which a swimsuit was named. I put that in back of my mind for future trips after the test.

Eniwetok was only 10 degrees north of the equator, and the weather varied from hot winters to hotter springs, then as the sun went north of us, it returned to merely hot. But the sea breezes made the nights good for sleeping in the open air. One Sunday, Lathlean, Garrigan and I went over to Japtan Island and explored. It was a magical place with palms and vegetation so thick it was difficult to move. There were tropical birds, crawling things and the famous giant lizards which were timid of intruders but otherwise seemed friendly. I wondered how all the radiation would change or mutate the future of this beautiful natural park. I still wonder.

It was near the end of the test program, and I had experienced as much testing and more fallout than I wanted. The last A-bomb test at Eniwetok had just finished and suddenly the wind changed 180 degrees; the fallout was coming right over our little island. There was some panic in the voice of the PA announcer as he advised everyone to seek any shelter they could find. A very serious crisis had occurred, and top level people were in a panic conference. I heard later in the bar from one of the top scientists that a decision had to be made quickly between two possible solutions to the problem: (1)

order a fleet of transport planes to evacuate the islands; or (2) by the stroke of a pen, raise the limit of radiation exposure a human could take with safety. We could only guess which one was chosen, but we weren't evacuated from the islands. The crisis seemed to be over as suddenly as it came.

It was now time to witness my first "super bomb" which was located at Bikini Atoll, some 200 miles away from Parry Island. It was early morning just before dawn, and we all settled at the picnic tables to witness this event. We were given the usual PA system countdown by the seconds, and I heard—five, four, three, two, one—we saw a light which got brighter and higher as I picked up a newspaper and read about the Cold War by the light of that awesome man made sunshine. Then it was dark again, and we sat in reverent silence as we pondered or prayed that it would never be used in anger. About 15 minutes later we felt and saw the shock wave roll by, and I returned to my cot for some sleepless meditation.

Two weeks after the last H-bomb test at Bikini, a party of half a dozen men was assigned to go in and reopen some of the facilities. One technical person from our group was to accompany them. I volunteered and Sid agreed. The flight up on a C-47 "Gooney Bird" took just over an hour. As we circled the atoll, the pilot pointed out where the missing island was replaced by a few reefs and lots of ocean. We landed on a runway of the island across the atoll. The place had been void of any humanity for some months, and there was no evidence of any other life. The trees and other vegetation had long ago been obliterated. We unlocked and entered the bunker where our electronic equipment was located. Walls and ceilings of the bunker were reinforced concrete six feet thick. The one door was arranged in a protected area to withstand the force of the blast and had remained intact. Inside, everything had survived as expected. The generator was started, and we had lights and were able to begin our task of turning on various transmitters, receivers and other communications equipment. We were contacted from Eniwetok and proceeded with instructions for additional activity such as replacing sensors. Everything outside the bunker was destroyed although the blasts had been more than 20 miles away.

That evening we abandoned the claustrophobic bunker and set up chairs and a light outside. We ate our dinner, which we brought with us, and tossed our garbage into a metal drum. We turned off the light and sat viewing the brightest starry night I had ever seen. It was eerie to an extreme degree knowing that not a soul was anywhere within 200 miles of this desolate place. Someone thought they saw movement near the metal garbage can so we turned on the light. A large rodent scurried away. Someone had an idea. We quickly rigged a trap by positioning a pivoted stick with some cheese on the lighter end. This was mounted over the drum. Then we spotted the light on the trap and sat in silence. After some time of quiet and no movement, we saw a giant gopher rat climb up, and as he approached the cheese his weight caused the pivot to lower, and he slid into the can. Others came and repeated the action. As long as the light was still and we made no noise, the rat parade continued. We could only surmise that these mammals could survive deep in the ground. I guess this proves it takes little to entertain people in the absence of civilization. Soon we unrolled our sleeping bags and tried to sleep in a place too quiet for comfort.

We left Bikini, returned to Eniwetok, and settled into a routine of operating the TV station. Then I received news that my brother Julian was not well, afflicted with near-clinical depression. I took the letter from Bea and reread it in the chapel. I sat there alone and meditated for some time, praying that he would be well again. On a long walk around the island, I thought about the times we spent in our young years, playing games and working together. Then the war came and we went our separate ways. I wondered if we would ever have the opportunity be close as brothers again. I hoped that we would.

Another Christmas came, and I was alone again as in the war years. I had sent gifts for the immediate family and talked with them on a phone patch. I felt we really were not that far apart at that special time. I received my gifts and felt close to my family as I opened them. A few days later I celebrated my 35th birthday, and the day after, Steve turned eight. I thought about how those two children were growing up, and I was not around to enjoy them and to give my support as they faced the questions and problems of school. But I knew that Bea was trying to be both parents and that their grandparents were there for them.

The next year, 1957, was the beginning of the International Geophysical Year, a time when the US and 54 other nations conducted research and experiments in the earth sciences and the nearby environment. It was a cooperative effort to gain new and useful knowledge. I was especially interested in learning more about the ionosphere and the troposphere, areas which were so important in radio transmission. Congress had appropriated $39 million for world wide studies, and we were included as a small contributor. It was also a point in the 11-year cycle of high sun spot activity which augmented our ham operation. We were able to operate on more high frequency bands which lessened interference.

The monotony of the winter season was broken in a negative way when a large number of people, myself included, suffered food poisoning. People were standing in line at the latrines to vomit. It seemed that I unloaded my complete stomach through my mouth, went to bed and slept. It was important to pinpoint the particular item of food responsible. An exhaustive survey of exactly what each person had for dinner proved ice cream was the culprit. Many of us had no use for desserts for some time after that sad experience.

It was time to begin planning to go home for the one time which my contract allowed. Bea and I decided to plan it just after the end of school in May. I asked her to talk with the two youngsters about where they would like to go on vacation. It seemed that they would like almost any travel, but the Great Smoky Mountains in Tennessee and North Carolina were at the top of the list. So that is what it would be. I was as eager as a kid to see the time come.

It had been a long and lonesome year on the island when I began the flight home. Again it was a military flight to Honolulu via Johnston Island. Overnight there, then another military plane to California and a quick transfer to a commercial flight to Birmingham.

The great looking threesome met me at the airport, and we all hugged and babbled greetings. Bea was still the beauty I had known. Lynda was looking more like the little lady and was always quite reserved. Steve was also growing and reported that school had been fun, but he was glad it was over for the summer. Then he asked a question I couldn't easily answer, "Daddy why do you have be away so long?" I could detect a bit of a critical look in Lynda's eyes. My eyes watered as I blinked and turned away and asked myself that same question.

Everything was exciting for me. Being with my family was the best, and driving the car for the first time in a year and seeing the normal mixture of men, women and children were awesome. It was almost like I imagined returning from outer space would be. But in a way it was scary. I was so completely out of practice in any of the things we take for granted, like traffic and shopping and eating in restaurants. All these normal activities made me nervous. Sometimes people seemed to look at me as if I weren't normal. I suppose I wasn't for some time. It was a challenge just to be civilized again.

The little apartment in Bluff Park was comfortable but small. Bea had put her usual magic touch into making it livable. I was interested in getting caught up on all the local activities and especially how the two were doing in school. Steve had breezed through second grade, and Lynda was ready for sixth grade. As expected, she had straight As for the year. The time in California only added to their education, it appeared. They both were happy to be back with their friends on Shades Mountain.

We visited all of my family and spent some great times with Bea's parents. It was always good to sit around that table of delicious food and talk with the family. I was able to give some idea of what it was like in the test area of the Pacific, but many things could not be told. The arms race was in full swing, and the Soviets seemed to be getting an upper hand in the development of bomb delivery systems. People were concerned about the possibility of nuclear war; many were building concrete bomb shelters.

Bea and I packed our bags with outdoor clothing and walking shoes. We loaded the Oldsmobile and drove northeast to Little River Canyon for a walk around and on to Chattanooga for the night. From there it was a short day's drive to the Smoky Mountains of Tennessee and North Carolina. We spent several days just being together and seeing some of nature's best sights. It seemed a universe away from the place I had called home for the last year. I felt I should build up enough good memories to last for the next year in Eniwetok, a name I didn't want to think about.

On the way home, we returned by Arley to spend some time with my aging father. He was 80 and still living alone in the same house. I thought he looked somewhat tired, but he never was one to complain. It was a sad goodbye to the man I admired so much. We then visited Bea's parents one last time before I had to go back to the mid Pacific for the finishing phase of my contract. As usual, I made the airport goodbye as short as possible to avoid showing too much emotion. I promised to be back before Christmas.

It was hard to settle down to the job in Eniwetok after the month away. The trip back was just a ditto of what I had already experienced. My work routine, plus the hours I spent at the ham station making contacts and arranging for phone calls to people at home, filled my days. The weather was always pleasantly warm, and we swam in the clear cool water to get exercise. One hazard was the presence of what were called stone fish, which were sometimes encountered on the ocean floor. They were hard to distinguish from a stone, but if stepped on, its spines would emit a deadly poison. However, I never knew of any sharks or barracuda. We did see many multi-colored tropical species which were interesting.

Bea wrote that my father was in the hospital, and I was concerned that he looked tired the last time I saw him. My contract would be finished in a few months, and I would be there with him. I wrote him a get well card, praying that he would be well and able to enjoy life again, but he was not one to stay in bed, and I wondered.

On September 25th I received a message from a ham operator that I should call my friend Arnold Sartain urgently. I did and he called Bea and put her on. She said, "Dear Spud, I have to tell you that your father has died." She gave me details about his illness; he had contracted pneumonia and had a short stay in the Jasper hospital before it became hopeless for his aged body to sustain. She seemed to want to talk with me, but I just couldn't. I said to Bea and Arnold, "Thanks to both of you, but I just want go to the chapel and pray."

I was sure they were concerned about me, but I just couldn't force myself to make conversation.

I sat alone in the little chapel and thought about the great man who had been my mentor and friend for my whole life. Sometimes when I felt troubled and needed help, he was the only one I could talk with, and I was 6,000 miles away when I needed to be there to say goodbye. It wasn't possible to schedule a flight to get home without delaying the funeral arrangements. Soon my faith revealed to me that he really had a great and long life. He raised 12 children who all lived and had been successful in their family lives. In his time he had been a school teacher, a postmaster, a merchant, a farmer and a minister; he never had an enemy I could name. I also realized that now that he was gone, I could not do anything for him except to pray for his soul, and I knew that was already a sure thing. In a way, I was lucky; I could see him as the living being that he will ever be in my memory. I decided not to try to have the funeral delayed for me. I knew it would be a celebration by a host of people. I finally felt some peace of mind and called Bea back and was able to talk again.

In the international news, the race to get a satellite into orbit was going on between the US and the USSR. The US Navy had a contract to launch the Vanguard rocket into space, but the progress was slow and well behind the Russians. On October 4, 1957, the Soviets successfully launched their first *Sputnik* satellite into earth orbit. They announced that the signal could be heard on a frequency of 20.005 MHz. I hastily tuned in and recorded the ominous beep, beep, beep, as it passed some hundreds of miles overhead. We put it on the TV newscast that evening. The large scientific community of Parry Island was not only interested but somewhat dismayed that we should let our adversary beat us to this breakthrough in space exploration. So was I.

Soon after the Soviet success in launching *Sputnik,* they put *Sputnik* 2 in orbit. This heavier satellite started some frantic action on the part of our country. A university group came to the island with a new project: an attempt to lift a rocket and satellite above the atmosphere with a giant balloon. The rocket would then be fired into orbit with less resistance from gravity and atmosphere. Unfortunately, the balloon kept failing to lift, and they ran out of helium gas used to fill the balloon. I remember the project leader ordering a new supply on our ham phone patch circuit. I thought, "It's a sad day when the Russians have two satellites in orbit and we can't even get a balloon off the ground." I find no record or news item about this project, and I can understand why.

It was December, 1957 and my contract was completed. I said goodbye to my friends of the last 18 months and left in time to celebrate Christmas with my family as I had promised. Aside from the isolation and being away from the children, it had been a very positive experience. I had a feeling of satisfaction contributing to the test program. The radiation I had absorbed was something of a worry, but as far as I can tell, it has not affected my health in any way.

Chapter 11
You Can Go Home Again

Our Christmas in the little apartment in Bluff Park was glorious, and we were able to spend some time during the holidays with our extended families. After January 1, 1958 we began looking for a house for the family and a job for me.

The house we were able to find quickly. It was a nice little three bedroom bungalow on Darlington Street on Shades Mountain. It was just what we needed and in a very nice neighborhood with nearby shopping, schools and easy access to downtown. The owner was willing to transfer the GI loan thereby giving us the low interest rate that I had not been able to get, not being a veteran. We bought it and moved in. Bea shopped for furniture while I looked for a job.

I decided to take a temporary job as a transmitter engineer with the State Educational TV system. The transmitter was located on a mountain top some 35 miles away so I had a 70 mile drive each day. I bought a little French Renault 4CVI mini automobile which was more economical than the Oldsmobile. I worked the evening shift from four to midnight. The drive home was through many miles of a remote forest with no houses. One night as I was on that road, I saw car lights coming up behind me. The headlights were flashing dim and bright so I pulled over to see what they might want or need. A new Ford stopped beside me, and a man got out and another was coming around the front toward me. One said that I had pulled in front of them, and they were going to "get" me. I could tell they were under the influence of some stimulant, and I acted quickly, stepping on the gas as one of the men reached for my door. My little car would travel up to 60 mph, and as I reached that speed, I saw the Ford's lights lift as it "dug out" after me. I knew that a mile ahead I would enter a highway with traffic which might help at least to offer a witness. But could I stay ahead that long? As I made a left turn into the highway I saw a flash of the car lights in my rear view mirror and then nothing. I breathed a sigh of relief, thinking they must have turned right on that road. When I arrived home I called the Highway Patrol and reported the incident. They told me the Ford had plowed into a bank across the highway, killing them both instantly. The next night I drove the Oldsmobile.

As the long commute and the late-night work became a drag, I looked around for other options. Someone suggested that I talk with Andy Spear at the University of Alabama Medical Center. Andy was a physicist who had a small experimental lab for maintaining and sometimes creating electronic aids for the doctors in the university's hospital. He was a very laid back and kind person and was interested in talking for what seemed hours about my work at the atomic test site of Eniwetok and Bikini. Then he went into some of his projects. I could tell he already had decided to hire me as an assistant so I listened intently. In addition to a large inventory of commercial electronic equipment to take care of, he was trying to develop instruments which the new heart surgery group wanted. It included preliminary design and development of a sonogram for internal vision of heart action and some diagnostic equipment for detecting heart flaws in young children. The art of surgery on a living heart was new and, at that time, restricted to infants and young children who could adapt to the shock better than adults. Dr. Leland Clark had been hired from the University of Cincinnati and was developing the school's first heart/lung machine. Andy was working with him on the electronic timing and controls. I filled out some forms, and as I left, Andy said, "I'll see you soon."

Bea was interested in my prospects for getting the job, and I said I thought I had it, but the pay may not be what we needed. As I drove over to the Cheaha Mountain site, I thought about how interesting the job at the University would be. I could immerse myself into a project and have time to think it through in that seemingly relaxed academic atmosphere. I decided to give it a try if the offer came through.

Andy called and said I should come down and do mornings there while working out my required notice at the TV Station. First I had to make the rounds and meet the young doctors in our wing and their boss, Dr. Frommeyer, head of the department of surgery. And I met Dr. Volker, a man with a vision. His talk was of how he had been surprised with the potential here as he had left the state of New York to teach at this small dental school. Under his leadership the University of Alabama at Birmingham (UAB) was destined to become the largest employer in the state.

Lynda was now in Homewood Junior High School, and Steve was in Berry Elementary. After school, they did their homework and went about their various hobbies. Lynda did a lot of reading of almost every subject, and Steve did some reading and a lot of sports. He was thinking about trying out for a Little League baseball team in the spring. Bea and I attended PTA meetings at both schools and had joined the Shades Mountain Baptist Church. In our neighborhood we made several friends. Robert and Trudie Adams lived across the street. Robert was a photographer at the Birmingham News Company, and they had recently adopted three brothers, aged three to ten. Next door on either side were a young couple, Roger and Donna Thompson, with a baby on the way, and a couple our age, the Shacklefords.

My work at the electronics lab was as interesting as I had hoped, or maybe more so. My first project was to help design and build the electronic timer and control system for the hospital's first heart/lung machine. Dr. Clark had already built and tested the system which consisted of a cart full of pumps, valves, filters, an oxygenating system, and associated connecting tubing. The electronic timing unit would control the rate of "pulse beats" by switching from pressure to suction at any setting of the rate. This would control the blood pressure of the patient. (Understand, this is only a layman's memory of the system and does not pretend to be a complete description of this elaborate heart/lung replacement device). These early developments and equipment, while revolutionary in the 1950s, may seem strange to modern medical teams.

I had finished and tested my control unit, and it was ready for the ultimate test. It was inserted into the system, and I was assigned to scrub and dress in white to be in the operating room when it was first used. I had seen the young patient diagnosed as having a congenital "heart defect" where the partition (septum) between the two pumping chambers (ventricles) of the heart had failed to close. In other words, she had a hole in her heart, and blood was bypassing the oxygenating function of the lungs. The child was pale and had not developed normally.

It was more than exciting to watch as the surgeons opened her chest and rapidly inserted the machine, filled with donated blood, started the pump and stopped the child's heart. I was very relieved to see my little control unit doing its job. The blood coming from the patient was a bluish purple, and as it passed through the oxygenation process, I could see it gradually become a crimson color as it re-entered the patient. The surgeon sewed up the hole between the ventricles and soon the natural heart was reconnected and restarted. As the big machine was stopped and was rolled away, I was perspiring more than the surgeon. It's hard to explain the thrill I had a few weeks later when I saw the patient with rosy cheeks, bright eyes and full of energy like any other youngster.

(At about this time, my sister Doris' daughter, Marta, had a similar procedure in Houston. She was five years old and had been diagnosed with a similar problem when she was six months old, but the operation was not possible at that time. My memory and her father's pictorial record of the Campbell reunions present a biennial snapshot sequence of how she grew into a beautiful lady and the mother of three healthy daughters.)

While I was enjoying the work and learning under my "tutor," Andy Spear, I was also catching up with world politics. Stalin was gone, and a younger, more energetic and somewhat boisterous premier named Nikita Khrushchev was leading the Soviet Union with efforts to gain influence in Asia, Africa and South America. The headlines were warning ominously of the Soviet buildup of long range missiles and thermonuclear weapons. The US's aerial defense and radar warning system, needed against the threat of heavy bombers, was no longer considered adequate and a billion dollar project had begun to build the most powerful long-range radar system possible. This system, the Ballistics Missile Early Warning System (BMEWS), would be anchored by a unit in Thule, Greenland that would be able to detect anything leaving the ground anywhere in the Soviet Union. Two other sites were planned—one in Scotland and another in Alaska.

At home, television was overtaking radio and newspapers as the source of entertainment and news. The video recorder was replacing film in these broadcasts. In sports, Bear Bryant, who had made a good record at Kentucky and Texas A&M, had responded to "Mama's call," and soon brought back the old days of winning football at the University of Alabama in Tuscaloosa. (The University had protected their investment by bringing this local hero to the medical school for a thorough physical examination.)

My work was fun, but Bea and I discussed the possibility of getting more income because we gradually were digging into our savings. We also wanted to start a fund for our two good students' complete education.

On Darlington Street, we were just enjoying being together with normal family activities. We had a dog and cat, and Lynda had a beautiful canary which unfortunately escaped when I was careless with the cage door while outside. Steve had some white mice, and Bea was not too pleased to have them in the house. Just a typical American family of the 1950s as the war hero, General Eisenhower, was serving his second term as president. The extended Campbell family was talking of another grand reunion of the clan. Although our parents were no longer with us, the number of their descendents was increasing rapidly and were scattered over much of the nation. However, a reunion was only a dream at the time.

Lynda was taking piano lessons and practiced in her bedroom as Steve shot baskets in the back yard, and he was on the Little League team called the Red Sox. He was especially good at bat. I felt lucky to be home to watch him play on the winning team that summer.

The year and a half I spent working with Andy Spear at the University Medical School was the most enjoyable of any of my many situations. In the summer of 1959, I went to Washington, D.C. to take part in a Medical Electronics Symposium, hosted by the National Institutes of Health at Bethesda Naval Hospital. Bea and I decided to drive up for a vacation with Lynda and Steve. It was the children's first trip to the area, and we had a great time seeing sights and points of historic interest. On the way we stopped in every scenic spot we could find, and we made many pictures to augment our memories. Bea and the two did a tour of Washington, D.C. while I was at the meetings.

It was a great show, and I was amazed at the new instruments that soon would be in use at our hospital. While in Washington, I called the firm Page Communications Engineers which I knew was doing various defense and international broadcasting projects around the world. Their personnel office suggested that I come by to talk.

I went by for the "talk" and found myself filling out an application. It was quickly reviewed by the personnel director who picked up the phone and called someone and turned back to me and said, "Captain Conaughty would like to meet you." As we walked down the hall, he told me Conaughty was a retired Navy captain who managed projects throughout the world. Conaughty was certainly typical of the sea captains I remembered. His kind looking face belied his steely eyes which seemed to gaze right through you at some faraway horizon. I could visualize him standing on a deck of a destroyer giving orders in a fierce battle. He introduced his assistant, Joe Ryals, who took my application and departed to another office.

The Captain talked in general terms and asked about my experience and my family. Ryals returned and I peripherally saw him give a thumbs-up sign to his boss. They then got down to serious talk about an offer of an assignment. My tropo-scatter experience from Eniwetok was needed for a system in Thule, Greenland. He said the project was almost completed and would be reviewed for approval in a couple of months. I would go there for a short time and then would be reassigned to another project. The pay offer was quite favorable, compared to my salary at the University. After an hour of discussions about the project and other details, I left, saying I would talk it over with my wife and call them back. Later I learned that Ryals had called the Holmes and Narver personnel office in Los Angeles, and I was pleased that I had a clean record there.

As we arrived back in Alabama, we had some serious talking to do. First Bea and I sat down and had a long discussion of the options.

I was very happy with my work at the University, and it had been great to live in Birmingham again. But the old bugaboo, economics, was the big issue. We both could see that more income would be necessary in the not-too-distant future as our two approached college age. Bea made it clear she wanted no more long separations and I certainly agreed. It would be only a temporary assignment in Greenland, and then I assured her we would go together to my next assignment. Under those conditions we decided I should take the offer. But then I had to break the news to my friend and boss and the university administration.

Andy was not pleased, but as a fair-minded gentleman he said he understood my needs for a better income and future. He even said he envied me to be ready to take on such a challenge. I agreed to work for two weeks while he hired a replacement. We parted as good friends and Andy was always glad to hear from me after I made the big change in my career.

I also went by and thanked Dr. Frommeyer for his friendship and support during my time at the hospital. Dr. Volker, the president, wanted to spend more time discussing every detail of my plans and was not only supportive but apologetic about not being able to match the financial remuneration of the new job. He assured me that he knew my education and experience far exceeded my formal degrees, but he was constrained in promoting me for that reason. He wished me the best as I left for unknown adventures.

As I worked out my two weeks' notice, we had a little time to shop for winter clothing. Weekends we visited our families as I prepared to see another of the most isolated parts of the planet. I vowed this would be my last separation from Bea and the two children. Steve seemed especially miffed as he asked, "Daddy, do you hafta?" I can only answer, "Yes I thought I did, Steve."

Chapter 12
One Night and One Day in Thule

It was another sad goodbye to Bea, Lynda and Steve on that September day in 1959. As I got on the plane to Washington, I came close to changing my mind and turning around before takeoff. If I had known the assignment would be half as bad as it turned out to be I would have; I'm sure I would have. (Now in 2003 as I reread my files from 1960, I find it impossible to overstate the problems both technical and personal. The chore of reliving that experience—including the worst winter weather on earth—is, even now, depressing.)

In the Washington office of Page Communications Engineers, I was rushed through the paper work and then came the final briefing by Captain Conaughty and Joe Ryals. The project was called "DEW Drop," because it was an extension of the communications from the Distant Early Warning, or "DEW Line" radar network which crossed northern Canada and alerted our Air Force about aircraft intrusions. However the DEW Line radar did not warn against the launching of missiles from Russia and that was the purpose of the Ballistic Missile Early Warning System (BMEWS) in Thule. Page was a subcontractor for the installation and initial operation of the system's communications to the US. General Electric was the prime contractor, with some personnel at the site in Greenland. Conaughty impressed upon me that it was of the greatest importance to get the equipment ready for the final inspection and acceptance by the Air Force officials which were scheduled for late November. There remained several problems with equipment which were aggravated by the severely cold temperatures and by winter winds. Complete darkness would come in early November, and the sun would not reappear until February. As they said goodbye, Captain Conaughty said, "Ernie, study and learn as much as you can about the system because it might not pass the acceptance tests." That statement was to haunt me in two important ways. The nickname, Ernie, he picked up from my first name, Earnal, was to stick with me for many years, and the part about possibly failing acceptance was prophetic of the future of the project and myself.

The flight to Greenland was an experience in itself. First I took a commercial plane to Montreal, Canada, and then was picked up by a military vehicle and taken across the airfield to board a military plane. This one headed due north to Goose Bay, Labrador where we stopped for refueling at this northern outpost. From there we headed due north once again for several hours over ice-covered Baffin Island, then the across Baffin Bay which was also mostly ice and icebergs. We landed at Thule Air Base, about 700 miles from the North Pole, in mid afternoon. It was already dark and very cold and windy, and I was given an olive drab fur-lined parka when I exited the plane. In the terminal I was met by Jerry Bunch from the Page crew. He said he worked on the "P" Mountain project, and we got into the cab of a 1½-ton Chevrolet truck which had the motor running. He explained that if he turned off the engine it would probably not start again without a connection to a power outlet for keeping the engine warm.

Figure 23. Thule

As he drove through the base I could see that all buildings were metal, and Jerry explained that most were made of aluminum panels which were insulated like a large refrigerator. As we passed the officers club, I was astounded to see two palm trees at the entrance. He said that they were real and were brought here by some enterprising officer; they survived because steam pipes from the

One Night and One Day in Thule

building's heating system were running through their roots. Jerry said he and others often spent an evening at the club to get away from the desolate "P" Mountain site.

I thought, "This place is some vacation spot!" Jerry was a retired Navy officer, about 40 years old, who had signed on to get some electronic experience. As we headed into the open road (if one could call it a road) he pointed to our left where we saw a silhouette of a large installation. It was the BMEWS super radar site.

This billion dollar installation was being completed, and our project would relay its data to an air base in Nebraska where it would be fed into computers. It was intended to give warning of any missile as it left the ground in the Soviet Union. Jerry mentioned that he had heard the pressure was on to get our project finished and working by the time this big system was completed. But he also expressed doubt our DEW Drop project would pass inspection. As we drove along the unimproved road, I noticed small buildings at intervals. Jerry explained that they were stocked with emergency food, water, etc and were located at each mile marker so that a vehicle would never be more than a half mile from one. He said that in winter the blowing ice off the cap sometimes would be blinding. It was a condition they called "whiteout," which sometimes caused vertigo when one lost all sense of direction, even up and down. Jerry said the emergency stations had heat available and a phone for use in bad weather. He assured (warned) me that it would be used several times during the winter. Jerry had been there for a year and wanted to remain long enough to qualify for tax-free status, but wondered if he could stand much more of the isolation. I hoped he would because he seemed to be someone I could relate to.

We began a steep winding road up the mountain, and I sighted some little animals which Jerry said were arctic foxes. They, and an occasional polar bear, were the only animals he had seen. Then we arrived at my new home.

The site included a large dome enclosing a radar station for aircraft observance and a building with some wings which housed the several dozen air force personnel who operated and maintained the site. Our dozen men and the few from General Electric were housed in one wing of the building. It also included all support facilities such as kitchen, mess hall, recreation room, heating equipment and the electric generator. Space was at a premium, and my room was barely big enough for two stacked bunks and a small desk. Our bath was another room which we shared with the whole crew. I had the upper bunk, and Tony Demao, from Philadelphia, was in the lower as he had seniority. The only other building was located a hundred yards away and enclosed the DEW Drop equipment. Nearby and connected by a "cattle pass" tunnel stood two huge parabolic shapes which were our antennae. The tunnel, I learned, was for getting there during inclement weather. The word *inclement* in this case meant when one could not breathe in open air because of the wind-chill conditions.

The DEW Drop system, which had been tested in the US between mountains in Massachusetts and North Carolina, was the world's longest tropospheric-scatter link. It stretched the state of the art to build a wide band ultra high frequency link for 700 miles over the frozen Arctic between Thule and Cape Dyer on Baffin Island in northern Canada. It was a single sideband, quadruple diversity, circuit utilizing at each terminal two 50-kilowatt klystron amplifiers feeding two 120-foot parabolic reflectors.

At dinner, a typical military café style meal, I met some more members of the crew. They were: Sullivan, a rugged individual from Massachusetts; Gilbert from Ohio; Ralph Gaze, a brainy young Page engineer; Jerry Bunch from Virginia; and the GE supervisor, John Fox. I listened as they discussed the project and its problems. The leaks in the building were not considered our problem because another contractor, Greenland Contractors, was responsible for it. But the diesels were not performing well, and some dehydrators had failed; the supplier was working on them. The biggest troubles were with noise spikes in the receivers caused by some unknown source, and some other technical problems connected with the cold and windy weather conditions. It appeared to me the morale of the working crew might be another area of concern. Many of them had been there for a year, and they seemed to be ready for a rest or perhaps another place to work. I could understand how this place could contribute to such feelings. After dinner I went to the recreation room and wrote Bea some of my impressions. However, I tried to keep them as positive as possible.

I went to bed and tried to sleep in that semi-private little room. It was a depressing situation, but I vowed to survive it, and I hoped it would only last a few more weeks. After the long trip I was exhausted, so sleep finally overtook me.

The next morning I accompanied the crew to the project station and got my first look. The big room was full of impressive high powered transmitters, racks of receivers and other equipment, and a big control console. But much of the equipment was in complete disarray in the haste of trouble-shooting by the crew. Everyone seemed to be occupied with no time for questions from a newcomer, so I sat down and began reading manuals.

At noon I went outside and saw Greenland for the first time in daylight. The sun was low in the southern horizon at midday in September, when daylight lasted about three hours. Looking east I could see the ice cap which seemed to stretch to the far horizon and from north to east and to south. The other half of my panorama included rugged hills, blue icy ocean and Thule, with a dim view of a glacier to the north. I wondered if I would get a closer look. It was an interesting view from our mountain top, but without vegetation or other forms of life, it could become depressing, I thought.

Figure 24. Keep Greenland Green

Greenland was discovered by early Viking explorers in the 10th century. They seemed to have abandoned it in the 15th century. Some 200 years later, after much temporary exploration by various countries, the Danes began settling some places along the southern coast. It is still under Danish control. The northern part around Thule had been explored, and a small Eskimo village was there. During World War II, the Germans occupied Denmark. Then the Danish minister to the US, Henrik Kauffmann, signed an agreement making Greenland a temporary protectorate of the US. A weather station and some bases were then installed. After the war, the Danish government allowed the US to establish a NATO airbase at Thule. At that time the 338 Eskimos were all moved to a place 50 miles to the north because they had little natural resistance to germs carried by outsiders.

Greenland, the world's largest island, is 90 percent covered by a permanent ice cap which is over a mile deep in places. The weight of this ice causes internal heating which creates glacial movement into the several fjords. These glaciers have been measured to creep at about an inch per minute, a movement not easily visible. However, it creates creaking sounds and loud cracking and splashes as huge blocks of ice break away and fall into the ocean.

The tropo scatter system was somewhat similar to the Eniwetok-to-Bikini circuit except much more powerful and sophisticated. I could easily understand it, and we all knew its shortcomings. In calm weather it worked fairly well, but when the wind blew, we experienced the spiking interference with reception that made the circuits hardly useable. The theory was that wind induced movement of the big six-inch coaxial transmission lines would cause resistance changes at the joints and with this the high currents and voltages created the spiking condition. This was worsened because the transmitters and receivers used a common antenna/transmission line to the common antennae. In order to make this possible the designers had developed a filtering system which was state of the art. Everything had to be tuned perfectly for this to work. Some of us thought if we could weld the joints of the transmission lines it would eliminate the problem. But that was a project that took time and

One Night and One Day in Thule

special welding equipment, neither of which was available before the acceptance date. The strategy seemed to be to just hope for good weather during the acceptance tests. I wondered if this was a valid approach. I thought we should just ask for a few months delay and do it right, but as a newcomer, I had very little input in the decisions. I was also not eager to delay going back home.

In late November, the sun was barely visible at noon. Soon it would disappear for three months. As luck would have it, the winter weather came as the officials and engineers arrived for the acceptance tests. The system failed on several counts. Some of the crew gave notice. Things were serious on "P" mountain. The BMEWS over-the-horizon radar was ready to go, but the weak link was our circuit down to Cape Dyer. I was sure there was great pressure from on high to start operating for the protection of our country. Everyone was sworn to secrecy about this delay, for obvious reasons.

Our phone rang and someone looked at me and said, "It's for you." Captain Conaughty's voice sounded solemn as he said, "Ernie, I would like you to stay up there as site supervisor and retrofit the system." I was dumbfounded and answered, "I'll study the situation." Then he started a rundown of personnel as he visualized it. He would hire new people as he could find them and would give full support from his vantage point in Washington. I knew he was well connected there and in the military around the world.

As I sat and considered the problem and jotted down some things that would need to be done, I thought of my promise to my family to get back as soon as possible. On the other hand, this was an opportunity that would help or hinder my career depending on how I could handle it. If I gave up and quit, it would certainly be negative. I had never walked away from a technical challenge. I wanted to discuss it with Bea, but that was not possible, and besides, I knew she would support my decision.

The biggest problem would be to keep skilled people up there during the darkness, cold and isolation of months of winter when a few drinks at the bar might cause one to decide it just wasn't worth it and to catch a plane south. The technical problem was solvable if we could get the fast cooperation of military people. But I had enough experience to know of the paperwork and other delays to expect in that area. I could expect some resentment from the crew, all of whom had seniority over me. The mixed crew of Page and General Electric people would require careful footwork as I dealt with the prime contractor group. It would be another winter of isolation for the holiday season.

During the Thanksgiving holidays as we ate the turkey and dressing, I began a survey of all the crew. Then I sat down and wrote Captain Conaughty my analysis of how each man would fit into the effort, and in some cases, the facts of why they would not be willing to stay through the winter. I expected to lose about a third of the crew. We could use four replacements if experienced people could be found, and I knew this was doubtful. We had a two-man crew down in Thule to handle terminal equipment and one, Gilbert, would be brought up to the mountain because he was one of the best. Old timer engineers such as Bernie O'Brien would be asked to come up for short stays. I was confident I could get good work from the GE technical staff.

On the Sunday after Thanksgiving I was invited to go down and take a tour of the huge BMEWS project. I had only seen it from a distance and knew it was the largest and most expensive electronic project in history. It included acres of super-gain parabolic antennae and what seemed like acres of the world's highest powered transmitting station. My memory is of some 64 klystrons, each at 75 kilowatts average power; each had more than a megawatt of peak power. The project had a system of radio frequency radiation locks for protection because of the health hazard. The area in front of the antenna beam was "no man's land" for many miles ahead. I had the thought that it could create some ice cap melting, but perhaps that was a stretch.

Here's a story I heard from one of the engineers on the project: the day they turned the radar on, it detected something moving westward from the direction of Russia at a tremendous speed. There was panic in the control room because it appeared to be something that should be reported to the Air Force as an unidentified vehicle of a very suspicious nature. Then a clever analyst was able to determine

One Night and One Day in Thule

that it was the moon! The system measured out to 10,000 kilometers and then would repeat this distance. So anything beyond would seem to be between zero and 10,000 km.

The engineers were interested in how long our retrofit would take so that the raw data could be transmitted to the US for expert and computer analysis. I could only say, "As soon as possible."

As winter moved in I was faced with a bigger personnel problem. Our reduced crew was stretched between station operation and daytime retrofit work. It became necessary to keep the big transmitters operating around the clock only for heating the building. Things would freeze up as the temperature was already well below zero Fahrenheit. The problem of finding a helio-arc welder (necessary for welding the aluminum transmission line coax) was becoming a farce. It seemed everyone was urgently trying to locate one, and we had false leads of one being in Thule. There was so much red tape in getting anything from the military, I was getting very discouraged.

Another Christmas away from family; this time up in Santa's neighborhood. I went with the new GE supervisor, Percy Jolotta and some others to the officers club in Thule to celebrate. Percy was someone with good knowledge and a great sense of humor, so I was happy to see him moved up from the other end of our circuit, Cape Dyer, Baffin Island. While at the club I ran into an old friend from Eniwetok, Major Rodby, who had been transferred to Thule as head of the communications unit, AACS. I said, "Hey, old friend, I would like to talk some business with you soon."

Figure 25. Christmas 1959 (on sofa, from left: Anita Stewart, Nell Stewart, Henry McCullar, Grandma Jones; on floor from left: Lynda, Bob Stewart, Steve, Robert Stewart, Clara McCullar)

We had been trying for weeks to locate a helio-arc welder. The GE people had taken over the chase and had gotten the same runaround from the military. The latest was that they would have to get the Pentagon's OK to study the need. Then it would have to be budgeted and ordered. I went down to Thule and had a talk with Major Rodby. I knew from dealing with him in Eniwetok that he was a man willing to stick his neck out to get things done. He made a call and wrote a memo. Then in three days we had a nice 200 amp welder which came just in time for the welder who was arriving soon. We had what we needed to get a major part of our fix done within a month, at practically no expense. Since I knew that I had gone outside channels, I sent a report to Captain Conaughty with an apology. He fired back a congratulatory answer with many kind words. This did wonders for my sagging morale there in the middle of a three-month night.

The Chevrolet truck we were using began to show that it was as poorly adapted to this environment as I was. The oil got so thick that, as the temperature reached 50 below zero, the starter would not turn over the engine. We had to push it down the steep hill on the way to Thule. Then the tubeless tires froze and would not hold air. All attempts to get service failed, and I had the pickup brought up from Thule. Everyone just had to walk down there for a few days while we were in the midst of the retrofit work. Then I was able to beg a Herman Nelson gas fired outside heater so that our work in the tunnels could continue.

The final three paragraphs from my weekly report of January 7, 1960, to Captain Conaughty read:

We made it through the Christmas holidays without too much trouble. One small incident that I suppose should be reported to you. We had a rumor going around that the mail service would be cut off during the holiday season. After a night at the club, Jerry Bunch decided to do something about it. After making several calls to try to find information, he called the Base Commander, Col. Compton. This would be all right except for the hour which was after the Colonel had gone to bed. I guess it didn't set too well with the good Colonel. Jerry called him back the next day with an apology and told me about it. I also apologized to him for the company and he said he would forget about it under the circumstances. Since the story had been making the rounds here I thought I should give you the straight dope on it.

During the Christmas Season I spent twenty dollars on steaks at the Thule Officers club for the Page and GE crews along with some Air Force people. I'll report this on my next expense voucher since I think it is for the good of the project.

Thanks for all the encouraging letters, Captain. I have told my wife that if it were not for your encouragement and understanding and hers that I might not make it here when things get really rugged. And as you know, this place has its little disadvantages at times. But I try to make up for my shortcomings with determination.

Signed,
Ernie Campbell

Site Supervisor

A running joke was the promise that we would have a party and celebrate when we first saw the sun. Every day Jerry Bunch would walk into the bar and announce, "I just saw the sun; the drinks are on me!" Then finally on a late January day, someone saw just a bit of it for a few minutes. The party began and even I had a couple of drinks. I made a picture of the glow from the sun under the horizon. I was looking through our antenna to the south at noon during January. I have a drawing I made of it as my only contribution to art and as a reminder of that horrible three months of complete darkness.

Just as things were looking good for the retrofit, the weather moved in with a vengeance. A wind which began on the first of February quickly reached gale force. In the cold air, it became impossible to breathe outside the building. It was my first experience with phase-three weather—when we were restricted to staying inside. All roads were closed, and we had two of our crew stranded in one of the emergency buildings half way to Thule. But they had heat and food and the phone connection, so we felt they were secure for a few days. The two on duty at our transmitter building that night were stranded without replacement for the duration of phase-three weather.

The next day the winds got stronger; by midnight of February 2, the one surviving anemometer was stuck at full scale, 175 mph, for hours. The other two had been blown away and never found. Then one wing of the building had to be abandoned because it was breaking up in places. All we could do was sit around and worry or in my case, pray. I was reminded of the severe arctic storm as the SS *Henry Bacon* rounded northern Norway in February 1945. Only this wind seemed stronger with the ice blowing off the Greenland Ice Cap and getting into our building through every small crack and crevice. One could only speculate about what would happen if the building collapsed.

On the third day the winds decreased to merely gale force, but it was a full week before we could get down to Thule and to rescue the two who were stranded. Some of us made a quick dash to the DEW

Drop building on the fourth day, and the two on duty there got relief and some rest and sleep. But, in a way they could have been lucky to be in that building. An inspection team from Thule determined that the main living quarters barely survived the storm, but the DEW Drop Building was stronger and not in any danger of collapse.

By March we were seeing a few hours of daylight and morale was improving. Some personnel were being given a few week's leave. However, my friend Jerry Bunch got upset and resigned after an evening at the club. Other people also seemed shaky. By April, as we were winding down the rebuilding program, it seemed the long dark winter and severe weather were taking their toll. An engineer at the Thule Base, Al Galuppi, wrote a long letter of complaint about a personnel transfer I had made along with other complaints about me. I tried to get it straightened out, but eventually he resigned and left.

My own nerves were tattered, and I took Captain Conaughty's offer of a few days leave and caught a flight out. There was no time to get word to Bea, and I was in no condition to think it through, so it was a surprise when I arrived after midnight to be greeted by her and a house full of Lynda's friends who were enjoying a sleepover.

It was great to spend a short time with my family and catch up on all their activities. Both Lynda and Steve were doing well in school, and Bea had kept active with the duties of a "single parent." Steve was growing and looking forward to another year of Little League baseball with his Red Sox team. The time was a great healer as I completely forgot about the horrors of living in the strange conditions I had experienced over the past eight months. Then suddenly my time at home was up, and I caught a plane to Washington for a day of conferences.

The project was going well, and we had set the acceptance tests for June. Captain Conaughty was happy to be back from the Far East where he had been on another project for a couple of months. He planned to go to Thule with the acceptance party. When the time came, though, he had other commitments and his assistant, Joe Ryals, stood in for him at the ceremony. Joe told me that I should continue in Greenland until autumn when they had further plans for me. I hoped it would be somewhere that I could take my family so I could continue with the company. Otherwise, I would once again look around for alternatives in the continuation of my career.

May was a busy month as we put the circuits into operation to the delight of the Air Force people. It was a great relief to get that pressure off our backs as we began to make the building spic and span. The acceptance tests were only a formality as everyone celebrated our success as well as surviving the toughest winter imaginable.

The combined crew from Page and General Electric had worked well. Percy Jollotta and I had become great friends and never allowed the petty personnel arguments between the crews to become a great crisis. Now that the construction phase was over, the two companies became rivals as they put in bids for the maintenance and operation contract. We at Page had the advantage of having more skilled people on site, but General Electric had been prime contractor, and the larger organization carried more weight with the government.

Percy started a training program, and I did the same with the Page crew. One can imagine the possibilities for problems as we worked and lived together. But I must say that he and I never had a harsh word, and we continued as good friends. The weather improved and as summer approached we had 24 hours of sunshine and temperatures in the 50s and even up to 60 on rare occasions. I built a flower box and transplanted some arctic cotton into it since that was the only flora we had within many miles of "P" Mountain. Each day I gave it water and some plant food.

On Sundays we often made excursions to the ice cap or just for long walks over the rocks and tundra. We saw many arctic fox which were desperately scrounging for food, but fortunately we never encountered a dreaded polar bear as some others had and were lucky to escape with their lives. On Independence Day, Percy and I took some of our crew on an excursion to the glacier north of Thule. We drove the Chevy truck as far as possible then began our hike. After an hour we reached the edge of a canyon and we could see the glacier. After another two hours of struggling down rugged rocks while slipping and sliding, we finally reached our destination. The glacier was a beautiful sight, with its hundred-foot sheer edge of multicolored ice. We heard the constant creaking and cracking as it inched its way to the Artic Ocean. At intervals we saw huge bergs of ice break off and cause waves as they sank and then floated to the surface as icebergs on their way to the open sea. I accompanied a few of the men around and up on top of the glacier. We waved to our more cautious friends who waited below. As we walked close enough to see pieces breaking off, we turned around and retraced our steps. We began to question the wisdom of this extra trek as we had to begin the long uphill climb with depleted energy.

Figure 26. Spud at the Thule Glacier

After an hour of climbing, I was so tired and out of breath that I remembered my day-long walk with my brother, Julian, as a ten-year-old boy in Alabama. I stumbled on, desperately fearing I would not be able to continue. Then suddenly I got "second wind," as I had experienced in high school football practice in my youth. My breathing was easy and normal, just as it was on that fateful day in the Arctic when the *Henry Bacon* was sinking. The strange sensation enabled me to continue with ease. As we reached the top, we found some signs of previous visits by Americans—some unopened cans of GI "C" rations. We opened them and our hungry crew enjoyed a meal that had been under natural refrigeration for a dozen years. This energized us for the remaining two hours of walking. It was nearing midnight when we got to Thule and decided to go to the officers' club.

We were experiencing the flip side of total darkness, and we watched the sun circle all day. At midnight it was low to the north, and at noon, high and south. All rooms were darkened at "night" so we could experience normal darkness. I can tell you it was a weird feeling after a big dinner at the officers' club and conversation over drinks until after midnight—then to walk out into bright sunlight.

In August, Percy Jollotta was transferred back to his home office. I said goodbye and we have had no contact since. I have often wished we had continued our friendship because we seemed to have so much in common. Then I began to seriously plan for my return to the US. Captain Conaughty asked me to stay until the end of September, and I did.

I departed Thule on October 1, 1960, which was the day the big radar system officially went into operation with everything apparently working well. My trip was good except for an incident as we left Goose Bay, Labrador and had traveled south for an hour. I noticed that one engine on my side suddenly showed oil leaking and was stopped. In a few minutes the other engine on that wing did the same. The pilot announced that we would be dumping fuel and would return to Goose Bay. We limped back on two engines and landed safely. In several hours another plane was readied and we continued on to Washington.

Chapter 13
Washington

In Washington I found a hotel and called Bea. She was thrilled that I would be home in a few days, and I was more than thrilled to be working in the US again. I told her I had heard about a house for rent and I would look at it the next day. Bea reminded me it should be near good schools; it was too bad that our two once again would be required to switch schools after the year had begun. I had her put Lynda and Steve on so I could talk with them. They were both excited about moving to our nation's capital, and Steve wanted to know if they played Little League up there. I said I was sure they did. I went to bed, thankful to be back in my own country again. Getting back home again was becoming the story of my life.

The next morning I was in the Page office at eight o'clock and had a great reunion with Captain Conaughty and Joe Ryals. They informed me that I was assigned to a team of engineers who were to design the Voice of America relay station destined for Monrovia, Liberia. Page had just been awarded a $12.5 million contract for this design project, and I would be in the transmitter and control group headed by an engineer I had not met named Wildermuth. The Project Manager was Bob DeHart. I was pleased to learn that I would share an office with Bernie O'Brien with whom I had worked off and on during the last year in Thule. After making the rounds of offices and discussing my new assignment, I got to a phone and called the owner of the rental house I was to see. That afternoon he came by and picked me up. We drove from the Page office on Wisconsin Avenue and across the Potomac at Chain Bridge. Then we passed through McLean and at Tyson's Corner turned on Highway 7 to Ashburn in Loudoun County, Virginia. The house was in a development called Potomac Farms, on the river. There were a few houses already completed and occupied. I asked about schools, and he told me Ashburn had an elementary school and the high school was in Leesburg. The best news was that the rent was well within our budget and it was available immediately. The drive out had taken only about 30 minutes but traffic was light in the early afternoon. I wondered how long it would take in morning and afternoon rush hours. But since the owner said he had other prospects, I made a quick decision and signed a one-year contract on the spot.

That evening I called Bea with the news: we would be moving within the month. She said she would be ready. Many things had to be done: our house on Shades Mountain would be sold or rented; we needed a car because Bea had showed her interest in economy by trading the Oldsmobile for a building lot in the area of Vestavia, thus she had been using the little Renault for her errands; our furniture would be transported to Washington, and Bea would have to contact a moving company for an estimate. There was school to think about and our friends to bid goodbye. Her parents would be unhappy; her sister had moved to New Orleans and her brother was married and living in New Mexico. But Bea had gone with me to California and was still willing to live our nomadic life. I said, "I'll be at the Birmingham Airport at seven tomorrow night." I went to bed thinking how lucky I was to have such a family and to be able to live with them again.

The next morning I was again at the Page office at eight and attended a meeting of the design team. The project was urgent and appeared to be ideal for my needs at the time. Bernie and I fixed up our common office, and I gave him deference in placement of desks because he was older and more experienced, and about the nicest gentleman I had known. As I left for National Airport I said, "Bernie, I'll see you in three weeks." I knew that was a short time, but I thought I should get with the project before I was left behind by others who were more experienced engineers.

My family was there at the Birmingham airport as I knew they would be. I threw my luggage into the little ugly bug, and we all went home as fast as the tiny engine would take us. Bea wanted to fix something to eat, but I declined as I had a meal on the plane. First I had to catch up on everything they had been doing. Lynda was a ninth grader at Homewood Junior High School, and Steve was in elementary school at Berry. They were not eager to leave their friends, but both seemed to look forward to living in a place as exciting as Washington. Steve had made the All Star Little League team as I had expected and was trying out for the school football squad. Lynda was taking piano lessons along with other activities. I told them about our house which was only a couple of hundred feet from the river. There was a wooden bridge to a wooded island and that was interesting to us all. We discussed many things we would be able to see in the most historic part of our country. Soon the two students went to bed, and Bea and I had some time to talk about all the things we needed to do before we got on our way north.

We visited Bea's folks in Double Springs and learned that Don, Laura and their two girls were being transferred to Madrid, Spain. Don had been serving in the Air Force for the last 10 years so they were happy to get the family some overseas experience in that pleasant country. My brother Julian and his family had been in London for two years, and they now had three girls as Jean Marie was born there. Don was not taking his Mercury with them to Spain, and we decided to buy it to get us to Washington. I would tow the little Renault behind the Mercury to have the two cars we would need in Ashburn.

My nephew Bill Campbell lived on Shades Mountain, so I asked him if he would act as my surrogate in getting the house rented. We listed it for rent with a real estate agency. Bill was doing us a big favor because of the many small problems which needed attention from time to time. Things were beginning to fall into place for us. In addition to visiting all of our families, we went by to see my friend Arnold Sartain and his family. Then I made a visit with Andy Spear and the people at the medical school and the electronics lab which Andy ran along with a new assistant. Andy was interested in all my activities, and we wished each other well as I said goodbye once again.

Our furniture was loaded in the moving van, which pulled out ahead of us. We hitched the little Renault to the Mercury and loaded the two cars with our personal effects. Our good neighbors were there to say goodbye, and we hit the road for Washington. The first day was uneventful until the Mercury ran out of gas in North Georgia. Don had not told me that the gas gauge was unreliable, and I got no warning until it started sputtering. That's when the little Renault became our lifeboat. I unhitched it and found the nearest station and came back with a few gallons. These things only tend to make life more interesting.

We were all tired on the second day as we arrived at our new home. Bea's first reaction was approval of the selection except for the distance to the city. I explained that I had considered that also, but because of the urgency and lack of other immediate prospects, I closed on this one. Lynda sided with her mother, but Steve and I could see adventure all over the island adjoining our house. A little paddle boat went with the house, and the lease was for only a year. Sorry Bea, next time I will wait for you before making a commitment.

Fortunately our moving van arrived the same day, and as it was unloaded, we began making it a livable home. While Bea and Lynda made beds and found dishes, Steve and I went to Ashburn for groceries. The little country store had most things we would need, but I told Bea that Leesburg might be a place to shop in the future. The following day was a busy one for us all. Bea took the children to their respective schools, and I headed to Page. Even though I left at 7:15, I was a bit late getting there. I began to realize what the traffic in Washington was like. In Thule I could walk to work in two minutes, but that job had other disadvantages.

My desk and the job of becoming familiar with the VOA design project awaited me. However, this was just what I had wanted. Something I could sink my teeth into and prove my ability. Bernie was a great help. He gave me books and charts on government procedures, military specifications and plans for other VOA installations which had been done in the past by Page. The assignment was different from any I had before when I worked with hardware or did troubleshooting by analyzing a schematic diagram of hardware. This was generating ideas and reducing them to symbols or other forms. I was determined to master it.

Washington

As I read government procedures and other manuals, I marveled at the detail we were required to study and record. When finished, the big station would be specified in every detail down to the smallest items. No deviation would be allowed by any contractor except by special permission, which was rare. We had a VOA engineer as liaison for the project; I asked if all this didn't tend to run up the cost. He agreed that it often did, but said it also prevented many cases of inferior product.

My first study was a layout of the control room, which would take days. I had to know the size and shape of many pieces of hardware, some of which had not yet been determined. I worked with other people to help with this design decision. Then finally the jig saw puzzle began to fall into place, and I turned out my first drawing. The finished product was done by a professional draftsman because drafting was never an interest or skill of mine. I continued to enjoy the job. November rolled around; John F. Kennedy was elected president, and there was an air of celebration in the whole city. Even those who opposed him seemed to be optimistic about his administration. Bea and the children remembered meeting Kennedy a year earlier as they ran into him in the tunnel connecting the Senate Office Building with the Capitol. They were impressed that he spent time talking with strangers.

On our first weekend, the whole family explored the island behind our house. A little wooden bridge crossed the short span of 50 feet to an island of more than a hundred acres. It included a 40-acre farm, completely enclosed by forest. On the other side of the island, we saw the main Potomac River and across to the state of Maryland. We were able to see many species of birds and some small animals like rabbits and squirrels.

Later Steve and I went hunting on the island. I had never been a fan of hunting, but it seemed the thing to do since I had a rifle and the game was there. I found a squirrel sitting in a tree and took aim and fired. As I saw the helpless little thing fall from the tree I turned to Steve, who gave me a look that caused me to swear I would never again fire a gun. I wondered why I found the need to do it at that time. We went rowing in our little boat, but no one suggested fishing.

In December the winter set in with a big snowfall that stayed with us through the Christmas holidays. We had a white Christmas and celebrated at home with a tree we had found in the island's forest. The snow restricted travel, and schools were closed for several days, although I was able to get to work most of the time. In the middle of January, 1961, as I was deeply involved in my design of the Voice of America International Broadcasting Relay Station, it again began snowing. By mid-afternoon we were notified the office would be closed and everyone was warned to leave for home.

As I left the parking lot of the Page office building on Wisconsin Avenue, the snow was a couple of inches deep. As the blizzard continued, it became more and more difficult to see. It reminded me of a year ago in Greenland except that the temperature was in the 20s while at Thule it was below zero. Driving was slowed, not only by the conditions, but also because the population of the District was composed of people from all over the country and from around the world who were not experienced driving in snow. As with ship convoys, the speed was restricted to that of the slowest traveler. My Thule and "P" Mountain experience only helped to the extent that I could get around stopped and slow cars. Many cars were already abandoned along the roads.

There were no means of communication from cars in those days, and I could only wonder what it was like at home in Loudoun County. The radio did give some information; I heard that snow removal equipment was inadequate but was clearing most main roads. By 6 pm I had made my way to Tyson's Corner where I turned west on Highway 7 toward Leesburg. Even though traffic was lighter on this two-lane road, it crept at an average of about three miles per hour as the snow continued to fall. At 10 pm I had reached the smaller turnoff road in Ashburn. That road was 12 inches deep in snow and had not been cleared. I abandoned the car and headed out on foot ; the road had few houses and reminded me of the emergency shacks at one mile intervals on the road from Thule to "P" Mountain. A large house halfway to ours was that of the Gore family, headed by a brother of Senator Albert Gore of Tennessee, and the uncle of Al who was later to become Vice President. I trudged on, and some minutes before midnight, I arrived at our house on the Potomac where I was greeted warmly by the three members of my family. Bea fixed coffee and a good meal, and I felt so lucky to be home safely again.

During most of the next week we were snowed in and spent time playing cards and keeping up with weather conditions by television. I was the only one who had played bridge and the family was interested, so we all learned that game with my limited knowledge and the book, "Goren's Hoyle." As our snowed-in isolation lasted for days, I wondered if I should have been more patient and looked for other rental options last October. Some days later we were able to dig out, and I went back to work. Lynda and Steve missed more than 20 days of school that year. That winter is remembered as the "Year of the Blizzard."

Figure 27. Lynda and Steve on the Potomac, 1961

Late January, and it was inaugural time for the new president. John F Kennedy was the youngest and the first Catholic to be elected to that office. Nikita Khrushchev, who had made blustering statements concerning the Soviet Union's increased importance in world affairs, seemed very confident he could out bluff this young man. Kennedy made his famous call for all to "ask not what your country can do for you—ask what you can do for your country." This president soon gained respect both at home and abroad.

The big thaw from the winter's snow and ice caused the river to rage and it came close to flooding our lawn. It didn't make it that high, but it did break the mooring line holding our little boat.

Lynda, Steve and I drove to a point downstream and asked people who might have seen it. One neighbor said that he thought it had been caught near the home of Senator Everett Dirksen. We went to his house and asked him. He was very nice and let us take it without even asking for proof of ownership. It was good to meet a famous person who seemed so easy to talk with. Lynda and Steve drove our little Renault around the open land near our house. They were only 14 and 12, so it was unusual for two so young to be driving, but it was an ideal spot for it, and the little car was almost like a toy; we all enjoyed it.

In March we had a call from Bea's sister, Nell, telling us the tragic news of her husband Bob's heart attack and death. We were stunned to learn that this great friend and brother-in-law had died so young. We immediately made preparations to drive to Birmingham the next day.

By April the Cold War was back on the front pages with Khrushchev making threats about our policy toward Cuba and the Soviets sending the first man into space. A month later the US National Aeronautics and Space Administration announced the sub-orbital flight of Alan Shepard. Once again it was obvious that we lagged behind the Russians in that important research area.

Figure 28. Robert Stewart, Steve and Poujay on the Potomac, Summer 1961

The school year was over, and we unanimously decided to look for a house closer to the city. We spent our weekends looking and chasing leads. In July we found what we wanted in Fairfax. It was larger than the one we had and was in a nice development. We bought it and prepared to move in August. Anita and Robert were visiting us in Potomac Farms during the month of July when we received a call from Nell that Bea's father was seriously ill with peritonitis following an appendectomy. She drove with the four children to Alabama and Don, Bea's brother, came from Spain, and I flew down. His condition worsened, and Henry McCullar died on August 5.

It was a sad time for her family, and Bea and the children stayed a couple of weeks after I had to go back to work. Then I, along with Don, who had returned with me on his way back to Spain, moved our furniture to the new house. Bea still kids me about how things were packed and labeled. It took some weeks to get things organized in the new place.

Living in Fairfax was better, having close neighbors and friends for the children. Shopping and commuting were much more convenient. Our children liked the Fairfax schools and said they would like to settle there for the rest of their school years. All these moves naturally had been tough on their social lives. Many of our neighbors were either military or government employees, and they also had moved many times, but we probably held the record for the past several years. Lynda was in Fairfax High School and was excelling in all subjects, including Latin. Steve was a good student and also enjoyed sports. He broke his finger trying out for football.

At Page, the VOA design project was nearing completion, and I was thinking of what I could be assigned to next. It turned out that the only jobs the company had were two projects which required duty in isolated sites. I began to look around for other opportunities in the Washington area. As usual, I was restricted because of my lack of a college degree even though my experience far exceeded that level.

At Christmas we were visited by Bea's mother and her sister Nell with her two children, Anita and Robert. We all had a great time, and they were interested in seeing all the attractions of the Washington area. But it was a sad time because of the loss of their husbands during the year. Bea kept them busy seeing the points of interest. At night we enjoyed discussing our many good times of the past when we got together at Clara McCullar's house for the greatest meals and when we often picnicked at her Smith Lake cabin. Clara's grandchildren would romp the wilds of the woods and pick wild flowers or swim in the cool water in the hot weather of Alabama summers. They were carefree days that came and went in all our lives.

In January 1962, I left Page and took a job as supervising engineer with a small company, Video Engineering Company of Washington. The president, Norman Selinger, put me in full charge of all projects which included closed circuit and TV cable contracts at various military bases, schools systems and defense plants throughout the eastern half of the US. I did everything from system design to proposals and bids to hiring and supervising the construction crews. When I went to work in the morning, I never knew if I would come home or be in Albany, Georgia or West Virginia that night. At lunch I ate a sandwich and answered the phone at my desk. I marveled at the contrast in my design work at the government project at Page and the way Norm's little firm operated. The differences between government and private company methods and costs would follow me for the rest of my career. Both had their purposes and advantages, but perhaps a combination of the best of both would be ideal.

The little Renault 4CV was beginning to show its age and the starter motor conked out. I found a used one at a junk yard and had it installed. It started again, but during a snowstorm, Bea was hit on one side then the other as she and the other drivers skidded on the icy streets. It was so badly damaged that I decided to junk it. Bea suggested the same junk yard which sold us the starter motor. They bought it for $10 less than I had paid them for the starter some months before. I bought a Volkswagen Karmann Ghia for commuting to work.

One evening in late March, Bea and I were watching our two students as Lynda was doing homework in Latin and Steve in Spanish. We talked of what a great place this was for them to be in a school where they could learn so many valuable lessons just by observing our government operation by sitting in on Congressional hearings and researching at the Library of Congress. Of course we were learning along with them about things we had taken for granted. We kept abreast of events by reading the Washington papers and by simply being in Washington.

One night, the phone rang and I answered it. The voice said, "My name is Perry Esten, You don't know me, but I know a lot about you."

He explained that he represented Radio Free Europe and that he wished to talk with me and my wife about taking a job with the company in Europe. We accepted his invitation to dinner and conversation at the Shoreham Hotel. Perry explained that RFE was a people-to-people radio broadcasting organization which had been operating since the beginning of the Cold War. They broadcast around the clock in six Eastern European languages from studios in Munich, Germany and transmitting relay stations located in Portugal and West Germany. The Portugal station was operated by an American owned company, incorporated in Portugal for political reasons. They had trouble keeping the American technical manager position filled, and that was what he wanted to talk with us about.

He was a bit flattering as he said a friend had recommended us highly as a stable couple who seemed to fit their profile. He said he had also used other means of confirming this information. He laid out a rather attractive salary and benefits package for us to consider. Then we spent an hour discussing the pros and cons of living and working in Europe. Perry had been in Europe for many years, and his background had been similar to mine before going over there. He was also an amateur radio licensee and was quite active on the bands, although I was not at the moment. Perry said he and his wife, Ida, had two young boys who lived with them and were going to school in Europe. Bea and I were interested in the schools and living arrangements in Portugal. He explained that there were three main options for American students: the so-called American School, St. Columbans, was private and was accredited by the New York state school system; the English school, St. Julians, was well attended; and the French *lycée*, Charles Lepierre, was also popular with some who wished to learn that language and culture. He thought his sons actually benefited more than they lost by being away from their native country for some years as they matured. Concerning living conditions, he told us that most foreigners lived along the coastal region west of Lisbon, and in our case, I would be transported by car and driver inland about 40 miles to the transmitter site. I liked Perry immediately and was interested in the offer, but I told him we would talk it over and call him back the next day.

On our way back to Fairfax we discussed the possibility. Bea was understandably cool to the whole idea because of several reasons, and I had to agree on most of them. The first and most important was our two who had been forced to move from school to school so many times in their young lives. We certainly would never again take them out during the school year. Although it never seemed to hurt their education, we knew it was emotionally disturbing for them to always leave old friends and have to fit in with new ones. Bea's mother and sister were both recently widowed, and she didn't want to be so far away from them, especially at this time. We had bought a new house and were settled in our neighborhood in Fairfax. Portugal was to all of us the great unknown. To me, however, that was more of a plus than a minus. We decided to call back and tell Perry we declined the offer, although it was difficult for me because it seemed to be just what I wanted and needed in my quest for settling into a good career.

In late March Bea and I took a few days vacation and flew up to New York City. We saw some Broadway shows and on the 29th had our 17th anniversary dinner at the Four Seasons. It was decorated for the spring season with live blooming peach trees, and our meals were the best. It had been a bittersweet 17 years as I had struggled to earn a living and to be a good husband and father. I thanked her for being so patient with me.

April 1962 was a very busy month for me, and I was on the road during the week. On weekends we drove around and enjoyed the area. I met an Eastern Airlines pilot who had formed a little flying club and was teaching the members to get their private flying licenses. I don't remember his name, but he convinced me this was just what I needed as I approached the midlife crisis age of 40. Flying was something I always wanted to learn to do. So on Saturdays I went flying with him in the little four-seat TriPacer plane the club owned.

The consulting partnership of Kershner and Wright called on me and at lunch they discussed the Radio Free Europe position I had been offered previously. These two engineers had a reputation of being the best experts in doing specialized short wave antenna and other systems used in international broadcasting. They had been retained to help fill the Portuguese position and specifically to offer me an even better salary structure. I listened and was convinced that it was what I needed to finally realize my goal of security and assurance of being able to educate two very bright young people. I talked it over with Bea and our students. I voted yes, Bea no, Steve no, and Lynda abstained. The motion lost, and I continued with my busy life of travel and flying. By then, I had soloed and had flown short trips with many takeoffs and landings at the little Rose Valley Airport in Prince Georges County, Maryland.

The next two months passed quickly with all the travel for supervising projects and getting in some flight time on weekends. Then in late June, the Deputy Director of Engineering, Meredith Kerner, of the New York office of Radio Free Europe called and notified me that they wanted to talk with me urgently. The message was that they were forwarding to me a "final offer" contract for me to sign if I wished to take the position in Portugal. Once again the pay offer was raised; I felt it would solve many of my problems, not the least of which was the fact that my present job had become very physically taxing as I was expected to handle too many things in a day. The family had another democratic session to discuss and vote on the proposal. This time the vote came out one yea, two reluctant yeas and an "OK, if you must" from the youngest. Steve wasn't too sure the athletic possibilities would be "All American" over there.

My flight instructor and I flew to Newark along with Lynda and Steve in the little TriPacer, then went into New York. There I signed the papers for working in Europe for the next two years. (Bea had agreed to that much time away from our beloved country.) I also was not sure I was doing the right thing by agreeing to move my family to an unknown situation in this very important time of their development. However, early on I had set my priorities to give them the best in everything including a good education. When I first agreed to go overseas to Eniwetok, the pattern for my career was set. At that time I thought this was the right course for us to have the good life I felt we deserved, and now getting this offer of having my family with me seemed great. The next few weeks were hectic. First we needed to put the house up for sale, and I gave notice to my employer.

RFE was sending us over by ship on the Italian line cruse ship *Vulcania* and this pleased all of us. It would bring back memories of the years I spent at sea, and I would have my family with me for a change. I was feeling very lucky with the big turn of events in our lives.

As I completed my work, Bea, Lynda and Steve went by car to spend as much time with her family as possible. Then I flew down and we all had a great time with both our families. While we were in Alabama, we attended the second reunion of the extended George and Martha Campbell family at the Holiday Inn in Jasper, Alabama. It was the first since that wartime day in 1944 when all 12 of their children got together for the first time. There were people there from many states, and the total number was close to a hundred. On the last evening we had a program, and as it ended, we planned to have another reunion in two years. We went back to Fairfax to prepare for the move. The house was advertised, "For Sale by Owner" in the following Sunday edition of the *Washington Post*. We sold many personal items like one car and the bikes to our neighbors. I had Friday and one weekend left to get in my cross-country solo flight and get checked out by an FAA official for being a licensed single engine pilot.

It was a typical July day with thunderstorms as I left on my solo cross country flight. The first leg down to Fredericksburg, Virginia was uneventful. I took off toward Cambridge, Maryland as the weather worsened, and I had to divert south to get around a big thunderstorm. As I crossed the Chesapeake Bay, my fuel was low. I finally saw the runway of the airport, but it had an "X" painted at the end indicating it was closed. My fuel gauge read empty so I landed anyhow and taxied up to the little building. A worker told me there was no gas available there, but across town the other airport had gas. Without too much thought I took off on an empty tank for the 10-mile flight, and luckily I made it. I told my story to the attendant. He introduced himself as the local FAA inspector. Oops! I had visions of this being the end of my flight career, but he only warned me to be more careful, and I took off again for the long flight over water back to Rose Valley Airport.

My instructor called several states to get me checked out on the next day, which was a Saturday. Finally he found one willing to do it on a stormy Saturday, but it was in Frederick, Maryland. He passed me, although he skipped the stalls because he didn't want to fly high enough in that weather to perform that exercise. Things seemed to be falling into place as the house sold to the third caller the next day. On Monday we made arrangements to store our furniture, and we packed the Mercury for the trip to New York. We also bought and packed several large steamer trunks with our personal items and shipped them to New York.

We first drove to Maguire Air Base in New Jersey for an overnight visit with my brother Julian, Marie and their three girls—Teresa, Martha and the young Jean Marie. The next day we drove to New York City and checked in at the Pennsylvania Hotel. From there I took the Mercury to dealers and finally found one who would give me a little money for it. I breathed a sigh of relief because we had only one day left before boarding the ship for Europe. I made a last quick trip to the RFE office for a final checkout. I was told that we would be met in Lisbon by Henry Lolliot, the head honcho who "Worked in marvelous ways his wonders to perform." I was later to learn what they meant by this cryptic remark.

Julian and Marie drove up from New Jersey, and we had dinner together at the hotel on the night before our departure. They gave us some ideas of what it was like living and working in a foreign country for an extended time. We and they were sorry that our overseas times were not simultaneous so that we could visit each other. We said goodbye to them and went to bed for the last night in the US for a couple of years.

Chapter 14
Portugal

As the taxi traversed the many turns through the busy New York streets, I thought of the other times I had boarded a strange ship for unknown destinations. I was very thankful that I could have my family with me this time. However, the other members probably had other thoughts and misgivings about this adventure.

The Italian liner *Vulcania* was not new. She was built in the1930s, and it appeared she had made this voyage many times. But our cabin was comfortable, with four single beds and a sofa. We stored our luggage, hung up clothes in the little closet and made a short tour of the ship, with its grand stairways of polished wood leading to the beautiful dining room and other recreational areas. Among people milling about and talking in many strange languages, we went to the outside deck and watched as the crew made ready for departure. The PA system blared, "All ashore who are going ashore." My emotions were mixed as I thought I observed a tear or two in our little group.

The ship's horn sounded loudly as we moved away from the dock and headed past the Statue of Liberty out of the harbor. As we ate a great meal, we headed up the coast toward our first stop at Boston.

As we entered Boston Harbor, I pointed out my previous home of Gallups Island to Bea and the two. We were too far away to see details, but I understand it was not being occupied at that time. In the historic city we saw many sights on the day we went ashore: "Old Ironsides" was impressive, as were the Old North Church and Paul Revere's home. I wished for more time to show them that great city where I had spent much time some 20 years earlier.

The cruise to Portugal on the *Vulcania* was fun for the whole family. The food was always good, and one tended to overeat and put on pounds. Each evening there was live music and other live entertainment. On the final night at sea, Lynda participated in a hat fashion show for the young people. She was dressed up and we were proud of her as she looked great. As we approached the European coast, the weather worsened and Bea got a bit of seasickness. As we entered Lisbon harbor the next day, she slept late, so we were among the last to leave the ship that day.

Figure 29. Dining Well and Often Aboard the Vulcania

We walked down the gangway to the dock to be met by Henry Lolliot and all the American employees of RFE along with their families. It was also our first meeting with Marty Oebbecke, Director of Engineering of that location, Mr. and Mrs. Earl Chubbuck with their two children, Mr. and Mrs. Bob Cotton, Program Supervisor, and Mr. and Mrs. Harold Bowman and their two girls.

We were all transported to a lovely outdoor garden restaurant for a late lunch. It was obvious that Lolliot was the man in charge as he herded us around and led the conversation in his French accent. During lunch we talked about our future life there. We were able to learn many things about the country and the company as we paired off and talked. The young folks were doing the same. Marty Oebbecke and Bob Cotton told us they were golfers and wanted to know if I played. I said I had, but that was many years ago in Birmingham and I certainly was not good at the game. They promised to take me out to the Estoril Golf Club sometime. By the time we got to the Hotel Florida to relax, I (and I'm sure the others) felt a bit overwhelmed.

The next day I went to the Lisbon office for a briefing by Lolliot. He gave me a rundown on the operation which began in the early 1950s. Portugal was selected for the main short wave relay transmitting station because it was an ideal distance from the target countries of Poland, Czechoslovakia, Hungary, Romania and Bulgaria. As a ham radio operator, I knew what he meant because short wave transmission was reflected off the ionosphere and would bounce back to the earth at a particular distance.

There were also other reasons RFE was in this country. The Portuguese government was stable under Antonio Salazar, their "benevolent dictator" for many years who was anticommunist. However, the law required all foreign corporations to be controlled by a local board of directors, so the company there was known as RARET, Inc., short for Radio Retransmissão. There was also a large group of expert advisors for everything from electrical engineering to transportation to security and many other areas. The company employed twice the number that would have been required in the US, but because of the lower wage scales, it was still a bargain for the purpose.

It became obvious that Lolliot's position was mainly political as were the other American positions of the technical operation to some degree. Of course, this was somewhat troubling to me; I had never been trained to be a diplomat. But I knew I could learn in time.

Soon Lolliot got around to discussing our housing, which would be paid by the company. The type and cost were not specified and would be considered according to our needs. He assigned his administrative assistant, Carmen Costa Pereira, to work with us as we got situated.

Carmen had started with the company as a young secretary and was now using her extensive knowledge and strong personality to handle a wide variety of tasks. Her first suggestion was to look at an apartment in Lisbon although all the other Americans, except for Lolliot, lived out in the suburban areas in somewhat of an international community. It was necessary to stand firm and to look in that area for a house. We got help from others to find what we were looking for in the little town of Parede. The house was not large, but was very pretty and well furnished to Bea's satisfaction, although not exactly the type she would have selected. The company signed a one-year lease, and we settled in. The house included a full time maid who lived in a small apartment in back and a part time gardener. Bea had to adjust quickly to a new way of running the household.

My first day of work, I was picked up at 7:00 am by Daniel, our driver, who already had my new boss, Earl Chubbuck, in the Peugeot sedan's rear seat. As he drove us through the heavy traffic of the Marginal (an express road along the waterfront to Lisbon), Earl gave me some insight into my new assignment. I was to become his backup and right arm in the many details of one of the busiest plant operations imaginable. Daniel was an expert driver, using his quick responses and the car's horn to wind through the Lisbon circus of traffic and north onto the Auto Estrada. As Earl continued informing me of the conflicts and pressures of his job, I saw he was overstressed as his brow was often wrinkled into a grimace. I remembered that someone had told me that this job had always been a stepping stone to a return to the US and other employment. I resolved to do my best to relieve some of his load.

Figure 30. Guard Swans at Gloria, with Antennas in Background

At the end of the only super highway in Portugal at Villafranca de Xira, our driver headed east and crossed the Tagus River, passed through several small towns and arrived at the transmitter site, located near the little town of Gloria. We saw a dozen company houses, one of which was assigned as my home when I needed to stay in Gloria. We also saw the 500-acre antenna field which contained high gain directional antennas for beaming our programs to all the countries of Eastern Europe. We entered an enclosed compound where the main transmitter and office building were located, landscaped with a reflecting pool of goldfish and swans. There were several outbuildings for shops, a motor pool and a guard house where a crew of Guarda National (government guards) lived. It was a very clean, impressive plant and larger than I had imagined. Earl pointed to my office and entered his across the hall. I noticed that his desk was loaded with mail and the in-box was full of paper. Mine also had a few memos and other things to read. I could see a steady flow of people going into Earl's office with problems and other matters. I could understand why he looked stressed.

By mid-morning Earl had worked through some of his stack of papers and invited me over to meet some of the staff. First and foremost was the plant superintendent, Engineer Horatio des Campos Neto, commonly known as Neto or just Net. (Titles and status were important in Portugal, but the Americans sometimes simplified them to a degree.) Neto appeared to be on top of everything on the site. Then came Engineer Aleixo Fernandes, who was Neto's assistant specializing in antennas and mechanical work. Joaquin Rodrigues, a distinguished man who spoke with a British accent, was Earl's and my secretary. He was very polite and knowledgeable.

We took a walking tour of the plant, and I saw the big transmitters and shops where people were working. Everyone was so polite and formal that it was beginning to make me think, "This is a bit much and could get old if it continues." (Fortunately it was to become more routine as they got to know me better, and I them. Even today, more than 40 years later, I still look on the Portuguese with love and admiration for their gentleness and good will toward my family.)

It was suddenly lunch time and we four—Earl and I, along with Neto and Aleixo—walked the hundred yards to the mess building. On the first floor, we stopped by the recreation room with its small bar, pool table and card tables. It also had a TV set which usually showed Portuguese language programs but sometimes American movies in English with Portuguese subtitles.

Portugal

Figure 31. Gloria Dining Hall

One flight up was the huge dining room with windows on three sides. In one corner was a larger table where the Americans and Portuguese superintendents ate along with invited guests or visitors. Our waiter, Senhor Maia, was very attentive and efficient. He had been on this job for years and hardly missed a day at work, according to Earl. As we ate the several courses of fish and cheese, fruit and dessert, we talked about the plant and its future. Our transmitters were old and needed more power. No one seemed to be in a hurry to get back to work, and after lunch Earl took me out to his house and showed me the one across the street which was mine. We both went to our respective houses and observed the ritual of *sesta* (the Portuguese *siesta*) by taking a rest or in my case a nap. The lunch hour was an hour and a half. I thought, "The first thing I will have to learn over here is how to relax and enjoy a meal." Back in Washington it was order a sandwich and answer calls as I ate. An hour was a long time to be away from the desk.

I got up from my nap and looked around the comfortable three bedroom house which would have been perfect for our family if it were in the city. Living this far from schools and shopping would not work with a family such as ours. However, we planned to visit it some weekends. We could use the tennis court, read or just stroll over the 500 acres of the antenna farm. I also would spend some nights there instead of driving an hour to get home every day. The after lunch *sesta* became a habit that I have continued to this day. After my first day at Gloria I went with Daniel back to my family in Parede.

It was time to decide the best school for our two. The consensus among Americans we talked with was that the French school was superior, and we decided to let them try it for the first year. We thought learning a foreign language would serve them well in Europe and in their future careers. In retrospect I was remiss in not getting more involved in selecting the school. I should have been more aware of what we were doing to them, especially the 13-year-old son who was so interested in American sports along with his education. He did rebel against wearing the school uniform, or *bota*, a smock which to him looked too much like a dress. Trying to learn a new language before anything else must have been a shock to them both, although I was proud that Lynda was as usual a top student, and Steve also did well.

Learning Portuguese was a high priority for me. I began studying the language with a tutor on the nights I spent in Gloria. It is not an easy language to learn to speak; although very similar to Spanish, the pronunciation is very different and is considered more difficult. We learned that the Portuguese can understand Spanish easier than the Spanish can understand Portuguese. Strangely enough after living there several years and studying Portuguese, I was able to understand Spanish as well or better than I could understand Portuguese.

The international community of the towns of Estoril and Cascais, and also Parede where we lived, included many Americans who worked at the embassy and at American companies. There were also many Britons who had lived in Portugal for generations while still retaining their British citizenship. Historically they owned the port wine industry, and to a large extent, controlled cork production. We met several at social occasions and soon had a good variety of friends with whom we could speak our language. We also had many Portuguese friends who spoke English. Their proficiency made learning the local language more difficult for us because we really could survive without it. But in shopping, Bea found speaking Portuguese was necessary, and daily communications with our maid helped her with this. Meanwhile our children were picking up the language quickly.

Transportation was not a big problem with me being driven to work and to business trips. The rail line to Lisbon was used daily by the students. But Bea needed a car for her shopping, and we looked around for something. A British family let us use their Austin one weekend, and we all four survived the hectic traffic on the *Marginal* to Lisbon. Everything was strange and confusing to me, and I soon found myself going the wrong way on a one way street. A policeman tried to get me to understand what he was saying and soon learned I had no identification. He took us to a nearby police station where no one spoke English. I wrote out the name of our company and the phone number, and he called. He took me all the way to Parede to get my passport and international driver's license while the family waited at the police station. We learned about living in a foreign country mistake by mistake.

We decided to buy the Austin, which was small but comfortable for the four of us. I was more careful about documentation and continued my efforts to learn the language.

My work was interesting and kept me fully occupied during the week. I was beginning to understand why Chubbuck was thinking about getting back to the States. I tried to avoid getting involved in the feuding between the Lisbon office and Gloria that appeared to be a personality conflict between the two offices.

Much of the routine work—such as the approval of all purchases and work orders—was routed to my desk. I was all over the plant as an observer of progress and eventually gained the respect and friendship of all supervisors.

By the weekends I needed a diversion so I joined a local flying club at the little airport at Sintra. We had one Piper Cub which I took up on short flights, but its conventional "tail dragger" landing gear made this more difficult than the TriPacer I had flown previously, which had an easier tricycle landing system. The Cub was so light it was more like a kite and seemed it didn't want to stop flying. One day Harold Bowman, the supervisor of our receiver site, asked if I would take him and his four-year-old son Paul for a ride. I was a bit skeptical because we had only one runway and there was a crosswind that day, making takeoff and especially landing more difficult. But I decided to go up anyhow. After viewing the area and the beaches for 30 minutes, I brought the Cub in for landing. As we touched down the windward wing was a bit high and was still flying while the left one was stalled as they both should have been. We heard the loud screeching of our tires as the plane spun around in a fast 360 degree "ground loop" and stopped within a few dozen feet to end up facing forward on the runway. Harold and I were so scared we could hardly breathe, and little Paul said, "Let's do that again." Needless to say I didn't—I decided to take up golf as a hobby.

October came and we had been in Portugal two months. In Washington, the headlines concerned the Cuban missile crisis. President Kennedy had given Khrushchev an ultimatum to remove the missiles or else. Khrushchev blinked, and the missiles were rapidly loaded aboard ships headed east. The young president gained more respect as the whole world breathed easier.

In Parede, Bea wistfully looked me in the eye and pleaded, "Dear, the vacation is over, let's go home." I realized I had been too busy to notice that her life was not as full as mine. We decided that she should investigate what other wives in similar positions were doing. She mentioned the English/Scottish group which ran a "Trash and Treasure Shop"—a sales campaign of used furniture and clothing to aid the English Hospital. We also decided to visit the Church of Scotland services the next weekend.

Russ Geiger, Director of Engineering of RFE in Munich, came down and I was able to meet him for the first time. Russ told us that Perry Esten had been on leave of absence from RFE and was in Liberia supervising the building of the VOA transmitter relay station which we had designed back in 1961 at Page Communications Engineers. He also had news that we at Gloria would be getting some new 250-kilowatt transmitters next summer and Perry would be back in time to supervise their installation. This was very good news to me and the rest of our crew. He told me that Bea and I would be brought up to Munich to visit the headquarters operation.

A few weeks later as our plane landed in Munich, we were met by Geiger's deputy, Bud Black, and his wife, Delores. They gave us a look at that beautiful city as we traveled to our hotel. We passed by the RFE building and through the edge of the big mid-city park, the *Englisher Garten*, which was a mile long and almost half a mile across. That evening the Blacks took us out to the huge beer hall, the Haufbräuhaus, where Hitler had many of his early gatherings. We began at the lowest floor where several hundred happy people were drinking liter-sized steins of brew, singing or talking loudly. Although it was November, it was similar to the *Oktoberfest* but on a smaller scale. We learned that the fest never ends in that happy city. (I hope they are still celebrating Hitler's demise.) People were dressed in *lederhosen* and work clothes or dressed to the nines. It was our first look at how these people were able to drink and have a good time without fighting, but now and then someone went to sleep. I can think of no better description than "peaceful bedlam." Then we went to other floors, and it became more sedate as we ascended to the top, where I had a delicious dinner of *wiener schnitzel*.

The next day I got my tour of RFE's big *Englisher Garten* building where more than a thousand people worked, including analysts, news specialists, writers, announcers, and many others in special or administrative support activities of this major information dispenser. It was too much to absorb in one session, but I remember seeing the 18 studios where people were talking in several languages with the huge master control routing it to two transmitter sites in Germany and to the largest at Gloria. I remembered many years before in Murmansk as the old interpreter told me how the people were kept in the dark without knowledge of the real world in order to protect the Communist form of government. I formed a mental picture of some Pole or Czech hovering over a small radio trying to understand what was really going on in the outside world through the heavy Soviet noise "jamming." I was proud to play a part in this effort.

I met Executive Vice President Rodney Smith, a retired Army general; Ralph Walter, Vice President of Programming; Hans Fischer, Administration Director; Russ Poole, at that time head of security; Don Brooks, Services Manager, and many others who were later to be close friends.

That evening Russ Geiger and his wife entertained us, and we met more of the people—Ralph Patterson, John Gurr, Varick Steele, Willi Kluehe, Ed Harrington, Ted Bergstrom and their wives, to name a few. As we traveled back to Lisbon, I had a better idea of what RFE was all about.

Back in Portugal, we settled into the winter as work took my time and strength while Bea became active with the Trash and Treasure sale group and our two students studied the French language. That winter I developed a bad case of the flu and spent two days in bed and missed work for that time. Dr. Guzmão came out and gave me some breathing medicine. I attributed it to the cold and damp conditions in our house but who knows. Anyhow, those were the only sick days I missed from work in 20 years at RFE.

As my health returned and the weather began to warm up, I went to the Estoril Golf Club with Bob Cotton and Marty Oebbecke. It was a first class course, and we saw celebrities among the players, like the deposed kings of Spain and of Yugoslavia along with the American Ambassador, Admiral Anderson. The club had no golf carts so we used the caddies who were always around looking to make a few *escudos*. They only earned about 50 cents for carrying a bag for 18 holes. We often tipped them another four bits. There were more foreigners than Portuguese playing the game. Steve took lessons from the Scottish pro and developed a good swing. Once when he was 18, he teed off on the par four 13th hole. His ball went over a hill toward the green which was downhill and some 300 yards away. When we got down to the green, we had not found his ball until his caddy finally found it in the hole. Steve is still gloating about getting a hole in one on a par four. Bea also got a hole in one before me, and she will never let me forget that either. I had to play some 60 years before I finally got a hole in one at Terri Pines in Cullman, Alabama, in September 2003.

Portugal

Figure 32. Estoril Golf Club

In late June 1963, we decided to take a three weeks vacation and do our "Grand Tour" of Europe. We wanted this trip to be special because at that time we had planned to be in Europe for only two years. We loaded the Austin and the four of us started out across central Portugal and into Spain at Badajoz. There we first used our students' language abilities at the border going through routine inspection by the customs police. It was a long day's drive through small Spanish towns to Salamanca where we saw typical Iberian churches and a castle and then found a hotel for the night. The plan was to drive until we saw something of interest, then stop for as long as we liked, and when night came, begin our search for lodging. However, Bea had researched the points of interest, and we went by the route she set out.

In northwestern Spain, we especially enjoyed the city of San Sebastian, where we ate some excellent seafood. We entered France, and our language specialists were useful as the French officials appreciated Americans who tried to speak their beautiful language. The coastal drive up to Bayonne was beautiful.

Our next points of interest were the vineyards and wineries of the Bordeaux region, where it took a whole afternoon to do the underground tour of the wine storage caves at St. Emilion. After our tour of the thousands of bottles and barrels stored in the cool caves, that variety became a favorite for years. The next day we drove to Limoges for a very special reason. Our boisterous young boxer dog,

Feia ("ugly" in Portuguese), had broken a lamp with the Limoges mark on the bottom, a lamp that was very expensive in Portugal. We decided to locate the factory and replace it, which proved to be an adventure; but with the help of our interpreters we managed to complete the mission.

In late afternoon, we started north toward the next goal, the fabled *chateaux* of the Loire River Valley. But it was getting dark, and we began looking for a place to sleep. Nothing was available in the small towns we passed through until we found one in Bellac. The town still stands out in our minds for its lack of proper facilities. Nothing worked in the dark hotel room with its lumpy beds. The toilet was a fright with a somewhat disguised flushing system. The food was something to try to forget. I hate to disparage a town based on our limited experience, but this one has always been synonymous with "bad" in our family.

We were glad to leave Bellac and looked forward to the contrast of the elegant palaces. The first, and one of the most interesting, was Chateau de Chenonceaux which was built over the Cher River in 1515 on the site of an old mill and given by Henry II to Diane de Poitiers, who no doubt had been a good "friend." It came into the possession of Catherine de Medici, who added a gallery above the bridge. The grounds were extensive and very formal. We saw another at Amboise, Leonardo da Vinci's burial site. At Blois, we spent an afternoon at Chateau de Chambord, huge and with a profusion of turrets, pinnacles, elaborately carved chimneys and dormers. The present building was begun in 1526 for Francis I, who spent his last days there, in retirement. These edifices depict a lifestyle of the elite in the 16th century.

We proceeded to Paris and its many points of interest, including Notre Dame, the Louvre museum and the Eiffel Tower. By this time the two students were sick and tired of interpreting, and we kept that to a minimum. Their language ability became increasingly less called on while we were in the non-French-speaking areas of Belgium, the Netherlands, Germany and Switzerland.

Our return was again across the southern part of France and into the principality of Andorra. From there we saw some more of central

Portugal

Spain. Our last night was in a hotel in Zaragosa. While there we saw a bus load of American tourists as they stopped for a meal and the night. Sitting in the lobby, Bea talked with one lady and when Steve came to us the lady said to Steve, "Ah ha, now I know." Then she told us of asking Steve if he spoke English, and he answered, "Ah leetle." Apparently he was tired of talking to strangers.

We arrived back in Parede a little tired but feeling good about all the things we saw and did on the long trip around the continent. Then we learned that Perry Esten was on his way down to install our new transmitters and would bring his family with him.

The year 1963 was a busy time at Gloria as we got our four new 250-kilowatt transmitters. Perry Esten arrived and moved into one of the houses in Gloria. Soon we began enlarging our building and installing the transmitters. Perry and Ida had their younger son, Chris, with them. He was Steve's age, and the two enjoyed the summer at Gloria.

During the summer, the boys proposed a rocket project. They ordered plans from a scientific magazine and built and fueled a rocket about 12 inches long. It was set up on our property with an ignition system which was connected through a switch to a battery. A crowd stood by as they moved 50 feet away for the countdown. At countdown to zero, Steve threw the switch. We saw and heard a blast, and the rocket disappeared. Someone in the crowd said, "Where did it go?" Fortunately another person saw the smoke trail as it zoomed up to a quarter of a mile and landed in the antenna field. The boys built another with similar results. This time we watched closer and saw it as the trajectory took it a half mile away.

Retired Portuguese Air Force Colonel Metello, who worked as our security contact, was interested in their next rocket project. That was to build one five feet long and four inches in diameter. Col. Metello thought this might be a hazard on our property if it traveled five times as high so he contacted his friend who was commander of the Lisbon Air Force Base. As was typical of our Portuguese friends, they were eager to support the boys' project so they invited them to fire it off at the air base. A rather large delegation of adults and young guys assembled at the base, and the rocket was set up. As they were ready for the countdown, the base commander, who had already halted all air traffic at the base, called the Lisbon commercial airport, and they held up traffic for the time it took for the test! This one achieved about the same height and distance as the small one, but everyone was duly impressed as the bigger one could be viewed more easily. However, despite its huge white vapor trail, we never found the rocket after its otherwise-successful maiden voyage.

Figure 33. Preparation and Launch

By the end of our first year in Portugal, our family had become well established in the Church of Scotland in downtown Lisbon. We appreciated Kenneth Tyson, the minister of St. Andrews, whose sermons were of interest to our whole family. Lynda taught a Sunday School class, and I was elected to the board of managers. On special occasions we attended St. Georges Anglican Church where the rector was a cousin of our English friend, Pat Eastwood. Pat and Dick Eastwood became our close friends then and remained so until their deaths. It was also at St. Andrews where Bea first met Gertrude Hunter at the weekly tea where the church women sewed baby clothes for indigent mothers.

By this time I had become well aware of the capability of the Gloria crew. Over the previous dozen years their skills had been honed by their efforts and the American leadership; the entire plant had been built by this staff, and was now self-sustaining. The many large buildings and the antenna field, which contained more than a hundred towers supporting special curtain antennas, were built using local talent and skill. This self-sufficiency was necessary because Portugal, and particularly Gloria, lacked many specialized professional services. Despite its isolation, the Gloria plant grew into a major relay broadcasting facility. We also had a foundry where brass, copper or aluminum castings could be made. I was impressed as I watched our 300 skilled workers, many of whom had been hired from the local village and trained on the job, complete the RFE transmitter expansion program.

Figure 34. Engineer Aleixo

Although all our family was busy, we found time to travel to Madrid where Bea's brother, Don, was stationed with the US Air Force. Their two daughters, Pattie and Debbie, and our two had fun talking about their experiences overseas. Don and Laura also took us to the Prado Art Museum where we enjoyed an afternoon. Later their family returned the favor and visited us in Portugal, and we toured the area with them. Laura especially wanted to see Fatima, where a young girl had a religious vision. We also enjoyed exchanging visits with the Paxtons, who had been our neighbors in Fairfax, Virginia and were living in Spain.

I had been working for RFE for several months when Earl Chubbuck announced he was planning to leave because of personal reasons. With four years of service, he had set the record for an American staying in Gloria, and the pressure was getting to him. I took over as Chief of Transmitter Facilities of one of the largest plants of its type. We now had 21 transmitters of up to 250 kilowatts in power with dozens of antennas beamed to the countries of Eastern Europe. Perry Esten was still there doing final testing of the four new transmitters, and I had the best superintendent in Engineer Neto. I felt confident that we could work as a team to beam these important programs to the information hungry people behind the Iron Curtain.

We had what seemed a constant stream of VIP visitors, mostly from the US. The American staff would always give them a tour of the major facilities along with an explanation of how Portugal had been selected and was built into the main transmitting entity of Radio Free Europe. Gregory Thomas, President of the American division of the Chanel perfume company, had played a large role in the original negotiations and organization of RARET, Inc. He made the trip over as a member of the RFE Board of Directors to Lisbon, where he would visit with his friends. The RARET Americans and top Portuguese were invited to a dinner hosted by these visitors. Mr. Thomas was considered a top American expert on European wines, even by the French. Like many of the early RFE officials, he had been active with the Office of Strategic Services during World War II.

Figure 35. Entertaining at Gloria (Bea, third from left, is between Engineers Neto and Aleixo)

In 1963, Hans Fischer, Director of Administration at Munich Headquarters, came down and briefed me about some of the lesser known operations of the company. He first made me aware of the fact that a major part of our funding was routed through the CIA;

Portugal

the annual Fund Campaign for private contributions was only a part of our support. But the CIA had no control over our broadcast policy. RFE's mission was limited only by our government's desire to "broadcast nothing counter to the foreign policy of the United States of America." The CIA did receive information gleaned from our monitoring of everything broadcast out of the Iron Curtain countries. Also at intervals, we were visited by an "auditing agent" who would not identify himself.

In the following year, President John Richardson of the RFE Fund Committee kicked off their annual campaign by bringing some 20 chairmen and their wives from all parts of the US to look us over before departing for the Munich headquarters. It was a full day as we divided them into small groups and assigned English speaking Portuguese to lead them. Sometimes this made for awkward situations. One young man who had learned his English from books had this assignment: An American lady in distress asked him, "Where is the powder room?" So he pointed over to the Guarda National building where the guards stored ammunition. She realized he misunderstood, so she asked, "Do you have a rest room?" "Yes we have one, but there is a man there sleeping now," he said. Then she exclaimed, "I need a WC!" And finally he got the message as everyone laughed.

The house in Parede was nice and we liked some of its features, but we decided to move to another more suited to our needs in the little town of Cascais. The house was less damp and the rooms were larger, but it had one major disadvantage: the water heater was a wood burner which had to be started and fired each morning. Many times I left before the water had warmed, and I had to make do with cold showers, but I rationalized by thinking, "This is better than Eniwetok or Thule."

At the close of the school year our two students were honored at an evening presentation of awards. Lynda won many first place citations, and Steve usually followed close behind with special mention. This was amazing because we knew how he felt about the curriculum and learning all those French poems. I understand that the *lycée* system is standardized worldwide, with each school giving the same lesson each day. This probably gives a certain discipline to students, but was "foreign" to Americans.

That fall, Bea and I went along with the wishes of our two students, and they entered St. Columbans, the "American" school accredited in the New York system, which was known as "McKenna's School." The private school was wholly owned and operated by Headmaster Anthony McKenna, an Irishman. He was an interesting character who ran a tight ship and often announced that he needed no PTA or other interference by parents. As one can imagine, there was often friction in that area, although the students seemed to like him, and he employed good teachers. The student body was mostly American with a dozen other nationalities also represented. Once he joked, "When I die, I hope to go to heaven and teach little Oriental children. But it will be my luck to go the other way where I will have to take American kids." He was always popular at social occasions because of his wit and candor.

Although our two had done well in the French school, they were more than happy to get back in a more familiar system. This was certainly the case of our young son, Steve. He was suddenly an honor student and found his sports niche in soccer, the top sport of Portugal and most of the world. Steve quickly made the team and sometimes played goalie. He was happy, although he often came home with bruises and stomped off toe nails from this very physical sport. Lynda was glad to begin preparation for her final year in high school.

As we finished dinner on November 22, 1963, the phone rang. Marty Oebbecke said he had heard that President Kennedy had been shot and had died in Dallas, Texas. Later, several of our friends from other countries called and gave us their sympathy and hopes for the future. It was a sad day when one mad person could so affect the history of the world in one senseless act.

A young Yale graduate, Dave Porter, had been hired as my assistant, and he was given some help in getting settled in. It soon became obvious that he would not last long enough to help relieve me of the load of paper work and the other technical and personnel decisions which filled my day. He did offer American coverage on

Portugal

times I was away, but lacked experience with decision-making. It was reported that once when there was a grass fire on the big property, he ordered the Portuguese to stop fighting it at our property lines. His wife and two small children never accepted the living conditions, and he left after one year. But he was still there when we went on our first home leave in 1964.

Our two-year contract would end in the summer of 1964, and we discussed our plans. In my mind the only practical thing was to remain on the job. I had no contacts for seeking employment in the US and was too busy to give it much thought. Bea and the children agreed that we were now "expatriates," so to speak.

Although I was free to leave the company after two years, Bea and I decided we would stay as we both had adjusted to living with the gracious people of Portugal and the international settlements of Cascais and Estoril. This group was enlarged by many Americans who came over to build a big suspension bridge across the Tagus River. We quickly became close friends with the Hunters from Pittsburgh. Bruce was a senior advisor with the bridge division of US Steel Corporation. Bea and Gertrude Hunter also were close, and we traveled with them throughout the Portuguese countryside and up to Oporto in the north of the country. In addition to bringing over people who enriched our social activities, the project was interesting to watch as it became a beautiful bridge, somewhat like the Golden Gate in San Francisco. It was like an extremely slow motion picture. Each morning while I was being driven to work along the *Marginal* to Lisbon, a new scene emerged.

Figure 36. Stormy Weather on the Marginal

In June 1964, Lynda graduated from St. Columbans with honors and she was looking around for a choice of higher education. Having been overseas for the last two years, it was a difficult decision. It was decided that she would spend the first two years at the American College in Paris. The curriculum was in English, but she would live with a French family, which would be interesting and educational in itself, so she applied and was accepted at ACP (now the American University of Paris). We planned that she would return to her school in Paris after returning from our summer home leave.

Figure 37. Lynda's Graduation, 1964

Steve had enjoyed his year and was fond of Mr. McKenna and the many students who were from all over the world. He and all of us were looking forward to taking our month of home leave during July.

As July 1964 approached, we were ready for a new experience, to board the big 707 jet at Lisbon Airport and fly over, instead of sail on, the Atlantic. Bea and the children went first and stopped in New York long enough to visit the World's Fair in Flushing Meadow, and I followed later. In New York as we boarded a local flight to Birmingham, it was a thrill to hear people speaking English in public places. Friends and relatives in Alabama greeted us warmly, and we quickly returned to feeling at home in that laid back environment.

We rented a convertible and visited all our families and some friends before driving down to Winter Haven, Florida for the Campbell family reunion. My brother, Bill, and his family had lived there for many years, and they hosted the gathering. The pattern of meeting somewhere in the country every two years had been decided upon at the previous reunion in Jasper, Alabama before we

Portugal

went overseas. The numbers held at about 75 with relatives coming from all over. It was an excellent way to get our visiting in over a weekend to learn about new births and other interesting occurrences in each of the "original 12's" families.

The younger children played games, romped and talked as they renewed their friendships with cousins. There were many interesting things to do in the area, including seeing Cypress Gardens with its water skiing show. Some of the men played a two day golf session where we competed for cups and bragging rights; on Saturday night we held a big banquet. There was a program of entertainment by the more talented relatives and speeches and jokes by some of the less gifted of us. We posed for group pictures and all declared it was great fun. On Sunday we said goodbye for two years, in most cases. My little family won first place for coming from the farthest distance. At closing, we planned to hold the next reunion in 1966 at a place to be selected later.

Back in Double Springs we had some time to enjoy Bea's family at the lakeside picnic area. Steve and his cousin, Robert Stewart, wanted to build a small rowboat. They found a plan in a magazine, and I helped them purchase materials at a local lumber company. I mostly watched the sawing, bending, trimming, nailing, sanding, caulking and painting before they proudly showed the rest of the family their handiwork. Success! It floated and served them many years of enjoyment at the boat dock at Smith Lake.

It was a good fun time, but also sad as we missed Bea's father and her sister Nell's husband. At the end of July, I returned to Lisbon, with a stop in New Jersey to attend my brother Julian's party celebrating his promotion to Lt. Colonel. The others stayed in Alabama for another month after which Bea and Lynda flew to Paris while Steve returned alone to Portugal. Lynda was established in the college, and Bea left her there to cope with getting into school and eventually moving in with a French family. There she learned not only to live with the language, but to appreciate the life in Paris. I can imagine some of the problems of adjustment she made, but she never complained. I believe she still looks on those two years as a positive episode. Steve reentered McKenna's school, and we all settled into a routine for the school year.

In international affairs, the Cold War worsened. Ten years after the French left South Vietnam, on August 5, 1964, President Johnson, citing attacks by North Vietnamese forces on US ships and planes, asked Congress to pass a resolution which would give him authority to conduct American military action to reinforce South Vietnam's opposition to the North Vietnamese regime. This authority, which was called the "Gulf of Tonkin Resolution," was passed by the combined Congress on August 7, 1964. Soon thereafter, President Johnson sent some American troops as advisors to assist in holding off the Communist North which was supported by China and the Soviet Union. The Vietnam Conflict began.

While at the RFE headquarters in Munich, Perry Esten returned to Munich, and soon replaced Engineering Director Russ Geiger, who retired. In Gloria, Dave Porter left and was replaced by Bob Beattie from Oregon. Bob was older and well experienced and was to become very helpful in keeping the place operating efficiently and within our control.

During the year, I decided to replace our old Austin A40 with what was to me a more exciting car, a 1957 Jaguar S type. It looked very much like the modern model. We used it to travel around Portugal on weekends and when we were able to take a few days off.

Figure 38. Gloria's Craftsmen and Spud's First Jaguar

When our house lease ended and the owner wanted to move back in, we had to find new living quarters. We found a rather large place on the hillside overlooking the harbor of Cascais. It was on three levels; the first floor contained the large living room/dining room combination, with windows and a balcony extending the whole length. The upper floor had three bedrooms with another balcony on the ocean side and another bedroom and a bath across a hall. That side also contained a three flight semicircular stairway all the way to the roof which was flat and could be used as a patio sitting area. We ordered our furniture shipped over from Fairfax and had our own things for the first time in Portugal. Although it was more house than we needed, the cost was reasonable and we came to enjoy living there.

Figure 39. The Campbell House in Cascais

We gave a dinner party for our Portuguese supervisors and their wives. As the large group began arriving, they appeared to be rather formal, and the party was too stiff for my taste. Although I knew the men well, Bea and I didn't know their wives, and the occasion began somewhat awkwardly. Then I heard some commotion upstairs, and I went up to find our 16 year old son, Steve, locked in the bathroom. He was getting ready to go out with friends so he could avoid standing around with these adults. But unfortunately, the door lock found this the time to fail, and he was stuck inside with only a towel, as he had undressed in his bedroom down the hall. Steve was quite "interested," even anxious, to get out without creating a scene. I tried in vain to get the lock to work, but the handle just turned around without any resistance.

Suddenly my maintenance supervisor, Jaime Costa Cabral, appeared and asked for tools, and I found a hammer and chisel. Jaime began to bang away at the door while others from the party showed up to watch. After some minutes of chiseling, he had completely destroyed the door, but the bathroom was empty with the window opened. I feared for the worst, because we were two floors up. Then suddenly Steve appeared, fully clothed, from his bedroom down the hall. He politely greeted all the guests and disappeared, we discovered he had moved along a very narrow ledge to get into his bedroom window while Jaime banged away. I gave him an A for audacity. He also can be credited for making our party come to life with laughter and conversation. Thanks to Steve, who always comes through when needed.

As the bridge project began to take shape, with the two support towers installed and the suspension support cables in place, Steve and his friends decided to "inspect" the job. At the north end, or the Lisbon side, they climbed onto the "catwalk" which was mounted on the cable and began a scary walk across. They walked all the way up the north tower in a steep climb and then made the descent to the middle of the river, then repeated the climb up and down over the south tower. They finally arrived at the south attachment point then turned around and in a similar way, walked back to the Lisbon point of the beginning about two hours later.

Figure 40. Lisbon, from the South Tower of the Tagus Bridge

Some changes in the top level at RFE and RARET came to pass. At the CEO level in Munich, William Durkee replaced General Rodney Smith who retired to his home in Washington. The death of Henry Lolliot in Lisbon created a vacancy there. Bud Black, who was an Assistant Director of Engineering in Munich, was transferred to Lisbon and Marty Oebbecke was moved from Lisbon to replace Black in Munich. The Lisbon contingent was reduced by the retirement of Bob Cotton and the departure of Harold Bowman. My job was unaffected except for the requirement of working with different personalities.

Bud Black and I were called to Munich for a series of planning sessions. CEO Bill Durkee, a swashbuckling type, opened a business meeting after a dinner party at his home by saying to his wife, "Dorkus, get the women out of here!" He then appeared to be instigating a feud between Black and Esten. I worked for both of them, who were now in different divisions—so it appeared that I was caught in the middle. Perry was the old friend who hired me, and Black was now my administrative boss. Durkee seemed to be pressuring Esten by trying to get me to take Black's side, but I refused to involve myself. Somehow I managed to survive and always stayed outside the feud. But it wasn't easy. Just one of the many little adventures we coped with at this "intriguing institution" known as RFE.

Another little diversion from the routine of my busy life at Gloria was the Pete Seveski experience. Pete had been employed off and on as a project engineer for the company. He was assigned to Gloria for some special work, and he needed transportation. Our motor pool assigned him one of our Opal station wagons for use in his work.

He was also allowed to use it for personal trips on weekends. Pete refused to turn it in for maintenance, at intervals, as requested. Soon he had run it low on oil and ruined its motor. I gave him strict orders about the next car they assigned him, and he took it personally and left the job in a huff. Then he traveled the world for some months and sent back postcards to Black in Lisbon and the Munich HQ which were always insulting about me. It didn't seem to upset anyone so we just let it play out. Years later Pete tried using some Washington influence to get back into RFE employment. Needless to say it didn't work as we had no need for his talents. It seemed that our operation was attractive to this type of person which made life more interesting but also tended to create friction at times.

Free Europe Fund President John Richardson came and spent some time with us at Lisbon. In Gloria he was interested in the educational system in the little village. He was told that the students in the primary school were bright children, but they had no possibility of continuing with secondary school in the immediate area. At lunch, Mr. Richardson, Bud Black, Engineer Neto and I discussed the possibility of the company establishing a small technical school on our property. Richardson picked up on the idea and within a year we had the school with our own Horacio Neto as headmaster. This outstanding person handled it, along with his many other duties, with great skill and thoughtful planning. Thanks to John Richardson, who later became Assistant Secretary of State for Cultural Affairs, the school continued to turn out students who went into the work force with good skills. I only hope it is still doing so.

Engineer Horacio Neto and I became close friends. On the many evenings in Gloria, as we played chess and discussed many things, I realized that he was a man of outstanding character and intelligence. I came to understand that without this guy the Gloria plant would never have evolved to its state of great significance. The RFE mission of giving information to people owes much to my friend, "Net."

In July 1966, I went to Paris for Lynda's graduation and then helped her to pack up all of her books and things which she shipped to the US in preparation for her entrance into Agnes Scott College. Bea and I, as parents, were disappointed when her excellent grades transferred as Bs, but she never complained. Her cousin Anita joined her in Paris, and they toured on Eurail passes before returning to Portugal. Later, they both entered Agnes Scott College in Decatur, Georgia—Lynda as a junior and Anita as a freshman.

The Vietnam "conflict" had become a war, and it seemed that the end was not in sight. We read of protests of the draft in the US colleges. Some young people were going to Canada to avoid serving, and this was hard for me to understand. I remembered how people rallied in support of the big World War II effort. My brother Julian had been ordered to serve a year in Vietnam, as were thousands of other military people. It seemed that our country was changing, and we were somewhat isolated from the change over in Portugal.

In the summer of 1966 we again went on home leave to the US. The biennial Campbell reunion was being held, once again in Jasper, to correspond with the time Julian would return from Vietnam. We all had a great time and had a picnic meal at their lot on Smith Lake. That big Campbell extended family was learning how to hold a celebration to the hilt. It seemed that there were dozens of young people running around. We had trouble keeping up with the names and ages with all the nephews and nieces who were so close in ages. Let's see—Calvin and Mae had three, W.G., Hazel and Dora Fay, but they were older and married; Tommy and Francis had two, Butch and Sandra; Bert and Madge had one, Bill, who was already married; Lee and Lecie had five, Harold, J.D., Ershel, Roanne and Judy; Bill and Kat had two, Jimmie and Keith; Evelyn and Arvel had three, Betty, Margaret, and Tommy and, after Arvel died, Evelyn and Milo had one, George; Ralph and Mary had two, Dick and Pat; Julian and Marie had three at that time, Teresa, Martha, Jean and later Robin; Bea and I had two, Lynda and Steve; James and Gloria had none; Pat and Joyce had two, Phil and Connie; Bill and Doris had three, Paula, Marta and Jana. What a gang! Of course there were many others as some already had grandkids running around.

Back in Portugal, I settled into the routine of the busy Gloria operation. Steve was getting ready for his senior year in high school and now had many friends in the international community of the coastal area. He had a Zundapp motorbike with a 50cc engine, which was the largest size not requiring an operator's license. However, he did take the driving test in the States and had his US license and an international license. This allowed him to take the Jaguar on short drives as we permitted. He had begun to think about college and wrote for information from some schools in the US.

Sometimes communication problems made getting proper medical treatment difficult. Once in Gloria, I developed a severe nosebleed. Daniel, my driver, rushed me to the Lisbon office where the nurse on duty, who spoke no English, attempted to stop it. She insisted that I lie on my back, but this caused me to choke on the blood in my throat. As I struggled to get up, she kept pushing me back down. Then I loudly said in Portuguese, "Get someone here who speaks English!" She left and returned with one of the English speaking secretaries. However, by the time she got back, she had already convinced the secretary to help hold me down on my back. Later I told Dr. Guzmão of this experience, and he blew his top at the poor nurse.

Bea and I planned a trip to Morocco during the school break in the spring of 1967. Steve was 18 and would rather not have spent that time with us, but we wanted him along to help drive. He enjoyed driving the Jaguar with his newly acquired international license, so he agreed to go if I would let him do all the driving. For half a day we saw the small Portuguese towns and entered Spain. The afternoon was similar, and we arrived at Algeciras, near Gibraltar, in time to get a hotel and spend the night. The next morning we took a ferry across Gibraltar Straits to Tangier, Morocco. This was their first time in Africa and my first since World War II. A native "guide" attached himself to us and went with us down to Tetuan where Bea shopped for brass and other gift items as she learned the Moroccan method of bargaining. Then we drove back up to Ceuta where we said goodbye to our passenger and gave him a small tip as we boarded the ferry back to Gibraltar to spend the night. We were warned not to drink the water and to eat carefully to avoid dysentery. We enjoyed the time in the British controlled "Free Port" where Bea did some serious shopping. There were bargains in clothing and many other things which were not available, except at high cost, in Portugal.

Figure 41. Spud and Our Guide in Morocco

Crossing the border into Spain was routine as the customs guard just waved us through. However, as we later entered Portugal at a very remote outpost, I went inside to wait in line then signed a card of declaration. The official looked at me and said, "Are you sure you don't have a bottle to declare?" I said maybe a Drambuie, and he sent his runner out with me to get it for stamping. I had to rummage through many packages and other bottles in order to find that particular bottle, while the guard stood there with a straight face. He went back in, and they stamped my bottle, and wished me a good trip as I handed the guard a few *escudos* for being so understanding. We had learned that this was the accepted practice in the country.

We heard that our great student, Lynda, was doing well at Agnes Scott in Decatur, Georgia. After the two years in Paris and living with two different French families, her mastery of that language was impressive. We learned of a time when, after her class presented a stage program in French, a Frenchman who witnessed the show asked, "Who was the French girl?" That was a great compliment for our Lynda.

The spring of 1967 was a time when college protests in the US were rampant. The war in Vietnam seemed to be going badly, and President Johnson was feeling the brunt of the nation's unrest. Lynda had done well at Agnes Scott in Atlanta and planned to remain for her BA degree the next year, although her cousin, Anita, wanted to transfer to another school.

Steve had enjoyed his senior high school year at "McKenna Tech" with all the other students of various nationalities and backgrounds. The soccer experience had been great as he mastered the "no hands" running and kicking game. At graduation, we were proud parents as he gave his valedictorian speech in the lovely outdoor courtyard ceremony. He and Headmaster McKenna had become friends for life, and he carried many fond memories of Portugal and the school into his adult life.

Now it was time for a decision about Steve's higher education. He had applied to two schools, Rensselaer and Georgia Tech. Georgia Tech accepted his application, and he spent the summer preparing to go to Atlanta. It was a big step for the young man. He had no chance to look over a campus and talk with other students about what to expect; he had been in Europe for the past five years. I guess it was quite a shock to him when he got there all alone. He soon realized that his major of aerospace engineering was a heavy load. The first quarter he squeaked by with a C average, which was not what we expected from this bright student. After two quarters, he was on probation until one of his professors helped him to get a bit more stabilized, and after the first year he changed his major to industrial management, which gave him more liberal arts courses. Then he began to find himself, and things improved.

With both of our children away in college, Bea and I found time to do some traveling. We went with our friends, the Hunters, on trips through Portugal. First we drove up to Coimbra and saw the famous university where the Portuguese leader, Salazar, served as an economics professor before getting into government and eventually becoming the permanent Prime Minister. Actually, he was a dictator, although not as ruthless as Franco, but austere in his own life style and autocratic in his actions on behalf of the Portuguese people. Someone told us that he was offered a new and larger TV, but refused it because his dust cover would not fit, and a new one would cost money.

Figure 42. Spud Between Bruce and Gertrude Hunter, in Coimbra

Bruce Hunter, the builder, wanted to see the bridge in Oporto which was designed by Alexandre-Gustave Eiffel, of tower fame. We traveled through the port wine country and sampled the product. We learned that the English families who controlled the port productions had kept their British citizenship intact after many generations of living in this lovely country. In the 17th century, the Cockburns, Grahams, Crofts and others had come to Portugal where they developed the process called "fortification," by adding brandy to wine to slow fermentation. This preserved the wine's sweetness and flavor, and it became a favorite as an aperitif, and in some churches in the sacramental celebration of the Eucharist.

Through the Hunters' friends, Mr. and Mrs. Schurz—who came over from their home in South Bend, Indiana every year for the Gulbenkian Foundation Festival—we were introduced to various cultural programs. Mr. Gulbenkian, an Armenian shipping mogul, had adopted Portugal as his second home. His foundation sponsored the festival season by bringing in artists from different countries. That is how we began to understand and enjoy opera. Our first introduction was Verdi's *La Traviata* with Renate Scotto singing the soprano part of Violetta. We were amazed at how much we enjoyed beautiful voices and the total experience. Later when we lived in Munich, we attended many operas and soon learned that the mystery of a simple story in a foreign language created the illusion of great drama.

Figure 43. Lynda's Driving Lesson

We took our third home leave in 1968. When Lynda graduated from Agnes Scott, we attended the ceremonies with Bea's family. As a graduation present we gave her a new Camaro even though she had never driven and didn't have a license. Steve was able to teach her to drive in two weeks. He had drilled her in parallel parking to the point that she passed the test handily. I rode with her as she drove her car on the interstate and through the city of Atlanta. Then as we arrived at the college in Decatur, I asked her to pull over to the curb and park. There were no other cars parked on the street, but she said, "Daddy, I don't know how to park like that."

Lynda had accepted a job teaching French in Broward County, Florida. I had to go back to work in Portugal, so Bea remained to help her move there. They rented a trailer for the Camaro and loaded it with her things, mostly books. Bea went along as she made the long drive in two days. It was quite a feat for her to do so soon after getting her first lesson. Bea said goodbye and made her way back to Portugal as Lynda began this new phase of her young life. Steve had reentered Georgia Tech for his sophomore year and seemed to be determined to find a major which would fit his requirement for a career. He seemed to feel this school was somewhat limited in the fields he now wanted to pursue, but he stayed with his commitment there.

The biennial Campbell reunion was held in California and hosted by my brother Tommy and his family. We were too busy with our own little family to make it out there. Several of my sisters went with their families and reported that they had a glorious time. The next one was scheduled for Cullman, Alabama in 1970, and we planned to be there if possible.

Back in Gloria, I learned that my assistant Bob Beattie had resigned after three years, which was about par for the course on the job in that busy place. My work then was more stressful, and I began to wonder how many more years I could remain. I passed my thoughts on to Perry Esten in a memo, and he wrote back a very understanding and hopeful letter about my future with the company. He was looking into some changes in the next year; I then settled into the busy routine. My Portuguese staff was still doing a great job, and although I appreciated their support, I knew that seven years there was my limit, so I let Perry know this.

The bridge was completed and most of our friends were gone. We still enjoyed Portugal and loved the people; however, as 1969 came around, I was glad when Perry Esten informed me that I would be transferred to the Biblis Transmitter Site in Germany and that Willi Kluehe would replace me in Gloria. It was sad leaving, and we were given a big party by the staff and workers at Gloria, who gave us a generous gift which we still treasure. Many people and especially Engineer Neto made farewell talks, and we left the party misty eyed. The seven years in Portugal had been a very rich experience for us all. We learned about the people and how they respected their government and the proud history of their country. That included the explorer Vasco da Gama, Magellan and even the Italian Christopher Columbus who set sail from Lisbon to "discover America." The mournful *fado* music reflected some of the attitude of the people who may still be grieving for the loss of a great empire centuries ago. The country and its people still hold a big, tender spot in my heart.

In May we began getting ready for our move to Germany. RFE housing was furnished for Americans, so the decision to sell as much as possible was logical. Steve needed a car at college and for the summer break in Europe, so we made a plan. We heard of a little Triumph Spitfire convertible with American driving specs that was for sale in London. We flew to England and I picked up the little car in the middle of the city and drove it to a hotel. That was my first experience of driving on the right side of the street, and I can tell you it was nerve wracking in that traffic. We spent some time enjoying that great city, shopping and seeing a show. We visited our friend Pat Eastwood on our way to Southampton. After a round of goodbye dinners and parties with our friends, we boarded a ship for Le Havre, where we disembarked and drove across France and on to Darmstadt, Germany, our new home.

Chapter 15
Darmstadt

With the move to Germany, some big adjustments in our lives were necessary. In Portugal, the lifestyle of a southern European culture was relaxed and unhurried while my job was very busy and intense. Now it was the job which was comparatively easy, while the German lifestyle was more rigidly structured, in a way, more like that in the US.

Our rather large two story house in Darmstadt was on a lot enclosed by a solid masonry wall with an iron gate. It was already furnished by the company and had been occupied by the current American manager of the Biblis transmitter site for many years. I was replacing Bill Simons, who was retiring and returning to the US. His assistant, Don Leonard, was being reassigned to Gloria, Portugal, as assistant to Willi Kluehe, who had replaced me down there. In reality, I was filling the two positions at Biblis as the assistant was not replaced.

Figure 44. The House in Darmstadt

A Mercedes sedan was assigned to me, but unlike Portugal, I had no driver. The drive down the Autobahn to the little village of Biblis took about 20 minutes. The plant was much smaller than Gloria and had only 30 employees, a tenth as many as Gloria. Eddie Krahe was promoted to be my assistant, and I soon learned he was very capable and dependable. My secretary was Fraulein Irmgard Dentler, who kept the paperwork organized in the typical strict discipline of that country. My adjustment to the new job was pleasant and easy. As I sat at my desk, I thought about what Perry Esten had told me: this was to be a period of decompression after the hectic seven years at the busy Gloria job. And I began to make a plan.

I was sure I could quickly master the necessary routines of keeping a tight budget and to retain American control of the operation. My spare time would be spent learning the language and customs of the people as soon as possible. Then my focus would be toward understanding all I could about the institution of Radio Free Europe. Getting information to the isolated people behind the Iron Curtain in their closed society had fascinated me ever since my World War II days; my trip to Murmansk many years before had showed me how some of those people lived and how they felt about life.

Darmstadt had a US Army Base which had been there since the end of World War II, the Cambria Fritsch Caserne. The US military newspaper, *Stars and Stripes*, was published in Darmstadt and was distributed all over Europe. We were invited to join the club which was maintained at the newspaper. There we met many people who became our friends as we settled into life in this foreign country. We soon became friends with *Stars and Stripes* editor Herb Scott and his wife, Nell. Herb was from Chicago and had written for the *Tribune* and other papers before deciding to go overseas. He and I discussed the world situation and exchanged views of the Cold War and other matters. We went to the annual wine festival at Bad Durkheim, Germany. The streets were full of visitors and it was difficult to move. Herb showed us a way to get through a mob which was going the opposite way. He turned around and walked backwards. It was surprising how easy he made it. Everyone moved away, and he always seemed to have an opened area. He was interested in RFE and the communications role in the Cold War. Sometimes we agreed and sometimes not, but I always learned from conversing with Herb.

The school year was over, and Lynda came to Germany to see us. Bea had bought a Mercury Capri for our private transportation, and we went with Lynda on a trip through northern Europe. We saw Denmark, then crossed by ferry into Sweden. We returned through some of Germany and home to Darmstadt. Lynda returned to the US and spent some time with her grandmother and her cousin Anita Stewart.

That summer, Steve toured Europe with his high school friend, Marc Owens, who was in school at Florida State. They first went to Portugal to enjoy that country once again and to see friends who were still there. Then they flew up to Frankfurt where we met them with Steve's little Triumph Spitfire. They were interested in touring in it but first they needed some cash. We hired them for a couple of weeks at Biblis to clean up areas where antenna systems had been taken down. It was manual labor and paid a minimum wage (four marks, or $1, per hour) but they seemed to enjoy it, and it gave them the opportunity to learn something about the German people. Steve seemed more calm and confident in his life than before and seemed to be happier at Georgia Tech. He also mentioned that he had met a girl, Nancy O'Neal, and he wanted us to meet her when we got back to the States the next year.

Figure 45. Marc Owens and Steve in Darmstadt

On July 20, 1969 we watched with Steve and Marc, along with some other people, as Neil Armstrong took that "small step for man and a giant leap for mankind" on the moon. The moon landing marked the time that the US space program moved ahead of the Russians and fulfilled John Kennedy's promise to reach the moon within the decade of the 1960s.

The Munich headquarters arranged for me to participate in a "total immersion" language class conducted by the US military at Rhine Main Air Base in Frankfurt. A large group of Americans were together for a full day every day for two weeks and were not allowed to speak a word of English during that time. We had excellent instructors who made the experience interesting and even fun. I had to learn the language or go nuts from boredom. That is probably the most effective way to force one to learn a language. Too bad I didn't continue the process afterwards, but in Germany so many people spoke English that it was easy to drift back into our language.

In a trip to Munich I spent some time getting to know the people responsible for getting RFE's programs out to the five countries of Eastern Europe. Director Ralph Walter gave me a tour of the building as he explained the various departments and their functions. Each language group occupied a section of the office building where they analyzed the flow of information and news, which was constantly available to them. The information came from various sources such as our monitoring station in Schleissheim, the central newsroom, or newspapers and other periodicals. This news and analysis was then voiced by announcers who were exiles from the various Iron Curtain countries.

I met Henry Hart who headed a department for determining the extent of listening for each language. He explained the difficulty of getting information from behind the Iron Curtain. He had various ways such as interviewing visitors from the countries or from surveys done inside by embassy personnel or from travelers.

The central news room was a busy place with a dozen writers working on stories which were put on line and fed to the various language desks. There the news stories were translated for the readers to present on air. The news room produced a million words a day just like the AP or any other news service. I saw the administration offices and the security people and the personnel department, where I had a long talk with Russ Poole. Finally, I had time to visit the engineering division which was headed by my friend of some years, Perry Esten.

The engineering division included about 700 people who were scattered all over Europe and the US. In the headquarters building, the director had a staff of Americans who supervised the entire network of people in Germany, Spain, Portugal and the US. Minor operations included some technical monitors in Greece, Austria and Germany with reports from Helsinki by Voice of America monitors. Their purpose was to monitor constantly the reception conditions, a tremendously difficult job because of the number of bands used and changes in frequencies and languages throughout the day. Reception had constant interference from heavy "jamming," noise signals transmitted from the east by the Soviet government. It was estimated that our adversaries spent several times RFE's budget in an effort to prevent the people from hearing news from the outside world. I remembered the old interpreter in Murmansk who told me that the Communist system would not survive if the people knew too much of how the outside world lived.

Transmitter sites were located in Gloria, Portugal (the biggest) and at Biblis and Holzkirchen in Germany. A monitoring station was located in Schleissheim, near Munich, where they constantly monitored everything transmitted from inside the Iron Curtain. This was fed by telephone lines into the Munich building where information was recorded and selectively transcribed for the analysts to read and digest.

In the US, Stan Leinwoll and his staff were busy making frequency schedules which would be effective in all times and seasons. Short wave conditions varied during an 11-year cycle as sunspot activities changed. Stan was the world's best expert in this field, and he also attended conferences where international broadcasters negotiated and agreed on schedules for each season of the year.

By now I was getting a better picture of the RFE operation and the way my division worked within it. Because of the distance from the audience and the jamming efforts of the governments, the biggest challenge of getting through to the people was technical. Over the next several months I spent many hours mulling over the problems and ways of making the transmissions more effective.

Back in Darmstadt, I met some chess players at the *Stars and Stripes* club. One night a week I joined them for a series of chess matches. I got back into a hobby that I started back in World War II in Murmansk. Some of us joined the US Chess Federation and attended weekend matches at military bases in Germany. Once a month we would play three matches on Saturday and two on Sunday. It was good mental exercise, but I found I often would get a headache by Sunday evening; after several months I quit the club for this reason. It was just too tense, and I wanted a hobby that would be both mentally and physically relaxing. I found that to be golf, a hobby I have enjoyed into my 80s with good results as far as conditioning is concerned. It is a game that I will never master, and therefore, it never becomes boring.

Bea made our big house in Darmstadt very livable, and we often entertained people traveling through and our local friends. However, she wanted some activity outside the home, so she got a job at the local Military Base Exchange Merchandising organization. She managed the special order desk and kept busy with contacting suppliers for customers who wanted something not available in the store. She also was able to buy some things for our use from time to time. She liked the job and, in my opinion, was well suited to it. Helping others has always been her specialty. We were happy to have a visit by my grand niece, Carolyn, with her two-year-old daughter, Lisa, and her husband Roger Hairston, who was in the military in Germany.

Bea and I flew home for Christmas 1969 and also attended the wedding of our daughter Lynda to Tom Cicero. He was a teacher at the same school where Lynda taught romance languages. They immediately left for their honeymoon, and we flew back to Darmstadt. While in Double Springs, Steve let us know that he was serious about his friend Nan O'Neal. We expected another wedding within the next year.

Our fourth home leave was scheduled for 1970. We flew to Atlanta where Steve had just finished his junior year at Georgia Tech. We were very glad to see how well he was doing in school, and we were pleased to meet his fiancée, Nan, for the first time. These two items of good news seemed somehow connected. Bea and I, along with Steve and Nan, had a very enjoyable meal at the Abbey Restaurant in Atlanta. Then we flew to Birmingham and drove to Double Springs where we spent some time with Bea's mother and others of her family.

In July, the sixth biennial Campbell family reunion was held in Cullman, Alabama. Julian and his family had moved there after he retired from the Air Force. It was the usual three-day affair with much talk and good food. Attending were members of 11 of the 12 siblings with their spouses and many grandchildren and some great-grandchildren. On Saturday night, a banquet was held with musical entertainment by the gifted and announcement of the results of the men's golf tournament with trophies presented to the lucky few.

In early September, we all attended the wedding of Steve and Nan at a beautiful chapel on the campus of the University of South Carolina where Nan had gone to school. We were able to meet many of Nan's family and friends at the wedding. Immediately after the wedding, I flew to New York and on to Germany. Steve and Nan were on the same plane on their way to Canada for their honeymoon. Bea drove her mother back to Alabama while Tom and Lynda made their way back to Fort Lauderdale, Florida.

The year 1971 was uneventful for us. We enjoyed the quiet life of Darmstadt, and the job at Biblis was routine. We managed to do some traveling around the area, and during the summer, we went to London where we saw some shows. By this time we had become adjusted to the life in Germany. But things were so strictly regulated and orderly that it was good to get away from time to time for a "clutter fix." Sometimes it seemed that in Germany, "Everything not forbidden was compulsory." The traffic on the autobahn was fast, but the drivers were predictable and the accident rate was relatively low. All in all, we liked the people and the country for its beauty, and I often told people, "It's just a big old park."

Then 1972 came, and things got busy again. First we had another home leave and attended the seventh biennial Campbell reunion at Huntsville, Alabama. This one was well attended; all 12 families were represented. These gatherings were important because our family was always close, yet was scattered over the globe. Getting around to seeing all of them was not practical except for reunions, which now had become an institution we hoped would continue. To my delight, Bea's mother had become an honorary member of the group and seemed to enjoy all the people and festivities very much.

After we returned to Biblis that summer, RFE Director Ralph Walter and Perry Esten made an inspection trip to the Biblis plant. Ralph was a brilliant young man who had the title of Director but was really the Chief Operating Officer of the big institution. The President, Bill Durkee, was positioned in New York and only came over for board meetings and other rare occasions. I always admired the way Ralph could keep the company operating without major controversy when it was composed of the most diverse types imaginable and a dozen nationalities. They included scholarly analysts, artistic performers, writers and others with a variety of technical skills—all working for one goal. It appeared to me that the mission was being accomplished, at least to the point of getting information into the airwaves. The number of people who wished to get the information was enormous. But I wondered how many actually could receive the information with all the deliberate interference created by the jamming. Then I learned that I might get a chance to be more directly involved in that regard.

I went home and told Bea that we might be moving again. She was a bit startled because of the many moves we had made, but we began thinking of what it would be like to live in the big Bavarian city of Munich. The summer Olympics were to be held there soon, and we thought that would be interesting. Then I was called to the RFE headquarters to discuss some shifting of personnel.

Perry Esten told me that he was moving Lynn Pease to Gloria, Portugal, and Willi Kluehe would return to Munich as a projects engineer. I would replace Lynn as Deputy Director of Engineering for Administration, and Biblis would be headed by promoting Eddie Krahe. Marty Oebbecke would remain as Deputy Director for Technical Facilities.

I spent some time with Russ Poole in personnel, then sat down with Services Manager Don Brooks to discuss my move and housing arrangements. He took me out to the little city of Neubiberg, where I saw and accepted a house. It was smaller than we had in Darmstadt, but big enough for us. The 15-minute drive into Munich was no problem, but I would need another car as none was assigned for Americans at the Munich Headquarters.

Chapter 16
Munich

We moved to the smaller house in Neubiberg which was comfortably furnished by the company. Bea was transferred to work in the special order office of the military exchange European Headquarters at Munich. We both started our new jobs in the first week of September 1972, the sad week of the terrorist attack on the Israeli team at the Olympics complex in Munich.

Figure 46. Bea at Work in Munich

I had been officially transferred as Deputy Director for Administration, Engineering and Services Division. My friend Marty Oebbecke was Deputy for Technical Facilities. Perry gave me a briefing on my new duties and told me to get on top of all activities of the department quickly. He planned to retire soon and had recommended me as his replacement. I immediately thought of the decade of working with Marty, who had been my boss when I began in Gloria. We always had been close friends, and I hoped we could remain so. Then I went to work reading and reviewing everything that came through the department.

Munich

In Washington, Senator Clifford Case of New Jersey had gone public with the method of funding Radio Free Europe and the sister operation, Radio Liberty. RFE had been broadcasting to the Eastern European countries, which were under the control of the Russians, for more than 20 years and received funds from an annual campaign to support the people-to-people mission of the radio station. At some point, the government began supplementing the budget to cover an expanded program. Radio Liberty, which broadcast to the Soviet Union in Russian and 15 languages of the nationalities under that empire, was entirely funded by the US government from the beginning. Senator Case proposed that both radios be funded openly, and Congress decided to appoint a committee to study means of accomplishing this change.

The study committee made recommendations which were accepted, and funding became an item in the annual OMB budget request. Another recommendation was that these radio operations should be overseen by a Board for International Broadcasting which would be appointed by the US President. This recommendation also was accepted, and one of the Board's first requests was to study the feasibility of combining RFE and RL under one corporation. These two entities had operated for a couple of decades with headquarters of both in Munich, but with little, if any, interaction. At first blush, I thought there was certainly a more economical way of operating two so very similar services. But I soon learned that many people at both radios had other feelings.

Our director, Ralph Walter, asked all support services departments to meet with their counterparts from Radio Liberty to discuss the feasibility of combining functions. Perry Esten and I met with George Herrick, RL Director of Engineering, and his assistant. Herrick immediately suggested that we should do a study to show all the disadvantages of such a combination. Esten was noncommittal since he was leaving soon. I felt we should probably go into a study with an open mind on the subject, and let the chips fall where they may. The meeting ended with no plans for a joint study. We had been telling visitors, "We are in the business of working ourselves out of business" for years. This meant that our mission was to bring down the barriers to freedom of information so that there would be no need for our service. Now we were given a chance to live up to that promise by working to eliminate some positions which could include our own. I for one resolved to accept that challenge.

Perry came in one day and told me that he had bought a house in Santa Barbara, California, and they would be leaving in February 1973. He also had bought a 1969 Jaguar XKE to take home because he thought his Mercedes was not built with American requirements while the Jaguar was. I knew he really loved driving his Mercedes, and I suggested he check to find out if he could take it into California without major reinstallation of the required systems of emission control, etc. He promised he would but then he asked, "What would I do with the Jaguar if I could take the Mercedes?" I quickly answered, "Then I would take it at the price you paid." Since owning a Jaguar in Portugal, I had always liked the cars and the little sports coupe looked exciting to me. Perry let me drive it home because I needed a second car since I no longer had a company car. I drove it home and asked Bea what she thought of it. She said, "It sure has a long nose." But I guess by now she understood that "boys will have their toys." The good news was that Perry eventually was able to take his Mercedes, and I got my XKE.

Figure 47. The XKE

Ralph Walter and the company sponsored a big going-away party for the Estens. Many people spoke of Perry's long and successful career as they said a tearful goodbye to all their friends at the company. I thanked him once again for the things he had done to help me in Gloria during the installation of transmitters, and in Germany during my time at Biblis and the past few months in Munich. Bea and I were invited to visit them in California, and we looked forward to doing so in the future.

My good friend and golf partner, Marty Oebbecke, was doing a great job supervising all the technical facilities in Germany. One of the most important functions was the Schleissheim station, where we had special receiving equipment and a big antenna field for monitoring radio transmissions from inside the Iron Curtain countries and around the world. The RFE program groups used this information in their analysis of what was happening in other countries, some of which their own people only learned about after we rebroadcast it.

The receiving station was located on an old Luftwaffe airport which was converted soon after World War II. Some people may have considered it a bit spooky because of its function under the Nazis, and also because of its proximity to Dachau. Marty told me that they were experiencing poltergeist activities there. I had heard of the "noisy, but playful, ghosts," which seemed to haunt some Germans and were somehow associated with young people. I didn't take the threat seriously until one day Marty called me from the site and said things were getting worse; the manager, Herr Erwin Straub, had told him that some damage had been done to furniture and pictures. Sometimes fuses had strangely blown in the power to receivers or recording equipment. Then Marty said into the phone, "That chair is moving!" Although I was getting a bit concerned, this somehow amused me, and I made some joking comment about too much Munich beer for lunch.

Upon his return, Marty came into my office and gave me a report of the incident at Schleissheim. He said the damages, while minor, had continued over the past month and had always coincided with the time a certain young summer replacement person had been on duty. Herr Straub and the operators had tried to catch him doing something but to no avail. Straub said these things would occur in another room from where the suspect was located at the time. The young man seemed to be as puzzled as the others. He said he had had trouble of this type at the last place he worked. I listened and told Marty to keep me informed of any more problems. I was beginning to get concerned that we might have a news item concerning this mystery, and we didn't need that kind of publicity with our type of operation in a foreign country.

My phone rang at home the next Sunday morning—it was Herr Straub. He said, "You've got to come out here; this place is a mess." He reported damaged furniture, blown fuses, pictures that twirled around on the wall, and other unexplained occurrences. I asked him to call our security officer, and I would be out soon. Marty and I arrived together to see the mess. We toured the area as Straub gave us a running commentary. Then we passed through the receiving room and saw the young man at work. He didn't show any sign of being concerned. There was a chair with the seat blown off and lying on the floor. Straub led us into the basement to see more damage. As I stood at the bottom of the stairs, the chair bottom flew down and hit me on the leg. I had seen no one throw it; the mystery heightened. The security chief had arrived by this time, so the four of us went outside the front door and stood talking. I told Marty we might get rid of the young man, and maybe that would be the end of our problem. Suddenly an object came crashing through the glass door and fell at our feet. I looked to my right where a window opened three rooms down, and the young man's head popped out, and he looked at us. I wondered how he could do this trick and suddenly be so far away.

It's still a mystery, but the trouble stopped with the kid's departure. His mother begged us to give him another chance since he was devastated and needed a job badly. We didn't, and fortunately, it never got into the local papers.

During the next months, I visited all the major engineering department sites, sometimes with VIP visitors, but always taking the opportunity to discuss with the supervisors their needs for increased effectiveness. A plan I had visualized while sitting in the lonely office at Biblis over the past three years was always in the back of my mind. At the risk of becoming too technical, I will try to explain it.

Short wave radio transmission, which was the main mode of covering the large distances to our potential listeners, gets around the curvature of the earth by reflecting off an ionized layer which is located some 200 miles above the earth's surface. This layer, a gift of the sun, changes at sunset. It disappears completely for some wavelengths during darkness. In order to "jam out" our programs, the Soviets use the layer to beam noise transmissions from somewhere in their territory which is necessarily east of the target.

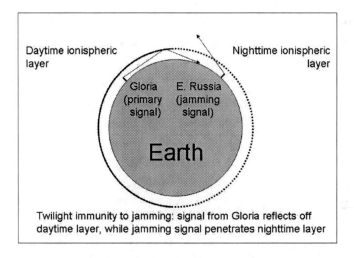

Figure 48, Twilight Immunity

The solar system's Creator must have liked us, because for a few hours during the prime early evening listening hours, we were given what we call "twilight immunity" to jamming. West to east transmission has a layer when east to west does not. To counter this, the Soviets had installed, at great expense, hundreds of small "line of sight" noise generators to cover the major population centers.

Over the vast areas of the big countries of Eastern Europe and the Soviet Union, however, these methods didn't block us out. I had imagined there was a chess playing technical expert, I'll call Ivan, sitting in an office in Moscow responding to our every technical move. I remembered my chess mentor in Murmansk in 1945 had told me to never make a defensive move, or as he called it, a wasted one. My plan was to play his game by adding power and numbers of transmissions to cause him to go on the defensive by matching our escalation. I knew they already spent three times our annual budget in this effort, and with their weaker economy, a sudden request for a doubled budget might make someone blink.

When the possibility of combining with Radio Liberty presented itself, I wondered if this would be the time to begin this technique by saturation programming to the time zone with twilight immunity and moving the beam and language each hour. I had explained this idea to Perry as we talked about consolidation, and he, wise old man that he was, suggested that I try to sell consolidation of the two radios on the basis of economy by saving positions, which was easier to explain, and might leave Ivan guessing about our plans. I agreed that we should use some good old American poker strategy to play his chess game.

I called a meeting of some of the people in the various support services to begin an effort to prove that consolidation was practical and could save money in the long term. Attending were Marty Oebbecke and Varick Steele from Engineering, Don Brooks from General Services, Hans Fischer from Administration

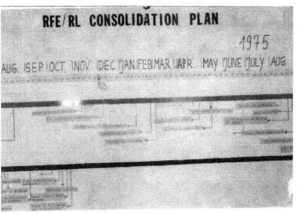

Figure 49. The RFE/RL Consolidation Time Line

and Russ Poole from Personnel. It was decided that my secretary would make a large time line chart showing six major categories of the effort. This time line would cover the years 1974 and 1975 with weeks and months listed at the top. When anyone came up with an item for study or plan or action, the secretary would type it and apply it to the chart at a time and place we decided would be feasible. Soon the chart began to take shape, and over the next months, we had over a hundred little notes spaced across the two-year time line. In the meantime, we had contacted an architect to study how we could add space to our already large multi-winged building. It was decided that with an increase of approximately 25 percent we could house both operations. A builder gave us an estimate of the time and cost of the enlargement. These items were placed on the timeline, which was now, by much joint effort, taking shape as a feasible plan.

Ralph Walter, our Managing Director, was impressed and invited some RL people over to discuss it. Some of them were opposed, but many signed on to it, and we presented it to the RFE Board of Directors. Eventually the new Board for International Broadcasting came over, and it was a big hit with that group. They even insisted we reproduce it and give them a duplicate for their Washington office. Our plan worked, and over the next two years my office was a center of much activity as we tried to, and did, live up to our "time line." Our building enlargement was completed in October 1975, and RL moved in a month later.

In some respects the merger was a "shotgun marriage" as a few people deeply resented the shock of making this sudden and radical change in their routines. The combined corporation hired Ken Scott, a retired RL executive and state department diplomat, as the new executive director of the combined company. The two broadcasting entities remained mostly unchanged. However, all the various support and administrative groups, including engineering, were combined with a saving of many positions. I had been so busy that I had not given my position much thought, but somehow, I was selected to head the bigger combined division of engineering. I became a member of a small group that had the difficult chore of reducing staff positions. Under the leadership of Ken Scott, the dissension was kept to a minimum by offering early retirements, and in some cases bonuses for people who left the company.

In the US, some changes were made: Bill Durkee was replaced by Sig Mickelson as president; the headquarters moved from New York to Washington; and the federal Board for International Broadcasting established offices in the building with the radios.

Some changes were necessarily made in the engineering table of organization: Paul North was moved from manager of the Pals, Spain site to Lisbon where he increased the American presence there; Tony Reigosa was promoted to manager at Pals; Varick Steele became Deputy Director of Engineering replacing Marty Oebbecke, who retired; and the studio manager position was filled by Dick Tanksley from RL.

With consolidation completed, our scheduling expert, Stan Leinwoll, could make better use of the combined transmitter and antenna complement to increase our effectiveness. Although there was more opposition to consolidation at RL, I knew they benefited more in increased effectiveness by the change than did RFE.

Ken Scott and I became good friends and played golf often at Dachau. The nine-hole course was located virtually in the shadow of the concentration camp, which had been preserved as a monument to infamy. I broached the subject of asking for capital funding for my plan of upgrading our transmitter and antenna complement. Ken thought it should wait for a year as we were still settling into the merged operation.

By mid 1976, Scott had managed to get the combined company operating smoothly, and he decided to retire once again. He was not a young man and wanted to spend some time living in the US with friends and family. A new executive director, Alex Buchan, was hired to replace Scott. Alex had been with the telephone company MCI and had a background in stateside broadcasting.

After meeting Alex and his wife, Bea and I offered to accompany them to dinner. We talked as we made the trip down to a lakeside restaurant where we had enjoyed a good meal before. I soon got an impression that Buchan, while having extensive experience in small town broadcasting in the US, was not interested in the details of how our operation differed from his experience. As we sat down to order, Alex seemed to feel the prices were high; he picked up his wife's menu and ordered for them both. I was amused and playfully took Bea's menu and began to order. She immediately informed me she was capable of making her own decision, and I gave her a wink. As we enjoyed our good meal and the Buchans ate the cheapest thing on the menu, we listened as Alex expounded on his recent good luck with his MCI stock: when the company won its case against AT&T, the value of his securities doubled and split. This experience indicated to me that we had a different boss from Ken Scott.

Ken and I had one last golf round at Dachau, and he was feeling great about leaving and beginning his second retirement. He played his best game, and I congratulated him as I left.

We prepared for our 1976 home leave. That year, the Campbell reunion was held in Cullman, Alabama where my brother Julian had lived since his retirement from the Air Force. Being once again with all those great people was a welcomed diversion from the frantic activity of the past few years in Europe, which seemed so far away. Although there was little local interest in the Cold War, the *Cullman Times* interviewed me and ran a story about my service at RFE.

While I was on home leave, I got the sickening news that my friend Ken Scott had suffered a heart attack and died in Munich, just a short time before his scheduled retirement. That reminded us of how our friend Bud Black had suffered a very similar experience as he retired in Lisbon and prepared to leave for his retirement in Florida. We decided to make a plan for our permanent return to the US at some time not too far into the future. I liked the small town, Cullman, where my brother and his family lived, and Bea and I wondered if it offered us what we would need when we retired. I had no other place in mind and wasn't interested in retiring to a big city. Bea was not willing to consider Florida, and I feared having to withstand the rigors of a cold climate. As a compromise, we decided to buy a residential building lot near my brother's house. He had a new career in real estate so he was helpful in the selection and arrangements for the purchase.

Back in Munich with the new boss Alex Buchan in charge, I found there was little interest in the technical division and our plans for upgrading and modernization of our transmitters and antennas; but the new boss liked to play golf. Alex had grown up near Edinburgh and learned to play the game with experts there; he played with a low handicap. Although my handicap was a bogie 18, I sometimes joined the foursome with him. He liked to bet small amounts, and as the boss, he set the odds so that he usually went home with a few dollars. The other players tolerated this arrangement, but I was also a stubborn Scotsman, and I rebelled. Sometimes we argued at the first tee for some time before he finally gave in and gave me the 12 strokes advantage I demanded. Once I won 50 cents, and he never forgave me.

Escorting visitors, who were usually board members or others with VIP status, seemed to be one of my job requirements. We usually made the loop to Lisbon and Barcelona/Pal and maybe to Geneva for a conference on international frequency allocations or to Berlin. In one case, we included Helsinki where we got reports on our effectiveness from the US Embassy. I used these visits to keep contact with the outlying engineering sites and to keep up with their progress and problems.

One interesting visitor was Paul Bartlett, a TV and Radio station owner from Fresno, California. After visiting some sites, he wanted me to drive him up the Czech border. We got into the XKE and headed down the Isar river valley through Landshut which he called "land shut;" I told him it sounded more like "lands hoot." As Paul was observing the beautiful countryside, I noticed a sign, "US Forces Halt" which I ignored. As we arrived at the border in the little village of Eisenstein, we parked and observed two towers with Czech troops armed with machine guns. Paul was excited and wanted me to take his picture as he placed his foot over the border. Suddenly we found ourselves surrounded by US military vehicles and soldiers with drawn guns. They pointed to my car with its green military plates and said I was not to drive that vehicle within five kilometers of the border. I explained our mission and that my car was registered that way because my wife worked for the US military, and I was a dependent. After some exciting conversation with his headquarters, we were allowed to go free but with a promise to head away from the border. Paul thought it was great drama, but I was just happy not to be in a jam.

By the end of his first year, Alex seemed to have few friends in the company, but the studio manager Dick Tanksley remained friendly with him. Alex complained to me that his friend Dick felt isolated in his office near the studios and wanted me to transfer him down to the executive wing. By this time, I was in no mood for his games, so I told him that my only reason for having Dick on staff was to supervise the studio operation. If Alex wanted him in our wing, he would report to Alex and not to me. He made some statement about making changes in my division and that he had a friend back in the States that he might bring over. I gave him my best glare and left. That night I told Bea we might not be in Germany much longer, and she smiled brightly. She had made the sacrifice of being away from family for a long time, so I just gave her a hug and said, "We will see."

Julian and Marie came over and spent some days with us. Bea was not able to get time off, so I took them around to see some of the points of interest. We went to Oberammergau and to some of the castles built by the mad King Ludwig. We had a good time traveling around and talking of how we had gone in separate directions and lived in various parts of the world. I suggested that we envied their retirement. We hoped to do the same before too many years. They asked us to think about the little town of Cullman when we decided to settle down, and I said we hoped to do that.

In the summer of 1977 the RFE/RL Board of Directors came to Munich for their annual meeting. Alex gave his report, and toward the end, he proposed a project of air conditioning the studios and offices. When it came my turn, I included an alternate proposal. I said, "The plan for air conditioning the building would cost a couple of million dollars. This is money we don't have, but if it should become available, let's use it for upgrading some of our ancient transmitting equipment. Air conditioning might make a few people more comfortable once in a while, but upgrading our transmitters would give us many more potential listeners. And this is the area that we have neglected over the past few years." Alex interrupted with, "There is not a radio station in the States that isn't air conditioned." I replied, "Alex, this is not the States. We get maybe six days a year when it is uncomfortable in this mountain area with low humidity." He was furious and I was a bit unhappy myself, but I was ready for anything. Perhaps I exaggerated a bit in order to make a case for my priorities, but I left that day with a resolve not to be intimidated by the guy whatever might come of it.

The good news, at least for me, was that Alex was replaced in a few months by Dr. Glen Ferguson, a member of the board of directors who had attended the last meeting. My dreams of getting the funding I had long desired looked to be a possibility.

With the arrival of Glen Ferguson, the president's office was moved from Washington to Munich, and the Washington office was headed by a vice president. Glen Ferguson's credentials were impressive: he came to us from the presidency of the University of Connecticut; he had served as ambassador to Kenya, and in his youth, he was in the Peace Corps; at Cornell as an undergraduate, he was quarterback of the football team. It appeared that his Washington contacts were good. Unfortunately, he had given up golf, but played a good game of tennis.

In his first staff meeting, Dr. Ferguson said he would be meeting one-on-one with all division directors to learn of their needs as he hoped to improve our effectiveness. I had a good feeling about our chances to do what I had been looking forward to for years.

My turn to present my case came last. He explained it was because he suspected that I would ask for more than the others, and he wanted to hear the others first. He also indicated that the technical operation was the area he least understood. After I gave my plea for bringing our transmitter plants up to date, he said he wanted to see for himself; we set aside the next week to tour the facilities.

On the flight to Lisbon, I briefed Glen on the big Gloria facility with its large number of transmitters and well trained staff which could be helpful in any capital improvement program. I gave him the basics of the theory of directing a mass of transmissions to an area with twilight immunity in the hope of exceeding the local jamming abilities in some cities. Granted, this theory was difficult to test and even more difficult to prove it was accomplished, because we had no way to monitor the effectiveness in cities deep inside the target countries.

We were met at Lisbon by Paul North who drove us immediately to Gloria where Lynn Pease and Neto were ready to give us the tour. Ferguson was very interested in the technical school which RFE built and operated over the past 10 years. Gloria is a very impressive place, and Glen quickly realized its importance to the combined radio operation. That evening we attended a dinner with the top people and their wives.

The next day we flew to Barcelona where Tony Reigosa met us and gave the tour of the beautiful Pals station. Although somewhat smaller than Gloria, it was more modern and the transmitters were more powerful. Pals was also a vital tool in our effort to reach the millions of listeners inside the Iron Curtain. Tony was a very interesting person, and he told us about his experience as a fellow law school student with Castro. He left Cuba at the beginning of the Castro regime.

As we returned to Munich, I gave Glen a word picture of the three transmitter sites in Germany and the receiving station at Schleissheim. Glen reserved his visit to these sites until another time. As we arrived in Munich, Ferguson told me to get my staff together and give him a proposal of what we considered to be needed and with a cost and timing estimate. I promised we could do it within a week.

Our team of engineers rapidly put together a plan for adding high-power transmitters at all the sites except Pals. The plan included: a study of the jamming problem; new antennas and modifications of others for the antenna fields; new switching equipment and building additions (Exact specifications and design of antennas would be done later.) .Costs and timing estimates were easily done by these experienced people. The project was estimated to cost about $16 million, and it would take three years after budget approval. We had most of the information we needed because, for some years, we had been thinking and working toward this day. A summary document was prepared for Dr. Ferguson to take to Washington for inclusion in the Fiscal Year 1978 budget. This plan would double the total power of the RFE/RL operation and add flexibility for scheduling languages.

Interestingly, the only "complaint" we received from the Office of Management and Budget was a query of how we could do this project at less than half the amount proposed for a very similar project by the Voice of America. It appeared that the bureaucrats in the government agency, OMB, had not counted on the efficiency of a private company as we were. The technical representative of the Board for International Broadcasting was very critical of me and the way we planned to do much of the engineering and installation of sophisticated antennas with our own talent. He also indicated that I should not be so worried about costs, as that was his area. I explained that our antenna construction team at Gloria would come to Germany and do the projects at Biblis and Holzkirchen. Transmitter installation would be done at each site by our engineers and technicians. I knew from my knowledge of the design and construction of a VOA site in Africa some 15 years earlier that the government method would have outside contractors do each job, which meant added costs. I wondered if the OMB had asked for an explanation from the VOA of why they wanted more than twice our request for their project. I must say that this was the beginning of some conflict between the BIB oversight group and my office.

Sometimes we needed an escape from the realities of the Cold War and office politics, and Bea was helpful in this regard. She had continued with her interest in learning about opera. With its two great opera houses, Munich was the place for it. Gradually I was indoctrinated into enjoying the pageantry and music by the likes of Puccini, Verdi, Tosca, Mozart, Richard Strauss and Rossini, and performances by the great artists who came to Munich each season. I was able to immerse myself in this fantasy because I wasn't handicapped by knowing the simple story lines. However, I agreed with Mark Twain's comments that Wagner "gives one too much for his money" but his music "is better than it sounds."

We learned that the opera *Aida* was being performed in Verona, Italy, in an ancient outdoor amphitheatre. Since this was the last year they were using elephants and other live animals, we decided to drive down. First we saw some of the mountains of Switzerland and Austria and then drove on to Florence. There we registered at a beautiful mountainside hotel and proceeded to enjoy some of the world's greatest art and architecture, interspersed with good Italian cuisine in that great city.

At the outdoor opera in Verona, we learned that every Italian seemed to be a great tenor or basso profundo as they joined in with the chorus, and sometimes one would solo at intermission. Everyone was having a great time. Venice beckoned nearby, but since we had visited that city of canals some years before with our friends the Blacks, we decided to "keep our good memories undisturbed!"

Back in Munich, I learned from Glen Ferguson that the OMB had included our capital request in the budget submission to Congress, and his contacts had given him some assurance that we would get the funds for the much-needed modernization of our technical facilities. This action soon came to pass, and our technical team got busy with specific plans for the big project.

New antennas were to be built in Gloria, Biblis and Holzkirchen. The Gloria team, along with Willi Kluehe and the consulting engineering team of Kirshner and Wright in Washington, got busy with electronic and hardware design. BIB staff put pressure on me to have the design, construction and installation of these systems farmed out to consultants and contractors, but my firm opinion, and our limited budget, called for this to be done by staff. Soon I was hounded by people who wanted me to give in and sign a contract with a certain California company. My position was that we had better designs and could do it for half the price of that company. Why should we pay more for less?

I was giving John Murphy of the BIB board a tour of facilities and accompanied him to an international spectrum allocation conference in Geneva. As we sat at breakfast in our hotel, we were approached by a representative of the interested antenna company. He sat down and began his pressure tactics when I interrupted him to introduce my companion as a very interested oversight official from the BIB board. At that point our new acquaintance ended his stay, and we enjoyed our meal as I gave Murphy my opinion of the issue.

The pressure continued, and as we attended the tenth Campbell family reunion at the Alabama State Park at Guntersville, I got some calls from company sales representatives using more high pressure tactics. This Campbell reunion was special because it was one of the rare occasions when all of the original siblings were able to reunite. These meetings had become standard with golf, lots of conversation, and the big Saturday evening dress-up banquet. It was always a good time to renew our closeness and to learn of all the births, marriages, and other big events in the lives of our great big extended "clan."

Figure 50. The 1978 Reunion (top row, left to right: Calvin, Tommy, Bert, Bill, Julian, Spud; bottom row: Lecie, Evelyn, Mary, Gloria, Joyce, Doris)

As I returned to Munich, I stopped over in Washington for a meeting at the BIB office. George Jacobs, who was the BIB technical staff advisor and had a background with the VOA, suggested that I was foolish to have these important projects done "in house" and that I should "cover my backside" by passing the responsibility on to an outside firm. He also reiterated his previous statement that the money question should be left to the government, meaning the BIB. I responded that RFE/RL had always operated as a private company and that money did matter to me as a taxpayer. I made one more giant step toward being alienated from the BIB staff. George was a GS 18 civil servant with many friends in the government. But he had no authority in making these types of decisions in my division.

As our project began and soon reached full steam, the media descended upon our offices, and it appeared that most ended in mine. NBC nightly news interviewed me, and it was seen by many of my family and friends, but I never saw it. Dan Rather did his newscast from our control room. I faced newspaper, TV and radio reporters from all over who all wanted to get the story of "What is going on at these radios?" I answered honestly without divulging anything not already known and published.

The media behind the Iron Curtain also reported on our operation and the modernization project. My name was being mentioned on Radio Moscow and in the Communist newspaper, *Tass*. Izvestia referred to me as the chief of the engineering department in Munich and said "everybody in RFE/RL knows that Campbell is a person connected with the American Special Service." Beats me what "Special Service" they referred to.

We knew the Soviets monitored our programs and matched each with noise modulation on our transmitter frequencies. As we analyzed the noise and how it covered our speech, we noted that it was designed to peak on the typical male voice. We saw that female speech, which is at a higher pitch, seemed to penetrate the jamming better, so we recommended the use of more women as speakers. We also did a study of the latest equipment for speech processing and other new products.

One March day in 1979, Glen Ferguson looked into my office door and asked, "How does the title Vice President sound to you?" I joked back, "Pretty good, but president sounds better." He grinned and said, "Watch it buddy, that one is mine." Then he told me that our board, headed by John Hayes, had approved his recommendation that my position be upgraded to Vice President, Engineering and Technical Services. He said in his announcement, "The vice presidential title reflects more accurately the nature of his important assignments." I thanked him and said that I would certainly try to live up to his expectations. Then he told me that my friend Ralph Walter had been promoted to Executive Vice President, RFE/RL Inc. I was very proud to be on a team with such people as Glen and Ralph.

In 1979 I traveled to Dallas to test our transmitters which were scheduled for a very warm day in July. They passed all tests and were made ready for shipment to Portugal and Germany. Our modernization project was moving along on schedule. On my way back to Munich, I stopped in Cullman and talked with my brother Julian about the possibility of building on the lot near his house. Bea and I were talking about retirement and were discussing the house plans we had selected. But that was a year or so away so no arrangements were made except to get Julian's agreement to oversee this project if we decided to build the house before we left Germany.

The new promotion mentioned in Glen Ferguson's announcement changed my day to day routines very little, but it clarified the line of authority in my division which had been somewhat hazy concerning the entire company. I also was appointed to the board of directors of RARET in Lisbon and attended their meetings. Glen assigned the acting presidency responsibility to me if both Ferguson and Walter were away. This was both an honor and a challenge with such a large variety of activities involved.

In 1980, our modernization project was completed within the three-year time estimate, and more importantly, within the budget. (I heard that the VOA had asked the OMB for more funds and time to complete their similar project. I wondered if they made any comparison with our success or if this detail was too small to get their attention.) As I gave the report to the board of directors, I gave major credit to our staff from Gloria and the German sites. They had worked diligently and with skills unmatched anywhere. Special mention was made of the efforts of engineers Neto and Fernandes and the crew from Gloria, Willi Kluehe from Munich, Eddie Krahe from Biblis, Eric Wisner from Lampertheim and Werner Franz and Oskar Mild from Holzkirchen. I also reported that we had evidence

Munich

that our effectiveness was greatly improved especially in the Russian and Polish languages.

In June of 1980, Bea and I decided to retire and move back to the States in 1982. I felt good about my time with the company and decided it was time to get back home for family reasons. I was very appreciative of Bea for staying in Europe when she had reasons for wanting to be closer to the family. I wrote my two-year's notice to Glen Ferguson, along with a complete review of what I considered his options for my replacement. In the end I recommended Hugh Fallis, who was my deputy in Washington, as a replacement. His background at both Radio Liberty and with the consolidated company seemed to combine with his other qualities to fit the requirement. Then Bea and I began our serious planning for the next few years. We had decided to retire to Cullman, a small town that met our basic requirements and could give us the simplified life we desired in retirement.

It was another home leave year, and I went home through Washington where I was debriefed by the National Security Council in the White House annex. I was questioned about our technical division and its successes and failures. I was happy to report that, on balance, we felt good about our present position, but recommended more upgrading of transmitter power in the future.

The 11th reunion of the large Campbell group was held, once again, at the state park in Guntersville. After the usual festivities, we spent time in Cullman where we planned the project to build our new home and selected a builder. My brother, Julian, would represent me in the process. The house would include a separate living area for Bea's mother who was in failing health. Our plan was that I would retire in 1982 when I was 60 years old and had completed 20 years of service with RFE/RL.

Then the morale of the RFE/RL team was given a blow by a staffer from the Board for International Broadcasting. James Critchlow from that staff came over and did a secret study of the program content of broadcasts in the RL languages. He also reported serious mistakes in the technical area at Holzkirchen. His report, which was leaked to the *Washington Post* columnist Jack Anderson seemed to have been aimed at Ralph Walter and me. It contained such exaggerations that I attributed his motive to a grudge carried over from the consolidation. Critchlow had worked for RL, and both Walter and I were from RFE.

To his credit, Critchlow came into my office and made an oral report to me. He said the monitoring in Holzkirchen found cases of wrong programs and language changes in the middle of a program. I asked if he had technical support, and he said he did it himself. I asked if he knew that trying to distinguish among different transmissions within close proximity of several high-powered short wave transmitters was not possible. The sums and differences of each frequency combination creates spurious image emissions, and with so many transmitters continually changing frequencies with a jumble of these images, it is impossible at short range to make much sense of what a receiver hundreds of miles away reproduces. It appeared to me that, although he knew something about the languages used in the transmissions, he knew next to nothing about radio transmission itself and didn't seem to want to know. I got impatient and asked him to leave so I could get on with productive work. I prepared my written report to answer his charges as did Ralph Walter, but the damage to morale was done, and innocent people suffered because of his allegations. Once again, I found myself at cross purposes with the BIB staff.

In Poland in 1980, labor leader Lech Walesa led a series of strikes and disturbances in the Gdansk shipyards, and our Polish language programs were given extra power to overcome the new jamming we monitored on that service. It appeared things were changing inside the Iron Curtain.

Meanwhile, back in Florida, Lynda's life had been difficult. Always a good student, she picked up a masters degree in languages from the University of Miami while teaching in high school. Teaching French and Spanish in high school became a problem, and she soon returned to college and received another masters, this time in special education. By this time, her marriage with Tom had failed, and she moved to Atlanta to try her new special education qualification in the inner city schools of that city. The extreme pressure of dealing with children with all sorts of problems, many of whom had problems at home, proved to be too much, and Lynda moved to Colorado to change careers. Steve lived in Denver after graduating from the University of Denver law school. Bea and I soon decided that we had lived abroad long enough, with isolation from the family and the changing society at home. Our retirement became a goal.

Figure 51. The Munich RFE/RL Building

It was February of 1981, and we had lived for five years in the apartment on the top floor of a building across the Isar River from the RFE/RL office and studio building. That Saturday night of the 21st of February, we heard and felt a blast so strong it shook our chandelier as would an earthquake. I rushed downstairs, and at the front of the ground floor some plate glass windows had been broken. People were gathering around talking, and I heard something about "Radio Freis Europa" (RFE in German).

Since the RFE/RL offices were on the opposite side of our apartment building and a quarter mile away, I couldn't imagine they meant that the blast came from there. But it did. I rushed back upstairs and called my friend Russ Poole, who had already heard about it on the radio. Then I made my way across the bridge and to the RFE/RL building, which already was cordoned off by police.

I pushed through a mass of people and showed my identification to the police. They allowed me to get into the building, and I accompanied the police as they took a flashlight and went through the darkened building. They were concerned that there could be a second bomb, and so was I. We found no second bomb, but one wing, near our master control room, had been largely destroyed. I was told that eight employees were seriously injured but none had been killed. Since it was a Saturday night, only about 30 people were on duty in the large building. The blast had barely damaged master control, and operation was still possible. However our technicians were ordered out, and programming was interrupted for a few hours. No one claimed credit for the bombing, although a woman witness saw three masked men running from the area before the blast.

The bombing was reported in all the major media of the world, and some pointed to the importance of our broadcasts to countries behind the Iron Curtain. The following day, we had resumed full coverage and we were already planning reconstruction of the damage including replacement of about a hundred broken windows.

Spring of 1982 arrived as Bea and I decided to take a week to visit Portugal and Spain once more before our upcoming departure and retirement. We drove through Switzerland, southern France and through Spain to our former home of Portugal. Although I had been there many times, it was Bea's first time there in 10 years. Our friends in Lisbon, and especially in Gloria, greeted us with an enthusiastic reception and showered us with gifts. As we were enjoying all the great conversation and celebration with some of the best friends we had known anywhere, I wondered if this would be the last time we saw them. Then we received a shocking phone call. Bea's mother had become seriously ill and was in the hospital in Alabama. Bea hastily made arrangements and flew home as I said my goodbyes and drove over to the Pals site on my way back to Munich. At Pals, I got the sickening news that my "second mother" had died, and it was too late for me to be at the funeral.

On the long and lonely drive back to Munich, I re-lived the many times we had enjoyed Clara McCullar's hospitality, and I thought, "She was in a class with my father, being as near perfect a human as I could imagine." As in the case of my father's death when I was 5,000 miles away in Eniwetok, I somehow tried to rationalize by being satisfied with my memories of an active person in good health. But gone were the dreams of having her live with us in our new home in Cullman and our hopes of repaying her generosity by helping her. Bea was thankful to her sister, Nell, for the care she had given their mother while we were away.

Back in Munich, I made preparations for our departure. Hugh Fallis had been transferred from Washington and was given some of my responsibilities. My workload was reduced, and I had time for the many chores of moving our furniture and two cars to Cullman.

Bea returned to report good progress on our new house which would be large for the two of us. However, Lynda was living in her grandmother's house in Alabama, and years later would come to occupy our lower floor.

Bea and I talked of how we had enjoyed our 20 years in Europe and especially all the visitors we had so enjoyed over those years. We especially treasured the memories of the visits by Steve and Nan when we toured Germany, "tiny" Liechtenstein, Austria, Switzerland and France with them. We had seen historic churches, beautiful castles, and had all that good food in some of the best restaurants. One outstanding meal was in Roanne at the Frères Troigros, early proponents of *nouvelle cuisine*. It was good to have all these experiences in Europe, and now we anticipated more time with our families and touring our native country we had missed so much.

We were given parties as we said goodbye to everyone. Dr. Ferguson and our Chairman of the Board Doug Mansfield wrote of their regrets that I was leaving at age 60 and thanked me for my key role in the important engineering phase of RFE/RL; they expressed an understanding of my desire to spend time with family. The BIB ignored my departure as they announced the transfer of Hugh Fallis to fill a "vacancy" at Munich. I appreciated their sense of humor. I also had a feeling of having saved taxpayer money by defying their efforts to control our modernization projects.

As we arrived in New York on a jumbo jet, and even though we had been home on regular visits, I felt like Rip Van Winkle who slept for 20 years and awoke to find surprises all around. In my last 20 years, I had lived a dream of fantastic adventures in a foreign environment, but I was "asleep" to what my own country had become. Our immediate problem was to adapt to these changes as I had to do when we first arrived in Lisbon some 20 years earlier. We made our way over to New Jersey, picked up our car and drove toward Cullman, Alabama—our new home.

Chapter 17
Retirement

Before leaving New York, I spent some time at the RFE/RL office where I said goodbye to the staff. With Stan Leinwohl, I discussed our common interests, especially the jamming and other matters of Stan's expertise. He planned to work for several more years before his retirement, and I was happy about that as much of the success of the RFE and later RL in reaching the anxious audiences inside the Iron Curtain had been due to this dedicated man's efforts.

We stopped by Washington and said more goodbyes to the bigger staff there. Mike Marchetti, Vice President for Finance, filled me in on the details of my retirement and insurance benefits. I thanked Mike for all he had done for me over the years and made a quick walk through the BIB offices as I waved goodbye and wished the best to them in their oversight activities. I thought their efforts over the past 10 years had been positive even though I disagreed at times with the staff about priorities.

We had two days driving across the hills and farms of Virginia and Tennessee, discussing our immediate plans. We would finish our house, and then we planned to see more of this great country which we had missed so much over the past 20 years in Europe.

Cullman is a small southern town, but not quite typical. It was founded by Colonel John Cullman, a German immigrant, in the period immediately after the Civil War. It was well laid out with wide streets and well-constructed homes and business edifices. The Colonel had convinced several other German families to move down from Cincinnati and even now the phone book contains many German names along with the Anglo Saxons and others who began arriving later. The Catholic and Lutheran churches are larger than in most southern towns, but other groups like Baptists, Methodists, Presbyterians and Episcopalians are well represented. The new private golf course, Terri Pines, played a part in my decision to settle in Cullman.

After a few days with Julian and Marie and visiting relatives in the area, we moved into our partially finished house. Our lower floor apartment was finished, but we waited to finish the main living area on the street floor level so that Bea could plan the decoration and the selection of furniture. We soon moved upstairs, and Lynda came over from her grandmother's house and moved into the lower floor.

Our first few months were so busy that we hardly noticed the big cultural change from living in the Washington area, Lisbon and Munich. I liked the slow pace of the south at this time in my life; I even suggested we change the stop signs to read "Mosey and don't mosey" to match the pace. Julian and I got more interested in golf as a daily exercise routine, and my readjustment to retirement had arrived. First we played nine holes; then as our legs became stronger, we did the whole course. Within a year we could walk the hilly terrain every day without much strain.

Figure 52. The House in Cullman

In the meantime, Lynda met and fell in love with Larry Sparks, moved to Colorado, and they were married. They moved back to

Cullman and on April 10, 1983 our grandson, Chris, came along and enriched our lives. I had heard of how grandchildren were so special, but I was not prepared for the experience. It seemed that he immediately managed to communicate his desire to be my friend, and this bonding continued. I became a typical Grandpa.

Over the next several years, I settled into a routine of spending time and energy at golf, doing chores around the house, visiting family and friends and always reserving time each day to enjoy being with Chris as he developed. His father, Larry, had problems of loyalty to two families, and soon he went back with his older children and his first wife. I tried to fill in on things Chris may have needed in growing up in a single parent home. My life seemed complete and serene as I had put the toils and troubles and isolation of past years in World War II, Eniwetok, Thule, Greenland and RFE/RL in proper storage of the subconscious memory. However, Russ Poole, who was now a Vice President, kept me informed of happenings with my last employer.

We met many new friends as we joined and became active in "the little white church with the red doors," which was Grace Episcopal Church. The people, the liturgy and the beautiful choral services were what we felt we needed in our spiritual journey. Bea joined the first hospice program in Cullman and kept busy as a volunteer care giver. It was a calling she must have inherited from her mother as she was able to help people who needed this service in their final months in their own surroundings. Hospice is a very worthy service, and Bea is a natural in that capacity.

Reunions with various families and other groups kept us busy with travel, mostly by auto, throughout our state and around the US. There was the biennial Campbell Clan fest, the annual Harbison/Lott cousins reunion and meetings with some RFE retirees. I also enjoy the smaller meetings such as a golf foursome—with Julian, Jack Lansford and Brent Hamner—that met for fun and for "serious" competition twice a year. With the RFE group: we met in Stewart, Iowa with Don Brooks' family; one was hosted by Russ Geiger in Washington; twice we met in Florida; another two in California with Perry Esten; and once here in Cullman.

Figure 53. The RFE/RL Reunion in Cullman

Over the years we had quality time with Bea's cousin Lois and her husband Elmo Brewer. How well we remember the fabulous fish fries with them and with the friends of Bea's mother, Clara McCullar.

I tried to keep up with things worldwide, and in 1984 I noted the death of Brezhnev; things seemed to be less tense as some minor figures took over in the Soviet Empire. A year later I was fascinated when one Mikhail Gorbachev became General Secretary. At 54, he was the youngest Soviet leader in modern times, and his personality and knowledge of the outside world gave hope that things would ease in the Cold War.

Bea and I traveled to Denver for some good times with Steve and Nan. Steve and I played golf, and I first experienced the feeling of exhilaration when the ball would travel so far in that mile-high atmosphere. It somehow made me feel that I was a golfer, and I kept hitting into the group ahead. When one guy hit my ball back, I knew to give them more space. We went on to California and spent some days with Bea's brother Don and his family in Fresno; then on to Monterey for some golf and fellowship with our friends from RFE/RL, Doug and Ruth Montando. With them we visited the points of interest in that beautiful area. We drove the 17 miles and then had a drink at the 18th hole at Pebble Beach golf club. As a very formal

German waiter asked for our order, Doug, with tongue in cheek, said, "Bring me a Perrier and water." And I said, "Make mine a double." The stern looking waiter doubled up in laughter.

As Chris passed the toddler stage and into preschool, he became fascinated with exploring in the lake and creek nearby for lizards, snails, minnows, and everything that swam or crawled. He even taught me to understand and enjoy snakes, and we would catch the harmless kind for his collection. But when one got loose in their house, Lynda ordered us to find that snake! We finally located it inside a floor heating vent, but had to place a board in it so it could get out after we left the scene. Lynda saw little humor in seeing his head sticking out from under a throw rug, and then she set some territorial rules for us "boys."

Chris was always protective of his reptile friends and couldn't bear to see one harmed. His father, Larry, once told me of his experience while walking through the woods with Chris. They came upon a large copperhead, and Larry found a stick and beat the dangerous snake's head in. He said, "I turned to Chris and he was saddened, so I asked him what was wrong." Chris answered, "Dad, I'll never forget the look on that snake's face when you hit it!"

Chris did well in school, but the long hours seemed to create some boredom. After the first day in kindergarten, I asked him how it was in school, and he replied, "It's long and l o o o n g." Then on a spring day as his mother was teaching in another school, I had a call from the office of Chris' school. The lady said that Chris was in the office and was sick. I rushed over and saw that he did look pale so I signed him out and as we walked down the school steps, Chris said, "Grandpa, let's go fishing!" I stifled my amusement and answered, "No Chris, I will take you home, and maybe your Gramma can find some medicine for your illness." He made a rapid recovery and was back in school the next day.

President Reagan and Gorbachev signed a missile reduction treaty in 1987 and vowed to work together for greater reductions. The Soviet leader began liberalizing the economy as he seemed to realize that they could not continue to compete with the free enterprise system of the outside world. For whatever reason, he soon ordered all jamming to be ceased on RFE/RL broadcasts by November of 1988. At that point his people were free to listen to all foreign broadcasts and almost immediately changes were demanded. On September 10, 1989, the wall came down in Berlin and people poured across, mostly east to west. That was the beginning of the greatest bloodless revolution in history. It all happened so swiftly that even the greatest experts were caught by surprise as suddenly several hundred million people saw a drastic change in their governing system.

Some said Gorbachev willed it, others that economic conditions forced him to act, and even others gave the sudden information availability some credit. At any rate, some "straw broke the camel's back" and the jig was up. Over the next two years, the great Soviet nation broke up into many small independent countries that were no longer controlled by the much bigger one, Russia. As I heard the "breaking news," I had visions of a great celebration going on in the big RFE/RL headquarters building on the edge of the park in Munich. For a brief moment I envied those who were still there. But most of all, I hoped that these hundreds of millions of people could make the most of this change. I envisioned a new and somewhat different role for the Munich radio station where I once worked.

I read in a newspaper that Lech Walesa, the Polish leader, in a Washington conference sponsored by RFE/RL, was asked how important these radio networks had been for the cause of Polish freedom. He replied with a question, "Would there be land and earth without a sun?" The article also mentioned that for almost 40 years the "sun" of these radio stations had illuminated the darkened lands of Eastern Europe. I felt pride at having a part of this effort. Soon I felt a bit of painful pride as our government finally recognized the Merchant Marine survivors as veterans of that great struggle for freedom.

In 1990, the year of my fiftieth high school graduation, my class held its first reunion in Cullman. Ten of the 11 surviving members of that class of 1940 attended along with wives and husbands. Of all the interesting experiences over the half century, I was sure mine was the most varied. I was interested in them all and only mentioned some highlights of what I had done. I skipped over the *Henry Bacon* incident as it had been buried deliberately deep in my subconscious memory. Then we went our various ways and made no plan for a repeat the following year. However, it did create an interest in the annual Meek High School alumni banquet which I began to attend, and there I saw a few classmates every spring.

My friend Russ Poole retired as Vice President of RFE/RL for Administration and Management on February 28, 1991 and promised to come by and visit us in Cullman as he traveled south from Ohio to Florida from time to time.

December 7, 1991 was the fiftieth anniversary of Pearl Harbor. And on the next day in the Soviet Union some leaders met and announced the death, at 70, of that once dominant union of nations. Although his programs and decisions would make him a cult hero in the West, Mikhail Gorbachev dissented and continued his efforts to keep the patient on life support. His work over the previous two years to reconcile a Communist government with the best features of a free economy failed, and a new leader, Boris Yeltsin, became the first president of the new democracy. President George H.W. Bush quickly recognized the new regime while praising Gorbachev for his bold moves of the past several years. However, many pundits predicted further turmoil in Russia and the adjoining small countries during transition to elected governments. RFE/RL inherited a new mission of trying to educate the people of these countries about how to live and vote in a free society. This being something we take for granted, often too lightly, but in these countries it must have been overwhelming as few had any inkling of how to think and act in such a free society. What a challenge and opportunity this presented.

Figure 54. Russ Poole Helps Dismantle the Iron Curtain

We were on our way to south Florida for another reunion of RFE/RL retirees when Bea and I stopped in Jacksonville, Florida to visit my sister Joyce and her husband, Pat Johnson. As we enjoyed the time with them I suddenly thought that I would look in the phone book for my friend of Gallups Island days, Bill Brewer. It had been 50 years since I had word of any of my classmates from that magical year on the little island, and I wondered if he would even remember me. Sure enough, I found the number and dialed, and when he answered, I recognized his voice immediately. Suddenly we both could not say enough and hear enough about our pleasure of getting in contact again. I asked him about Art Sheddan, who had also lived in Jacksonville, and he gave me his number. We had to leave, and I told him I would call again on my way back north, and maybe we could get together.

The RFE/RL reunion went well in Pompano Beach as we met with the Estens, the Brooks, the Millers, Russ Geiger, Fran Sherwood, the Pattersons and our hosts, Harold and Lilo Kane.

On our way back we called the Sheddans and had lunch with them. While Bea and Inez talked in the kitchen, Art and I sat on the front porch and caught up with our separate lives since 1942 when we last met. Art had some experiences similar to mine as he lost a ship off Florida and also made a trip to Murmansk. The meal Inez fixed was great, and we left with thoughts of getting together again sometime.

We spent some good time with Pat and Joyce before calling Bill Brewer again. Bill arranged a reservation at a nice restaurant where we met that evening. We had a good meal and great conversation as Bea and Pauline got to know each other, and Bill and I had a ball talking and laughing about our times at Gallups. Then we shared our wartime and career experiences over the past half century. Bill had left the Merchant Marine and gone into the Navy. He seemed to have had a great time, but was a bit wild until he came home and married Pauline. Then he settled into a more serious life of working with a Ford dealership for a long and successful career. He had become interested in church work and was now a devout Christian. He also had been in contact with some others of our classmates and gave me some addresses. That was the beginning of my thinking of the war years again. We left with a promise to keep in better contact.

Figure 55. Bea, Spud, Chris, Lynda, Nan and Steve at Campbell Reunion at Twin Pines Conference Center, 1992

In 1992, I was asked to speak to the Cullman Kiwanis Club of my RFE/RL experiences. I gave the members, representative of the Cullman population who were most interested in the community and world affairs, a 15 minute summary of my 20 years at RFE/RL. I answered the questions they had about this phase of the Cold War, and I was glad to see that much interest in recent history and the world outside our small community. I met and talked with some of the members who invited me to come back as an invited guest. As I learned more about the purpose and activities of this group, I decided to join in their efforts to serve the community and especially to help students and young people. I became an enthusiastic supporter of the range of activities of this group. These included: the international program for getting iodine in salt in countries of the less-developed world, resulting in prevention of goiter and some mental deficiencies in newborn infants; and supporting student clubs from elementary school through college as well as helping students and others in many ways. Our Cullman club gives scholarships to four high school Key clubs and sponsors a middle-school club. By joining this effort I felt I could give back to my community and the world a bit as appreciation for what my country has given me. The weekly meetings always include interesting programs and good food and are held on Monday when the golf club is closed.

In the fall of 1992, I received an unexpected invitation from the Russian Embassy in Washington. It was an official document from their government inviting me to come to Washington in December to be presented with a Russian medal for my part in helping that country in World War II. It sounded to me like a joke since I had spent almost my entire career countering Soviet interests. I wondered if they had checked their media files to see that I was on their list of most hated people during the Cold War. But further checking proved that the offer was genuine and that their new government carried no grudges. After some months of discussions, Bea and I decided that it would be a novelty to be the only one on our block with a Russian hero medal. I felt I had gone full circle from suspicious friend to enemy to cautious friendship with these people.

On a Saturday morning in early December, we began our drive to Washington. We still enjoyed driving rather than flying in the US, and on this beautiful day we discussed our good fortune of being in good health as I entered my 70s and Bea, three years younger. She had taken up golf in her retirement so that we could share that hobby. She had become a good golfer, playing weekly on the ladies' Wednesday golf day. I had been on the course about four days a week for the past 10 years. The regular exercise of walking briskly with a 30-pound golf bag kept me in fairly good physical condition. But this was a big day of a different sport—football. The first Southeastern Conference playoff game was scheduled, and our team, Alabama, was matched against Florida with the winner to go to the Sugar Bowl against Miami for the national championship. We decided at 3:00 pm, just north of Knoxville, to stop at a motel and see the game. When we finally saw a suitable motel I drove up, rushed inside and asked, "Could we rent a room by the hour?" The man looked at us and responded, "That's the first time someone who probably also wants a senior rate has made that request." We got a good laugh out of that one as we explained our plan. We saw the game and our team won, and we proceeded into Virginia for the overnight stop.

As we drove up through Virginia, Bea and I talked about how much had happened since the 1960s when we last lived in that state and I worked in Washington. I began thinking about the way my life had taken so many turns taking me around so much of the world with such a variety of adventures. I silently wondered if I was ready to dig deeply into my memory for the details of that trip to Murmansk in 1945, which I had purposely tried to forget for the past 47 years. Ready or not these memories would soon come back to haunt my days and nights.

On Sunday we arrived and registered at the Savoy Suite hotel. We discovered that many others who were getting the award were staying there. All of them had interesting stories of their adventures as they made the difficult voyage through horrible weather and even worse enemy action while delivering war materiel to the Russians in World War II. Some had heard of the *Henry Bacon* and told me they had read an article by the maritime researcher and writer Ian Millar which told the story well. I also learned that Millar had been largely responsible for convincing the new Russian regime to recognize the people who helped halt the Nazi advance toward Moscow by delivering essential goods. At the hotel, I met Ian Millar, who was eager to talk with me. He said he had seen a dozen accounts of the *Henry Bacon* trip and the Norwegian connection. I told Ian that I was surprised, and that because I had spent most of my career overseas, I knew nothing of these writings and had no contact with anyone from the era during that time.

As I met and talked with several other people who had made the trip to Murmansk, some details of my own experience, which I had long ago forgotten, began to come back. With the memories came an uneasy feeling as I remembered the loss of many friends on that horrible day of February 23, 1945. That night, I began to wonder what I was getting into.

The next day was Monday, December 7, 1992, the 51st anniversary of the attack on Pearl Harbor and the war that began my adventures. Bea and I drove up to visit the beautiful National Cathedral, and I made a call at the Norwegian Embassy which was close by. There I talked with Stig Lorentsen about my experience and also requested a replacement for my Norwegian War Medal which had been lost in my travels. He very kindly agreed to do what was necessary to get it replaced, and it soon came to me through the mail.

On Tuesday our group was transported to the Russian Embassy, and at 10:30 a.m. the ceremony began in an auditorium. After some preliminary talks, Ambassador Vladimir P. Lukin said he represented President Boris Yeltsin in thanking us for our assistance in fending off the Nazi army in World War II. The Ambassador gave each of the several dozen honorees a handshake and the Russian Commemorative Medal. Afterwards we had a grand reception and much conversation with the embassy staff and other participants.

On Wednesday we were transported to the Memorial Statue of the Lone Sailor and went through an elaborate screening process, then were greeted by our own president, George H.W. Bush, who also made us feel proud of our World War II contributions.

As we prepared to leave on Thursday, Ian Millar asked me to give him my memories of the *Henry Bacon* for an article he was writing. I promised I would send it to him by mail. We returned to Cullman and read the story of our little adventure in the *Cullman Times*.

I pondered how to write the details of my long ago experience for Ian Millar as I walked the golf course in our usual foursome of Julian, Norman, Bob and me. Concentration on this subject affected my ability to control my golf swing and more disturbing was a sudden loss of equilibrium at times. I managed to get the letter off to Millar and continued the routine of walking the course four times a week as I had done over the past 10 years. Someone suggested I write a longer story of the adventures of the SS *Henry Bacon*, but I passed it off as "not my style." Actually, I had a feeling that for my own peace of mind, I would have preferred to leave these memories undisturbed.

It had been more than five years since I had gone to Dr. Bill Peinhardt for my "annual" physical. Dr. Peinhardt was a believer in running and other strenuous physical routines for keeping the heart strong and healthy. He asked me about my exercise program; I said, "I play golf." He indicated this was not real exercise, but as I walked the treadmill in his stress test, he was pleased that I could do the full routine; at the conclusion he said, "Let's see if you can handle a few more minutes." He increased the speed and inclination, and I ran for some more minutes as he watched my heart rate, breathing and other indications. Then he said, "Whatever you are doing, keep it up." I told him of the occasional times when I lost balance and he had no answer except that it might be connected with the recent trip to Washington and resurrecting some long-buried memories.

Ian Millar finished his article and sent me a copy. He also gave me the addresses of Bill Herrmann, Chuck Reed, Dick Burbine and Robert Tatosky who were my shipmates on the *Henry Bacon*. He included the address of Len Phillips who was a member of the crew of the British destroyer, HMS *Opportune*, which picked us up from the lifeboat back in 1945. I called Bill Herrmann and we had a good chat for the first time in 48 years, and I sent letters to the others. I wrote Len Phillips, and we began a correspondence which brought back many details from my memory. Len had been to Sørøya Island in the extreme north of Norway and had spent time with some of the Norwegian refugees from that event. He sent me pictures, and he was especially excited about seeing 50-year old Sofie Pedersen who was two years old in the lifeboat. He said the Norwegians had always wondered about those Brits and Americans who were responsible for their being alive.

In December 1993, I had a call from CNN in Atlanta. Bruce Beffa, a features producer, told me they were setting up to broadcast the Winter Olympics from Norway during the following February. They had heard the story of the *Henry Bacon* from some of the survivors. Somehow he had gotten my name and phone number. He asked if I could come to Atlanta for an interview. I declined to go, and he offered to come to Cullman to interview me. He described this as a good human interest story which had a Norwegian/American connection and it would be telecast during the Winter Games

Bruce and his crew spent half a day in our house listening to my answers to his questions. From hours of tape, he got a couple of minutes which were included in his five-minute feature. He also interviewed Norwegian survivors Nils and Bjarne Mortensen, who were 8 and 4 in the lifeboat in 1945. I managed to get through the ordeal of the interview, but some days later I awoke with a severe case of vertigo. It was the first time in decades that I could not get out of bed. It was New Year's Eve and no doctor was readily available, so I just slept until noon and gradually I returned to normal. Then by night time I was back to normal and went to a New Year's Eve party as scheduled. I decided it was time I accepted the reality of remembering and discussing the bad parts of World War II along with the fun parts.

The five-minute feature about the *Henry Bacon*'s last voyage to Murmansk and the disaster and loss of life on the return trip aired on the TNT network of the Turner Broadcasting Group. It was broadcast worldwide on the 23rd of February which was the 49th anniversary of the sinking of the ship. I soon heard from many friends, some of whom I had not seen in many years. Bruce Beffa put me in contact with the Norwegians in Hammerfest and Sørøya Island, and we communicated by mail.

In that same year, Russ Poole from RFE/RL reported that he accompanied Jan Novak, the legendary director of the Polish programs of RFE, to a special ceremony in Pozen, Poland, with Lech Walesa, the Polish leader. Russ reported that Walesa got a good applause and Jan Novak received a standing ovation as the people remembered him for his broadcasts during the Cold War.

Later in 1994, Bea and I and our family received an invitation from the mayor of Hammerfest, Norway to a big celebration of the 50th anniversary of the Norwegians' return home after World War II. My first thought was that it would be a great vacation for the whole family, but Bea reminded me that Lynda would still be teaching and Chris would be in school as the celebration was scheduled for early in May. However, Steve and Nan were for it, and Bea and

I decided to help them make a plan for the "trip of a lifetime." It was to include every means of transportation from air to car to ship and train, taking us as far north as man can travel commercially. Unknown adventures lay ahead as we would see some friends of long ago and meet some new ones.

They say planning is half the fun, and we generously left most of that to Steve and Nan. They researched the flights, sailings and hotels, and over the next five months the plan was made. On April 30 we began the trip which was also a delayed celebration of our 50th wedding anniversary which had been on March 29th.

Our flight to Newark was on time, but our plan to meet Steve and Nan for the Oslo flight failed as their fight from Denver was late. The SAS trip to Olso was routine, and, as is the case of most Atlantic flights, it was a short night. We had made this trip over the Atlantic many times, and we managed to get some sleep on the plane. From Oslo to Tromsø, which is halfway up the 2,000 mile coast, we were in another SAS plane. Then we transferred to a small Widerøe Airlines Dash 8 turboprop for an exciting leg over rugged snow covered mountains, fjords and glaciers to the most northern city in the world—Hammerfest. We took a rental Volvo to the hotel and got a bit of rest; then we went back to the airport to meet our straggling traveling companions. They reported an "exciting" diversion to Frankfurt, Copenhagen and then to Oslo because the plane from Denver was a few minutes late. We all saw a bit of the city of the midnight sun as we proceeded back to the hotel. Actually, at that time of the year, Hammerfest has about 23 hours of daylight, and by the time we left it really did have a midnight sun.

At breakfast the next morning we were joined by Mayor Kåre Rønbeck of Hammerfest, and Magne Nedregard, editor of the local paper. The mayor presented us with invitations to a series of ceremonies on May 3rd and the editor had arranged a meeting with the press at a mountaintop restaurant the next day. We had time to see the town as it was getting ready for the King and Queen to visit and the big celebration in a couple of days. We also visited a museum where we saw a painting of the SS *Henry Bacon* and many other artifacts from World War II. We joined the Polar Bear Club, which required one's presence in Hammerfest to be eligible. I couldn't help wondering how these people could be so normal while living in a place where it was dark for half a year and daylight the rest, such as I had experienced in Thule for one year. We learned that some of them went south for the winters.

At the mountaintop restaurant, we met two of the survivors of the 1945 disaster: Bjarne Mortensen, who had been interviewed by CNN, and Sofie Pedersen who was the two-year-old child in the lifeboat. Neither spoke English but Ingrid Jacobsen, our assigned interpreter who stayed with us for two days, made communications with our friends possible. Bjarne, who was four in 1945, had vague remembrances, but Sofie had none, of course.

We were filmed and interviewed outside with an awesome view of Hammerfest below. It was a busy place with TV camera operators, radio and newspaper reporters milling about. The crew spent hours with the interviews, and I felt like a would-be celebrity but I thought of my friends like Captain Carini, Bob Hunt and all the ones who died; they were the real heroes. However, I was impressed at how much the Norwegian people appreciated what the Americans and British did for them in 1945.

Figure 56. Ingrid Jacobsen, Bea and Spud at Isbjornhallen

Afterward, we went inside the restaurant for a good meal with all the participants. We returned to our hotel, and I had a rest from too much limelight for an old man.

On May 3rd we ate breakfast as the radio and TV in the restaurant presented the story of the *Henry Bacon* and our interviews on the mountain top. The story was in both of the newspapers, one a local and the other a regional paper. We then got ready for the big day as our interpreter arrived to escort us to the Isbjørnhallen, an auditorium where a large gathering of people were seated. The Prime Minister of Norway Gro Harlem Brundtland (later Director-General of the World Health Organization) spoke and introduced King Harald and Queen Sonja. We enjoyed a concert and an elaborate program onstage. We were introduced along with other survivors of World War II. Then a small group of invited guests, including the King and Queen, made a trip on a catamaran to the caves where many local residents hid for months during the Nazi occupation in World War

II. As we ate our boxed lunches, we were amused to see the King open his box with his teeth; I suppose even a king gets that hungry sometimes.

Figure 57. Spud with King Harald

We returned to Hammerfest, and King Harald laid a wreath before the memorial plaque at the town hall. The King gave a speech in memory of those who gave their lives during the war.

In the evening we attended a reception and dinner of specially invited guests at the Rica Hotel. After the President of the Norwegian Parliament spoke, the King and Queen made the rounds and spoke with each group. They were unexpectedly conversational, and we talked for a few minutes. I mentioned that the King's late father had met our ship in Scotland and had presented the medal, which I proudly wore on my chest. He said he had often visited friends in Minnesota, and I asked if he knew about Garrison Keeler, who talks and writes about his Norwegian friends. He didn't, but he said he would ask about him on his next trip to the US.

Steve and Nan were talking with Queen Sonja, and I heard her say, "Steve is so handsome." Bea told the Queen that we would be in Oslo for their big National Day Holiday on May 17. Queen Sonja replied, "We'll wave to you." They were two very nice down-to-earth people whom we enjoyed knowing for a short time. We asked our interpreter why they could go anywhere without bodyguards, and she answered, "They have millions of bodyguards and that includes all the Norwegians." They certainly seemed to be loved by all the people, and we could understand why.

After only a few days, we were so well known in Hammerfest that people would stop us in the street to tell us they appreciated what we did in the war. Some asked for autographs. It was also graduation time and dozens of students were in uniform singing in the streets. They even serenaded our hotel room late into the night.

Figure 58. Spud with Captain Lebaron Russel Briggs

The next day, Thursday, May 4th, we drove south to Alta, famous for its prehistoric rock carvings and as the site where German warships hid in World War II. On May 5th we took a small Widerøe Twin Otter plane for the 15-minute flight to the island of Sørøya. There we were met by Ulf Jacobsen who owned a small hotel in the town of Hasvik. Ulf had invited us to stay with him and to entertain our friends in his dining room. There we met five people who were children in the lifeboat: Inger Pedersen Falk, Sofie Pedersen, Torild Pedersen Angell, Monrad Pedersen and Torild Pedersen Amundsen. We later learned to our surprise that Elbsjørg Pedersen (Monrad's sister who was there) was the 20th Norwegian aboard the lifeboat, as she was in her mother's womb. None of the Norwegians who were adults at the time of the rescue are still alive.

Figure 59. Spud, Monrad, Ulf, Bea and Steve at the Hasvik Airport

The next day Monrad drove us to Sørvær where we boarded a small Norwegian Navy torpedo boat that took us to the inlet at Børfjord where the people who had hidden in the caves were picked up by British destroyers and taken to Murmansk. After our excursion, we returned to Sørvær where scores of people were meeting for a banquet and commemoration ceremony. After a good meal there were many speeches by survivors and local officials. I was included as a speaker with help from an interpreter. After I cut my allotted time short of the 10 minutes scheduled, I received an ovation, partly because of my brevity, I was convinced. Ulf played a big part in the arrangements, and we could see that he was a respected local leader.

The next day was Sunday, and it was a busy one. After attending church in Hasvik, the four of us went with Monrad, Elsbjørg, Torild and her granddaughter Kaylen to see the site of the Sørøyans' bitter winter of 1944-45. We walked for what seemed miles over snow, rocks and tundra where the only living things were tiny cloudberry plants and lichen. At the edge of the sea was a cave about 35 feet wide and 50 feet deep where about 35 islanders hid from the Nazis from November 1944 to February 1945. The Norwegians survived in caves like this with the worst conditions any human could survive. As they came aboard the *Henry Bacon* we had no idea of the suffering they already had experienced.

Figure 60. Sofie, Ulf, Heldur and Torild in Hasvik

After our long walk to the cave, we celebrated Bea's birthday with a meal served by Ulf and his wife, Heldur. The next day, May 8, we boarded another small plane for Kirkenes, next to the Russian border. There we had planned to travel by car or plane to Murmansk as we had been invited by the mayor to attend a ceremony commemorating the 50th anniversary of VE Day. (To prepare for this trip, our hosts in Hammerfest spent hours arranging our visas.) However, our plans were thwarted when we were informed by the officials in Kirkenes that auto travel was restricted to one way one day with returns the next, to protect the secret Murmansk naval facilities. The only flight to Murmansk each day was a turn-around flight at midday. The Norwegians warned us that spending the night was not recommended as the "Russian Mafia" controlled the city and crime was rampant. So we spent our day in Kirkenes learning about the area and especially the Sámi people (Laplanders) who had lived in the far north of Finland for centuries. A museum contained the works of Sámi artist John Savio and had many other artifacts and writings. We also participated in a commemoration of World War II in Kirkenes and had a chance to talk with the Russian consular officials about the history of the war in the area.

On May 9, we boarded the Norwegian Coastal Line ship, *Richard With*, for a six-day voyage around the North Cape and down the rugged but scenic coast to Bergen. Our accommodations were very comfortable, the food was great and we were given an active program of entertainment and education about the many fjords and harbors where we stopped for passengers to depart and board. At some stops we participated in tours.

We spent a night in Bergen visiting the city's museums and soaking in one of Bergen's 300 days of rain. The next morning, we boarded a train which crossed the country over the most scenic mountain route imaginable and arrived in Oslo on May 16.

As Bea promised Queen Sonja, we were in Oslo on May 17, Norway's National Day; the queen kept her promise and waved to us amid the 100,000 others watching the colorful parade pass in front of the palace balcony. It was a great celebration with parades of bands that seemed to last all day. I celebrated with them because by now I felt that, "Ich bin ein Norwegianer."

Over the next two days, we toured Oslo, including Frogner Park, the Viking Ship Museum, the Kon Tiki museum and the Folk Museum; when we left the Folk Museum and were unable to find a cab, the museum's chairwoman stopped and offered us a ride back to our hotel. By a few minutes we missed the closing time of the Munch Museum where we hoped to see the Edvard Munch painting of "The Scream."

We arrived home on Thursday, May 18. Although we were very tired from the long and active trip, it was not time to rest. I was scheduled to be the main speaker at the Meek High School Alumni Banquet on Saturday evening. I revised my notes to include some of the highlights of our trip along with the summary of my career which I had previously prepared. I struggled through an hour of the talk and included some video clips of Norway as I proudly accepted the Alumnus of the Year award. Then we relaxed and had time to savor the memories of our most active three weeks. Later Bea put together a very nice album of the events for our collection.

During the lulls of activity concerning that event of 1945, I was able to serve on the vestry of Grace Episcopal Church, where I was Junior Warden for one year and Senior Warden for another. I also worked on two search committees of that church during the 1990s. I continued to enjoy my civic duties by working with Kiwanis and served on jury duty as foreman in a murder case. A year later I was called to serve in Birmingham for six months duty on a federal grand jury, and I was appointed foreman by the judge. I had missed out on these civic duties during my many years overseas, and felt I should catch up. Certainly it was a time to learn something of our country's legal system and its law enforcement problems.

My physical exercise needs were well served by walking the golf course at Terri Pines four times a week with my brother and others. I also still enjoyed my daily fun times with Grandson Chris as we walked the creeks and sometimes practiced hitting golf balls. So my life was full as I approached my 75th birthday. Bea continued her service in hospice and also was an active golfer in the women's group. She got her hole in one, and also won the net score championship. In both these areas she had eclipsed me as I became the only adult golfer in my immediate family without a hole in one.

My communications with Russ Poole by e-mail were constant and almost daily. He kept me informed of his activities and that of other RFE/RL retirees and some still active in the reduced service of that company. By mail and e-mail we had many communications, especially at Christmas, with our new Norwegian, British and Portuguese friends. I also made contact with the few American survivors from the *Henry Bacon* story.

The biennial Campbell reunion tradition continued and was again held in Cullman in June 1996. It was hosted by my family with Steve and Nan doing most of the work. Chris participated in the entertainment as he played in a small band and did some magic acts, two of his hobbies at that time. The Saturday night banquet was held in the All Steak Restaurant with a good turnout of more than 70 people. However there was a sad note: my four oldest brothers had died, and Julian and I were the only sons of George and Martha Campbell still surviving.

In 1997 we got the urge to see some more of our own country. We drove to South Dakota to see Mt. Rushmore and other scenic areas and on through Montana and into Canada. We especially wanted to see Banff, Lake Louise and on up to the Ice Fields. We crossed the Rockies at Jasper and returned to Vancouver where we met Steve and Nan for a tour of that city. The four of us took a ferry to Victoria and another down to Seattle. There we visited friends, Jo and Sid Stoltz, from Munich days. Steve and Nan returned to Denver by air, and we drove down to Portland for a visit with the Brooks and Pattersons, two ex-RFE families. Don and Dedda Brooks led us on a tour up the Columbia River valley. It was a beautiful drive with hills and cliffs and the spectacular view of Multnomah Falls. Then we drove up the side of Mt. Hood. It was good to visit with these two families once again.

As we left, we traveled south and swung by to do the exciting drive around Crater Lake. When we reached the rim, we suddenly were on a narrow two-lane road with a steep drop-off on each side. It was breathtaking, and Bea kept moving over to my side of the car to avoid having too much weight near the cliff. I recommend that drive to anyone who passes that way for its sheer beauty and excitement.

In Monterey we visited our good friends, the Montandos, and saw Pebble Beach again. We never tire of that beautiful peninsula; then to Fresno to see Bea's brother Don and his family. We made the long drive home to rest and to get back to Terri Pines for more walking the golf course. It was a great 7,500 mile trip and, as always, it was good to get back home.

That year we heard from Bill Brewer that he was hosting a reunion of our Gallups Island class of 1941. The timing matched our annual trip to Orange Beach, Florida to be with some family members, so we were pleased with that. From Orange Beach we drove to St. Augustine and spent some days with our old friends.

The group included: Bill and Pauline Brewer; James and Mae Smart from North Carolina; Coleman and Adele Barbour from San Antonio; Sam and Bea Notaro from Long Island; Art and Inez Sheddan from Florida; and C.W. Rampy from Texas. We had a great time and could have enjoyed many more days listening to wonderful stories of their adventures and trials during the 59 years since most of us had been together. Then back to Cullman and a return to the routine of our life there.

By this time we were thinking of restricting our travel as we were in our late 70s, but this was not to be. In March 1998, I received a letter from Harald Hendriksen of Oslo. He said he had researched and written a small book on the Allied convoys to North Russia in 1941-45 and the *Henry Bacon* story was included as a chapter. He was a retired banker and government official and had been awarded a government grant to do a preliminary study for a TV documentary of that era as it affected Norway. Harald asked if I would agree to participate if he should be given the money to complete the project. I told Bea that the *Henry Bacon* drama had taken on a life of its own. I wrote him back and agreed to help as I had great respect and affection for the Norwegians.

I had been elected (drafted is more accurate) to serve as president of Kiwanis for a year beginning October 1998, and we traveled to Montréal in July of that year for the annual International Convention. We went with 90-year-old Raymond Yost, who was a legendary member of our club. He had more than 60 years as a member and had received every honor imaginable. He was up early and stayed active late, and we became exhausted trying to keep up. But the convention was interesting and very helpful as I needed to learn from these people in order to preside for a year. Montréal is a great city, and we saw much of it thanks to Raymond and his eternal enthusiasm and energy. We returned in time to attend the big Campbell reunion in Guntersville State Park.

Chris was 15 and had his learner's permit. After his busy days at school, he and I spent hours together as he drove on his permit with me riding shotgun. We made the rounds of all the used car dealerships, and after some 50 hours, we found what he wanted. He had saved his money and could pay most of the cost (supplemented a bit) and he bought a used Saturn. Then he waited for some weeks before his birthday. On that Monday, he was first in line for his driving test and passed it easily. He was well versed in driving when he soloed for the first time.

In August Len Phillips, our English friend from the destroyer *Opportune*, wrote to tell me that Jack Harrison, a Navy veteran of World War II, had visited the little harbor of Loch Ewe, Scotland where the convoys had formed in the war. Jack was so taken with his trip that he had started a move to establish a museum in the town of Poolewe. He said Jack was very interested in contacting me so I wrote him a letter of encouragement in his project.

Jack wrote me with complete information about his plan for the museum at Loch Ewe. It was to be submitted to the Scottish Museum Council in Edinburgh and would tell the story of the convoys to northern Russia with pictures, text and artifacts from crew members. The story of the Norwegians and the *Henry Bacon* incident would be featured along with other events of World War II. Board members would represent many of the facets, and he asked if I would represent the American Merchant Marine. He was trying to get an exception to the Council regulation that no board member could be over 75 years of age. It all sounded like an exciting challenge, and I agreed to do what I could to help.

Serving a year as president of Kiwanis and keeping in physical condition walking the golf course filled my time. However, in midwinter Harald Henriksen called from Oslo with the news that he had his grant and wanted me to come over in April for a series of interviews with other survivors of the *Henry Bacon*. Bea wasn't eager to undertake another strenuous trip, and we put the plan on a back burner. I told her I would only agree to go if she accompanied me.

Meanwhile Jack Harrison arranged a meeting of his museum committee and the Scottish Museum Board in Poolewe in April. We mentioned it to Steve, and he said he would like to go with us to the Scottish meeting. I submitted Steve's name as my successor on the board because of my advanced age.

Unfortunately, Lynda and Chris once again would be in school, and I was sorry they couldn't go. Steve took over the planning for the Scottish phase, and the Norwegians planned the Norway part. I wondered if this *Bacon* story would ever go to sleep again. Around this time, the public relations person from Kiwanis arranged with the Birmingham TV station, Channel 6, to film a Kiwanis meeting in Cullman. They also came to our house and got a scene of Bea and me and a promise from me to come down for their morning show. This I did, and they presented me as a hero, which made me uncomfortable. Soon I had invitations to speak to various groups, but I declined; it was not my desire to complicate my life more than necessary.

In April I arranged with Seth Thompson, our president-elect, to preside over the Kiwanis meetings while we were away in Scotland and Norway. Steve worked out a plan to tour Scotland on our way to Loch Ewe. Bea and I packed our bags and headed to Europe once again. We arrived in London and took a train through the Midlands to the city of Derby where we were met by Jack Harrison. He loaded our luggage in the back of his car and drove through his hometown of Belper and on into the countryside to a bed and breakfast in an old farmhouse. The farmhouse was nice and modern, but one part of it dated back several centuries. On the way he pointed out a road which was built by the Romans when they occupied England.

After we had some rest, Jack picked us up again, and we met Jeanne, his wife, and we all met many of Jack's friends at his golf club. Our meal was great, and the conversation at dinner was about our plans at Loch Ewe. Then we went to a reception at the home of Jack's friend and our e-mail go-between, Stanley Suggitt.

The next morning Jack took us to the train station, and we were on our way to Edinburgh where we would meet Steve. He flew directly to Edinburgh, rented a car, and met us at the hotel. We drove west to Inverary and the Duke of Argyll's main Campbell castle, then traveled up the Great Glen, past Loch Ness to Inverness and the Cawdor castle, another Campbell landmark. We spent two more days on the road, traveling through the starkly beautiful highlands and islands region of northwest Scotland.

Retirement

We arrived in Poolewe and found the hotel. It was too early to check in so we drove over to the big park, known as Inverewe Garden, where we walked around to see the many flowers and plants, some of which were almost tropical. We were told that it was possible for this flora to grow and flourish this far north because of the Gulf Stream currents. The park had been developed by Osgood Mackenzie in the 19th century.

Steve drove us out to the point at the entrance of Loch Ewe. I stood and gazed at the smooth calm water, empty of ships. I was at peace and so was the world at that time. Then I closed my eyes to visualize the hundreds of ships laden with the tools of a war that seemed never ending. In 1945, when Captain Carini and I returned from the convoy conference, we joined the crew to enter a sea so rough we were unsure if the ship could survive nature; it did, but then it failed to be so lucky against the human storm. My good captain together with Bob Hunt and a couple of dozen of his crew and millions of others met their final fate because of a mad dictator and his willing followers. Then I felt dizzy so I opened my eyes and tried to forget once again.

At the Pool House Hotel we were greeted by Peter Harrison, the proprietor. Bea and I were given the bridal suite and treated royally during our entire time at this nice little hotel. We soon met Jack Harrison, Jim McHugh and Chris Tye and discussed the next day's meeting with the people from the Scottish Museum Commission. The plan was to build the museum on the grounds of the hotel. In addition to the main museum, there was to be a "Henry Bacon Bar" where the story of the ship would be depicted on the walls. On the following day, Steve and I met with the group and had a chance to speak of our part in the proposed museum. The meeting lasted for a couple of hours and ended without a decision by the Scottish officials.

Figure 61. Spud, Jack Harrison, Chris Tye and Jim McHugh in Poolewe

The following day we said goodbye and thanked the Peter Harrison family for their hospitality. Then we departed for Edinburgh for Steve to make his scheduled flights back to London and Denver. It was a more direct and better, if not as interesting, road so we made it back in one day.

We spent that night in the Bank Hotel which was in a building which was formerly used as a bank. It was an interesting scene as we entered through a very noisy and active pub where we later had dinner. Each room was named for a famous Scot; ours was named for Robert Louis Stevenson.

That evening we took a long walk along the wide and active Prince's Street. And we wished for more time to really see this city of so much history.

Steve left, and Bea and I were so thankful for his thoughtfulness to accompany us on this memorable tour of Scotland, the land of our ancestors. Then we boarded another train for the run down to York. There we took the circle tour which follows the site of the ancient wall, some of which still exists. The Roman conquerors had used the city as their military capital during the 2nd century, A.D. The city survived Viking raids and the Norman conquerors and then became a northern center of ancient Britain. We enjoyed the city, and Bea did some shopping and bought me a white shirt for our Norwegian trip, as we had run short on dress clothes. The next day we took the train to London.

We booked into a hotel near Gatwick Airport and took a walk through a big park, then found an interesting restaurant on the grounds of a church. Our last dinner in England was very good.

We were met at the Oslo airport by a surprisingly large contingent of people including TV producer Harald Hendriksen, his director, Jan Horne and others including Per Danielsen, who played a vital part in the escape and rescue of the Norwegian survivors from Sørøya in 1945. There were so many that it was difficult to get them sorted out as we went through the chore of picking up luggage and loading it and ourselves onto the two or three vans waiting outside. We were rushed to the hilltop hotel Leangkollen in the Oslo suburb of Askar, which had been the retreat of Vidkun Quisling, Hitler's Nazi collaborator who ruled Norway during the German occupation of World War II.

Soon we were ready and were picked up and driven to a downtown hotel where we met the 24 other banquet guests for a semi-formal reception and dinner. We found we had the "guest of honor" seats at the big oval dining table. We were flanked by Col. John Bilyeu and his wife Nina, representing the US Ambassador who had to cancel at the last moment. At the other end of the table were: Kjell Alvheim, Norwegian Secretary of State; Rear Admiral Jacob Borresen; Naval Captain Eigil Abrahamsen; Naval Capt. Marcus Osen; economist Hendriksen; Per Danielsen and their wives. Others included some of the TV production crew. It was a very interesting and informative dinner, and I tried to keep up with the conversation and enjoy my meal and to do my part in the after dinner speeches. I expressed my appreciation to Mr. Hendriksen for the honor and gave credit to the real heroes, those who had not survived. Then I spoke of the horrible ordeal of the Norwegians in World War II and the bravery of the survivors from Sørøya. The evening was memorable, and I felt humble and a bit overwhelmed by it all.

On the next morning, May 3rd, we flew with the Hendriksens to Bodø where we were transferred to the coastal liner *Midnight Sun*. At the airport we were met and greeted warmly by Monrad Pedersen and as we boarded the ship, we had a joyous time with Inger Pedersen Falk and her daughter Christine. *Bacon* survivors Monrad and Inger had somehow gotten word of our travel plans and came from their homes to spend a bit of time with us. We were first thrilled and then amused when our traveling companion, Harald, joked, "This is my country, but you know more people here than I do."

Our charming host and hostess, Harald and Guri, left the ship at Lofoten Island to visit relatives, and we continued on to Hammerfest where we were met at 5:30 a.m., by another old friend, Ulf Jacobsen. Always thoughtful, he had arranged a hotel room for the day so we could rest before taking a ferry with him to Sørøya at 4:00 p.m. By noon we were awake, and Ulf took us to lunch and then to a World War II museum. Some high school students were touring the museum, and one of them ran up and greeted us with a hug and began speaking in English. It was Torild's granddaughter Kaylen Karlsen, who could speak no English when she walked to the cave with us four years earlier

At 4:00 p.m. we boarded a ferry with Ulf, and again we saw Kaylen with her friends. So the short run to Hasvik, Sørøya was a time for talk with friends. Ulf assured us we had a full schedule for the next two days, and Kaylen asked if I could speak to her high school English class. I told her I would try to do so if I could find an hour.

At Ulf's hotel we were met by the TV crew: Jan Horne; cameraman Erik Lindbom; audioman Runar Grendar; and Per Danielsen, who had come up with the crew. After dinner we were invited to a reception at the home of our friend Torild and it seemed like a family reunion. These people wanted to express their appreciation for just being alive; I accepted these kindnesses in the name of our country and the *Henry Bacon* crew.

The next day the TV crew, Per Danielsen and I made the trip by PT boat once again to the inlet where the refugees were picked up in 1945. The water was rough, and I was embarrassed by becoming very seasick again. Then I had to face an hour of interviews and filming on the bow of the little boat. On the way back I got some needed sleep.

Back at the hotel, I recovered enough to walk up to Keylin's high school where the teacher, who had been my interpreter in 1995, introduced me to her class. They had been studying World War II history and were prepared to listen as I told them of my experiences with their friends and relatives as we shared a lifeboat. They then presented me with a little cap on which they each had signed their name and nickname.

When I returned to the hotel, I had time for a couple of hours of work with the TV interview crew. Then it was time for our dinner and, as in 1995, it was again Bea's birthday, so Ulf and Heldur had prepared a big party for everyone we knew in this town. Bea received many gifts, including two beautiful handmade dolls from Torild, a hand painted plate from Elbjorg, candles and a figurine from Keylin and her friends, and a handmade tablecloth from Sofie. That little island of Sørøya holds a very special place in our hearts and memories.

We made the return trip to Oslo and once again enjoyed those great breakfast buffets at the Leangkollen Hotel. In Oslo, we met two more *Henry Bacon* survivors, the brothers Mortensen—Nils and Sigvart—who had come in for interviews with me. It always took hours of answering questions in order to get a few minutes of useful footage. Nils was nine years old in the lifeboat so I was eager to get his remembrances. I asked him if he remembered how seasick I was after the strenuous task of erecting the mast for the antenna. I was delighted that he did remember it as he gave me a big smile. This was done through an interpreter because neither of the brothers spoke English.

After two more days filled with interviews, tours and a big party on the last night at the hotel dining room, we finally said our goodbyes and wished Harald and Jan success in getting the documentary completed and on TV.

At the airport, anti-terrorist precautions required that we walk our bags to the next flight at the Paris airport as we changed planes.

Because we were late arriving, we missed our connection so we were put up for the night at a hotel. This was not our desire; we wanted to get home with family and just rest, but these are the perils of flying in these times.

Back in Cullman, I completed my year as president of Kiwanis and was unexpectedly given both the Kiwanian of the Year award and the Barnett award for outstanding achievement. I passed the gavel to Seth Thompson and moved on to the best office of all, Past President, where I could sit back and enjoy the programs and the meals at meetings.

In October 1999, my Royal Navy friend Jack Harrison came over and spent a week with us. He was interested in seeing this part of the country. One of his primary interests was the Civil War. I enlisted my good friend Howard Williamson, an expert on the subject, to lead us on a tour of the battlefield and museum in Franklin, Tennessee. As we returned, Howard invited us to his home to see his full room of artifacts and information on that war. Jack was very impressed. I thanked Howard for his service as a tour guide. We also made a tour of the space museum in Huntsville and returned by Tuscumbia to visit the home of Helen Keller. On another day we traveled to Tuscaloosa and visited the Japanese garden at the Warner paper plant. We stopped for a short tour of the Mercedes plant at Vance on our way back.

In January 2000, the three-hour documentary, "Russian Convoys," was completed by the Norwegian Broadcasting Company and was aired in that country. It also was shown in some other European networks, but unfortunately the History Channel in the US did not air it, probably because it is a bit long for the attention span in our society. Maybe someone will condense it to an hour in the US and show it because it fills a very important gap in our appreciation of the war as it concerned the Norwegians. Mr. Hendriksen and Jan Horne are to be applauded for their efforts and the quality of the documentary.

During the early part of 2000, I learned of a book about the *Henry Bacon* which was being finished by Dr. Robert Alotta, an historian who was a professor at a college in Virginia. Co-author Donald

Foxvog had conducted many interviews in the sixties with *Henry Bacon* survivors. At the time I was living in Europe, so I had no idea of this activity. Dr. Alotta sent his book to me on-line, chapter by chapter, and I suggested changes and insertions, as I remembered the events. Many of them were included and the book went to press in early 2001 as *The Last Voyage of the SS* Henry Bacon. These writers did a great job of painting a word picture of one of the most dramatic sea adventures of World War II. I recommend anyone who has interest in that war to read this comprehensive volume.

At about the same time, I was contacted by a Scottish TV producer, Elly Taylor, who was interested in doing a documentary story which included the *Henry Bacon* story. She had already received a grant for a preview of the project and was to come to the US to visit the American survivors of the tragic event. Her preliminary work would be used in a request for a further grant to do the complete documentary. Bea and I assured her she would be welcomed if she came to Cullman. The story of this ill-fated ship was still occupying a part of our lives. Elly came by and spent two days with us. She taped an interview with me to be used in her presentation and request for funding the documentary project. She also visited two other *Bacon* survivors and a couple in Seattle who were the primary subject of her story.

In June we got word that Bea's brother, Don, was gravely ill and was not expected to live much longer. We decided to drive to California to visit him while he was still able to enjoy some time with Bea. We asked Chris if he would go, and he agreed, if he could drive. He did most of the driving and got some more valuable experience with freeway and traffic conditions. At Fresno, we found Don in a military rehab hospital and spent some time with him. He and Bea talked about old times and he had a marvelous attitude for one who was terminally ill. Bea said he talked of how it would be after death, and remarked, "Bea, I wish I could come back and tell you how it is after I die." It was a good time to be there with Don, and also with Bea's sister, Nell, and her husband, Lee Wetzel, and we thought it was better than going to a funeral. Don died in July, and we were happy to have spent some quality time with him and his family, along with Nell and Lee.

On our way back we stopped overnight at Las Vegas. With 17-year-old Chris, we walked around and saw some of the sights. Chris was not too interested in the lifestyle in that city and neither were we. But we did enjoy being there with all those celebrating people. The food and lodging were inexpensive and good. Then we drove on through the beautiful mountains of southern Utah and into Colorado. In Denver, we had a couple of nights with Steve and Nan, and that was a special treat as they always find time in their busy lives to be great hosts. There we had a good outing and meal with Steve's friend and colleague of many years, Robby Robinson and his wife, Beth.

The last year of the second millennium was also a transition year for our teenager Chris. His best friend Dallas Estes and his family were moving to Springdale, Arkansas, and they wanted Chris to accompany them. So Chris, after much discussion with his mother, grandparents, friends, and also with Jim and Bea Estes, decided to spend his last high school year with Dallas in Arkansas. Lynda was becoming overstressed with her teaching and having a discontented teenager in the house added further stress. It was decided among all interested parties that Chris would move to Arkansas.

In 2001 the Alotta/Foxvog book was published by Paragon House and received good reviews in the *New York Times* and many other publications. It created much interest among people who were interested in World War II but unfortunately it was not available in most book stores. It is available on-line at Amazon.com.

After Chris graduated from Springdale High School in Arkansas, he and his friend Dallas Estes came to Alabama to spend some of the summer. They needed to earn some money for a vacation on the Gulf Coast. Jobs for students weren't easy for them to find; most were taken by the locals. I remembered that my brother Julian was trying to get a contractor to rebuild a crosstie retaining wall which had been destroyed by heavy rain during the past winter. I asked Julian if he would give the boys a chance to do the job at half the bid price of a contractor. I promised to help with the planning and to supervise their work which would be guaranteed to meet his approval before they were paid. Julian agreed, and the deal was sealed with a handshake.

It was obvious to me that if the wall were rebuilt as before, it would once again be destroyed by the first heavy rain. I drew up a plan to give it support by burying "deadmen" of concrete, like those used to anchor the guy wires of power poles. A cable or rod could be tied from the wall back up to the buried concrete. This meant a lot of heavy digging and lifting of the heavy crossties. The weather was hot as is common in the Alabama summers. But we had fun as these boys, who had hardly ever broken a sweat at labor, followed my lead to dig, lift, nail, pour concrete and backfill for five days. Sometimes we could only work a few hours in the morning, and sometimes we worked after the sun went down, but we finished the job. Chris and Dallas were two happy boys when they finished and got their pay. It was a good lesson for them as they go into college to prepare for a career. They know what the alternative could mean: hard labor!

Soon Dallas returned to Arkansas and Chris began considering his options for college. He rejected the local community college, Wallace State, and then he and his friend Daniel Waugh visited Montevallo University along with Bea and Daniel's mother, Susan. It was decided that this was their best choice, so they applied and were accepted. In late August, they moved some of their personal items into a dorm and began the rigors of this sudden change in their routines. On September 11th, the whole country and much of the world were given the greatest wake-up call since December 7, 1941.

As a 79-year-old, I wondered if I would ever see another peaceful day as I suddenly became a pessimistic optimist. The whole country reacted with shock, then anger, followed by immediate drastic action by the government. In a way it was a repeat of the time when I, like Chris, was just out of high school, and the world was smoking.

We called Chris and found him also in an angry mood. The 9/11 disaster, plus coping with a myriad of problems, seemed to confound him. I felt helpless in the whole situation. What followed can be classified as "The winter of our discontent" which continued for more than a year.

Chris did poorly in school; he tried to solve his personal life by moving from a dorm into a house with a friend, but that was not the answer, so he decided to transfer to a junior college in Arkansas for the next year. His car was troublesome; so we helped him to trade for a better one.

Two months after the 9-11 disaster, my beloved sister Evelyn died after a prolonged illness. It was a sad time for the family and I told her in her last days how much she had meant to me. As a confused young man, I received much hospitality and encouragement from Evelyn and her husband, Arvil, as World War II approached. I am forever grateful to her and have love and compassion to her family and especially her daughter Betty and family who supported her so faithfully in her last years.

Since my retirement the Campbell clan has seen the passing of my four oldest brothers, one sister, four brothers-in-law, four-sisters-in-law, a nephew and a niece. It's sad to say goodbye, but in a real sense I celebrate them for what their lives have meant and for my good memories of them all.

Christmas of 2001 was not a time for big celebrations. We had a quiet celebration with many prayers that the world could soon find a solution to the problem of dealing with people who seemed so desperate. This is a new and on-going problem.

Bea and I needed a diversion so we accepted the invitation from Steve and Nan and left on Christmas Day for a drive over to the little town of Bamberg, South Carolina where they were celebrating a family reunion of Nan's great extended family at the ancestral home of Nan's mother, Clarice Brabham O'Neal.

We had picked up Steve at the Atlanta airport and spent a night with him at Augusta, Georgia. It was good to see Nan's parents at Christmas, as well as many of her extended family and friends.

On December 27th we went to Columbus, Ga. and then to the Victoria Inn at Anniston, Alabama. On the 28th we were joined by Steve and Nan to celebrate my 80th birthday. Along the way I had been trying to master the technique of photographing with the great digital camera they had given me for my birthday.

In 2002 Elly Taylor received her grant to film the documentary and asked that I meet with the other two American survivors of the *Henry Bacon* in San Francisco for interviews aboard the Liberty ship *Jeremiah O'Brien*, which is identical to the *Henry Bacon*. Steve and Nan met us in San Francisco and took us to the home of Nan's sister and brother-in-law, Mary Carlton and Tim Lull; Tim was President of the Pacific Lutheran Theological Seminary in Berkeley. Their house, on top of the hill overlooking San Francisco Bay, was more than impressive and we enjoyed a few hours visiting with him and his son Chris and grandson, Taylor. Mary Carlton was away in the South at the time.

It was like boarding a ghost ship as we ascended the gangway and walked through the Liberty ship which was so much like the *Henry Bacon*. Even after 58 years, everything seemed so familiar. It was good to have my family with me while we toured the ship. Once again all those memories came back.

It also was good to be once again in San Francisco, the great city by the bay, especially with Steve and Nan, who are such great traveling companions. We just sat back and let Steve do all the driving as we did in Scotland. He never seemed to mind doing it. After they had to return to Denver, we got down to the business of the interviews.

I still had not met my shipmates, Chuck Reed and Dick Burbine. Elly wanted to film our first meeting on the ship the next day. We were interviewed together as well as separately for some hours. On the last night, we had another good meal and talked around the table with the group which included Elly, her film crew, Chuck Reed and his daughter. The next morning, I was busy for two hours being interviewed as we rode the cable cars. As usual, it always takes hours to get minutes of usable footage.

Figure 62. Aboard the SS Jeremiah O'Brien (from left: Dick Burbine, Chuck Reed, Rodney Bowden and Spud

Back home, Lynda decided to simplify her life by changing her career as she had often considered in the past. She resigned her stressful teaching job, sold her house, and moved to Colorado. However, that wasn't the answer, so she came back and settled into the lower level of our large house. This worked and she soon became an active member of our family, which has enriched our lives. She began a new and different career as assistant director of the conference center at the Benedictine Convent.

One night in August 2002, we experienced an electrical storm so severe that our world was a constant roar of thunder with flashes of lightning. I was in bed when I heard rapid footsteps at our front entrance followed by someone banging on the door and sounding the chimes. Bea said, "Don't open the door." But I did to see Julian and Marie in night dress. He rushed by me, saying, "Our house is on fire," as he headed for the phone to call 911. By the time the firemen arrived, his house was so full of smoke and heat it was impossible to get into the basement to deal with the fire. The interior was destroyed along with their furniture and a lifetime's collection of treasures.

Investigation revealed that lightning struck a tree and traveled through its roots to the copper gas line and followed the gas line to Julian's furnace room. The force of this charge exploded into a gas-fired blow torch. It was too late by the time he knew it. Julian and Marie eventually got back to normal by moving into a "maintenance free" condo.

It had been a difficult year since the 9/11 terrorist attack. We decided to go to Orange Beach with other family members, a gathering we missed the year before because of the disaster. Bea and I decided to take some time off and stay a few days. We also were to meet Russ and Renate Poole for dinner while we were there. On our second evening in Florida, we received a phone call from Lynda telling us that Chris had been robbed and stabbed in Fayetteville, Arkansas and was in the hospital. We left almost immediately for Cullman and arrived at 3:00 a.m. We slept three hours and, with Lynda, drove straight to Fayetteville—arriving at 8:00 p.m. Chris had gone through surgery and was still asleep. His friend Dallas told us what had happened.

Chris was returning from work when he was paged by his girl friend. He stopped at a service station in a well-lighted area to call her at her home. The phone booth was occupied, and he sat in his car waiting. A young man came to his car and asked Chris for drugs. He had none, and the guy pulled out a knife and put it to Chris' throat, demanding money. Chris gave him his wallet, but the robber sliced him from the ear down his neck and fled in a waiting car. The newspaper reported the incident, but neglected to mention the robbery, leaving the impression that it was "a drug deal gone bad." I insisted the rumor be cleared up, so I contacted the detective on the case who told me emphatically that he had impounded Chris' car, and it was searched thoroughly with nothing illegal in it. The detective was very complimentary of how well Chris had described his assailant, a description that led to the man's capture in California. He also said that Chris gave this information in spite of having lost five pints of blood. In the hours after the stabbing, there was doubt that Chris could survive the wound. The detective also said there was another witness who stated that the culprit had approached her car around the same time. We were proud of how Chris handled this tragic event.

Chris recovered rapidly, and although he lost a semester in school, he has continued to pursue his education with renewed determination and energy. His physical scar is almost gone, and it appears that the wound and scar to his faith in humanity has been replaced with a strong faith in God, beliefs strengthened by his association with Dallas, another friend, Josh, and other supportive young people

In 2002, Dr. Bob Alotta asked his US senator and others to consider introducing a resolution in both houses of Congress to name the SS *Henry Bacon* a "Gallant Ship." This rare honor would show our country's appreciation for the Navy gunners who bravely defended the ship and its human cargo by holding off a vastly superior enemy force for half an hour. The designation would also honor the memory of Captain Carini and the two dozen crewmen who lost their lives while saving all the harried Norwegian refugees on that frigid arctic day in February 1945. I thought it would equate all the attention and honors bestowed by Russia, Norway and the British governments and their people. The resolution was introduced, but it failed and was substituted by a mild statement, showing little interest in a small group with no power to lobby.

The Norwegian Embassy had supported Alotta's efforts, and they gave a big party at the Army/Navy Club in Washington in honor of the ship and its crew. Many people from the US and overseas were invited to the two-day event. Bea and I were included, along with our son Steve and 150 others from all over the world.

On February 22nd a delegation of 16 including: Dr. Bob and Alice Alotta; Elly Taylor; Norwegian survivor Monrad Pedersen; Chuck Reed and his friend Marjory Steenwyck; along with Norwegian and British Embassy officials and Bea and I went to Baltimore to tour the SS *John W. Brown*. The *Brown* and the *Jeremiah O'Brien* in San Francisco are the only two sister ships of the *Henry Bacon* still functional. Once again I was able to relive my service time on the *Henry Bacon*. We were given a very complete look at the ship including its engine room. I also was able to see inside the cabin on this ship which was identical to mine on the *Bacon*. The one on the ship in San Francisco was locked when I was there.

The following day was Sunday; Bea, Steve and I attended services at the beautiful National Cathedral along with Chuck Reed and Marjory Steenwyck—later to become Mrs. Chuck Reed.

On February 23rd, which was the 58th anniversary of the sinking, we participated in a lecture ceremony. Maj. Gen. Jan Blom, the Norwegian Military Attaché, gave the opening talk as he said, "Welcome to the first annual *Henry Bacon* day." He introduced Ambassador Knut Vollebaek, who spoke of his country's wish to pay tribute to the Army/Navy Club, the American crewmen, and the US Navy Armed Guard who died while saving all 19 Norwegian refugees. Elly Taylor presented a clip from her recently completed documentary, "Come Hell and High Water." Dr. Alotta and his coauthor, Mr. Foxvog, told how they came to write their book and also paid tribute to the lost crewmen. Captain John Gower, Naval Attaché at the British Embassy brought greetings from Len Phillips of HMS *Opportune*, the rescuing ship. Lastly, we three survivors, Norwegian Monrad Pedersen, Chuck Reed and I, had a chance to say some words. I thanked the people involved and also gave Ulf Jacobsen, who was also there, a word of appreciation for all he had done over the years

After the program, we enjoyed a reception where I was able to talk with some of the families of my lost shipmates. I also was honored to sign many of the books and had the authors and survivors sign mine. That evening we attended a large formal dinner at the Washington Hilton hosted by Naval Attaché Captain Tom Egil Lilletvedt and other members of the Norwegian Embassy.

On the 24th we said goodbye to Steve as he flew back to Denver. Then I had time for a short visit with the people at the RFE/RL offices and a one hour interview with a military broadcasting service. Bea and I arrived back, somewhat tired, that night in Cullman.

Chapter 18
The Happy Ending

Being over 80, and with an ancient memory so full of the emotional highs and lows of a long and active life, I decided to give my story an old fashioned "Happy Ending." We all know that happiness, by definition, is only a temporary state of mind. Some wise person said, "Things are never as good or as bad as they seem." With that philosophy, an optimist with the future in mind can opt to be happy.

I looked in Webster's Collegiate of 1949(!) and found that the word *happy* has five meanings. I opt for the third: "Enjoying well-being, peace, and comfort." Or the fifth: "In a dazed, irresponsible state of unpredictableness, as in trigger-happy; also obsessed as in pun-happy!" So, shall I be obsessed and "take the fifth" or not? Let's just leave it and go on.

Chris came home for a week in June. He is a much happier student now, as in the third meaning of the word, "Enjoying well-being, peace and comfort;" therefore so are we. We had some good conversations, and he insisted he could cook us a meal. He shopped for all the ingredients and prepared a gourmet Thai dinner.

The Happy Ending

Figure 63. Chris the Culinary Artist

Chris later showed me how he had developed in chess by beating me easily. He returned to Arkansas for some summer courses, eager to catch up after losing time last year after the attack. In his communications course, Chris needed to interview someone he admired. I was flattered and humbled when he asked me for an interview. I gave him a summary of my career, and he told me, "Grandpa, you have had the most interesting life of anyone I know." It gave me a good feeling even though I realize how subjective that comment was.

Steve read and complimented Julian's book, *Memories That Must Not Vanish*. He asked me to write my own memoirs. I first thought it was just not my style. I also used the excuse that I had not kept a journal, nor did I have adequate records and files. I would have to work with an old memory, one which deliberately used the "delete" button for some of the horrors of World War II and other unpleasant sojourns overseas. I wondered how much time it would take to put down a hundred thousand words. I really had some questions about whether I could spare the time from my family and our busy life. Certainly I didn't want to give up the nightly Scrabble games with Bea and Lynda.

Then we got the disturbing news that my sister Joyce had been diagnosed with inoperable cancer that had spread. We all kept in touch by phone and by our prayers. This, plus the miracle of modern medicine, has given her hope and us a promise of much more of her treasured company. We later had a great visit with her and Pat, along with Bill and Doris and Julian and Marie as we made our annual trek to Orange Beach. While there, we had a great evening with Russ and Renate Poole, who were down from Chillicothe, Ohio. Together we relived our many experiences in Munich.

As I walked the course at Terri Pines for what could have been the 3,000[th] time with Julian, Frank Blanchard (whose remaining Boston accent reminds me of that city in 1941), Roger Stewart and Bob Hawley. I thought about my past. My life has been quite varied and with some successes as I lived and worked with a lot of very fine people.

Many people ask me why I walk the golf course in every season from very hot to freezing cold. My answer is that I'm not particularly interested in the score, but do it mainly to keep in shape. My brother and I are determined to test the theory that exercise and an active mind with a good outlook are conducive to meaningful longevity.

Would doing the research and writing steal time we enjoy with our many relatives and friends? Since retiring to Cullman, I have made contact with dozens of cousins who are named Harbison, Lott, Calvert, Campbell, Methvin, Willoughby as well as with many others in this area. At Grace, the little white church with the red door has been replaced by a beautiful edifice reminiscent of one in an English city. Much of the credit for realizing this "dream come true" goes to our multi-talented rector, Brent Norris and to our building committee chairman, Paul Bussman. We spend quality time with a hundred fellow worshipers like the Drains, with their annual Tide/Tiger party, the Drouets who host the Cajun crawfish boil, the Arndts, Williamsons, Smiths, Strandlunds, Prehers, McDonnels, Maleskis, Jacobs, Folsoms, Adamses, Moyers, and—gosh I can't name them all. There's that large Cursillo family we love so much. The weekly reunion sub-group of Phil and Pattie, Bill and Martha, plus others, where we search our souls for worthiness and find that one's contribution is returned at least five-fold. Then there is the weekly Kiwanis meeting and program where I enjoy George and Dean and Carl and Jack and Martha and Stan and Betty and 50 others, including those inspiring Key Clubbers. We didn't want to miss the regular evening out with Clint and Marion Frey, whom we like so much; always a good meal and hours of good fellowship and conversation across a generation. Also, there are those great meals and conversations with the Stewarts—Robert, Carol, Will and friends at their lakeside house.

And most important, would writing take time from our visits with the Campbell clan?

I talked it over with Bea and Lynda, and they said go for it—and I did.

It was a slow beginning as I struggled with my old computer—then bought a new one. By August 30, 2003, I had an outline and some tentative writing. On the fifth of September I went to Terri Pines for our regular round as Julian and I were joined by Roger Stewart. I swung my nine wood on the 140-yard eighth hole and watched as the ball soared high and gracefully came down to land in the middle of the green. Then, to our surprise, it turned slightly left and rolled slowly to the edge, paused, curtsied and disappeared into the hole. Thanks were due my guardian angel for the nudge and patience with me, and it was back to earth and high fives from my two startled golfing friends. After all these years I, like Steve and Bea, had my hole-in-one!

Soon I discovered that the only way for me to prod my memory for all the details of my past life was to do it chronologically. As I remembered one detail of an era and dwelled on it, some other facts would be uncovered by the process of association. Pictures, letters, some files and conversation with colleagues from the times all helped tremendously. I also soon learned that reviewing old newspaper headlines and other sources refreshed my memory of events of the hot- and cold-war eras. I decided to include some of those events because they had often determined my career choices.

It was like a rewind and then fast forward as I condensed some 82 years into virtually reliving it all in four months of writing. The story began on a December day in 1921, and now it is the same cold month in 2003. While reviewing these 82 years, I learned so much about myself—some good, some not so good—as I saw a kid grow up and impatiently go on a worldwide journey of many adventures, extremes of weather, isolation, problems, thrills, disasters, love and some success, then a welcomed return to his roots, near where he was born. On balance, it has been good, and as I told a friend as he wondered what I had to show for walking 15,000 miles at Terri Pines with a load of clubs on my shoulder, "I'd do it again tomorrow."

And now Bea and I, who have shared three score years, are still bonded and by our faith, we with "Grace," optimistically look to the final, "Happy Ending."

Figure 64. Still Optimistic

Index

A

Adams, Robert and Trudie 139, 290
AEC (Atomic Energy Commission) 112, 114, 115, 118, 120, 121, 126
Africa 30, 35, 45, 140, 204, 234
Agnes Scott 202, 203, 205, 208
Air Force, US 35, 36, 61, 97, 103, 106, 112, 144, 152, 155, 158, 163, 189, 191, 217, 229
Ajaccio, Corsica 60
Alabama 5, 7, 11, 21, 25, 27, 33, 35, 51, 60, 69, 87, 88, 92, 100, 101, 106, 115, 116, 117, 118, 138, 139, 141, 142, 159, 169, 170, 174, 196, 197, 218, 236, 242, 243, 255, 280, 281, 282
Alabama, University of 7, 106, 138, 139, 141
Aletti Hotel 47
Algeria 38, 45, 46
Allen, Capt. 55, 58, 59
Alotta, Robert xii, 78, 278, 279, 280, 286, 287
American College in Paris 196
Anderson, Admiral 186
Anzio, Italy 56
Arctic Circle 81
Arley, Alabama 1, 3, 9, 25, 35, 36, 38, 49, 52, 58, 64, 76, 89, 93, 103, 106, 109, 123, 134
Arndts 290
Atlantic 25, 27, 28, 38, 41, 49, 55, 58, 68, 72, 196, 260
Atomic bomb 99, 112, 119, 121, 128, 129
Auburn, Alabama Polytechnic Institute 7, 8, 22

B

Bailey, Buddy and Nina 111
Baptist ix, 4, 50, 90, 104, 109, 113, 139
Barbour, Coleman xi, 270
Barron, E.B. 6
Barron, Mollie 2
Barry, Dave 59
Bartlett, Paul 230, 231
Battery Park 41
Battle of Britain 44
BBC (British Broadcasting Corporation) 60, 99
Bea ix, x, xi, xii, xiii, 52, 53, 54, 55, 58, 64, 65, 66, 69, 70, 72, 74, 81, 88, 89, 90, 92, 93, 96, 97, 100, 101, 102, 103, 104, 105, 106, 107, 108, 109, 111, 114, 115, 116, 118, 119, 123, 124, 128, 131, 132, 133, 134, 135, 137, 138, 139, 141, 142, 143, 144, 149, 151, 157, 161, 162, 163, 164, 165, 167, 168, 169, 170, 171, 172, 173, 174, 176, 177, 179, 182, 183, 184, 186, 187, 189, 190, 191, 192, 194, 195, 196, 197, 199, 202, 203, 204, 206, 208, 213, 216, 217, 218, 219, 220, 222, 223, 228, 229, 231, 234, 238, 239, 241, 242, 243, 246, 247, 248, 252, 253, 254, 255, 256, 257, 259, 262, 263, 265, 266, 267, 268, 269, 270, 271, 272, 273, 274, 277, 279, 280, 281, 282, 284, 285, 286, 287, 290, 291, 292
Beacon Street 20
Beattie, Bob 198, 209
Bellac, France 188
Bergstrom, Ted 186
Bible 2, 4
Biblis, Germany 209, 211, 212, 213, 216, 218, 219, 223, 225, 234, 235, 238

BIB (Board for International Broadcasting) 221, 227, 228, 234, 235, 236, 237, 239, 240, 243, 245
Bikini Island 112, 120, 121, 126, 129, 130, 131, 138, 150
Birmingham, Alabama 8, 9, 10, 11, 14, 36, 37, 38, 44, 52, 53, 54, 55, 58, 64, 65, 70, 89, 90, 92, 102, 103, 105, 106, 107, 112, 116, 120, 124, 126, 132, 139, 143, 162, 168, 177, 196, 217, 268, 272
Bjerregaard, Capt. 39, 48, 49
Black, Bud 184, 185, 201, 202, 229
Blanchard, Frank 290
Bluebell, HMS 79
Bluff Park, Alabama 106, 113, 115, 116, 117, 119, 128, 133, 137
BMEWS (Ballistic Missile Early Warning System) 140, 144, 147, 151, 152
"Boris" 74, 75, 76, 79
Boston, Massachusetts x, xi, 8, 10, 12, 13, 16, 18, 19, 20, 21, 23, 24, 25, 37, 38, 51, 66, 67, 69, 70, 83, 176, 290
Bota 182
Bowman, Harold 177, 183, 201
Brewer, Bill x, xi, 13, 14, 20, 21, 22, 24, 33, 252, 253, 269, 270
Brewer, Lois and Elmo 248
British 29, 30, 34, 35, 44, 46, 59, 73, 77, 78, 80, 85, 86, 99, 100, 180, 182, 183, 204, 207, 258, 261, 265, 268, 286, 287
Brooks, Don 185, 219, 226, 247, 252, 269
Brundtland, Gro Harlem 262
Buchan, Alex 228, 229, 230, 231, 232
Budweiser 48
Buena Park, California 116
Bulgaria 110, 178
Bunch, Jerry 145, 146, 147, 148, 155, 156, 157
Burbine, Dick xii, 86, 258, 283, 284
Burns, Cortez 110
Burt, Lt. 55, 56, 57, 58, 59, 60
Bush, George H. W. 251, 257
Bussman, Paul 290

C

Campbell, Bert 65, 92, 203, 236
Campbell, Bill 52, 53, 54, 65, 196, 203, 236, 290
Campbell, Billy 92, 163, 203
Campbell, Calvin 37, 38, 65, 89, 93, 203, 236
Campbell, Doris 36, 54, 65, 103, 106, 140, 203, 236, 290
Campbell, George and Martha ix, 8, 37, 65, 174, 269
Campbell, Gloria 18, 23, 35, 36, 52, 54, 103, 106, 203, 236
Campbell, Jimmy 52, 53
Campbell, Joyce 36, 54, 103, 106, 203, 236, 252, 253, 290
Campbell, Julian x, xiii, 1, 2, 25, 35, 36, 37, 38, 44, 47, 51, 52, 56, 64, 88, 93, 97, 102, 103, 106, 112, 115, 131, 159, 163, 175, 197, 203, 217, 229, 231, 236, 238, 239, 246, 247, 257, 269, 280, 281, 284, 285, 289, 290, 291
Campbell, Lecie 65, 107, 109, 203, 236
Campbell, Lynda x, xiii, 104, 105, 107, 108, 111, 112, 113, 115, 116, 117, 119, 124, 128, 132, 133, 139, 141, 144, 154, 157, 161, 162, 163, 164, 167, 168, 169, 170, 173, 174, 176, 182, 190, 193, 194, 196, 197, 202, 203, 205, 208, 213, 217, 218, 240, 241, 243, 246, 249, 254, 259, 272, 280, 284, 285, 290, 291
Campbell, Mary 3, 23, 35, 107, 203, 236

Campbell, Nan ix, x, xiii, 213, 217, 218, 243, 248, 254, 259, 260, 263, 268, 269, 280, 282, 283

Campbell, Spud ix, 6, 7, 21, 51, 92, 99, 101, 107, 109, 114, 115, 117, 125, 134, 159, 198, 205, 207, 236, 254, 262, 263, 264, 265, 274, 284

Campbell, Steve ix, x, xii, xiii, 107, 108, 110, 111, 113, 115, 116, 117, 119, 124, 127, 128, 131, 133, 139, 141, 143, 144, 154, 157, 161, 162, 163, 164, 165, 167, 168, 169, 170, 173, 174, 182, 186, 189, 193, 194, 196, 197, 198, 199, 200, 203, 204, 206, 208, 209, 213, 214, 217, 218, 241, 243, 248, 254, 259, 260, 263, 265, 268, 269, 271, 272, 273, 274, 280, 282, 283, 286, 287, 289, 291

Campbell, Tommy 8, 64, 65, 96, 102, 115, 116, 117, 118, 203, 208, 236

Campbell, W.G. 203

Campbell castle 272

Camp De Soto 12

Cape Palmas, SS 100

Capri 56, 213

Cardiff, Wales 58, 59

Carini, Capt. 66, 70, 71, 73, 74, 76, 77, 81, 82, 87, 261, 273, 286

Carmen 178

Casablanca, Morocco 44, 45, 46

Cascais, Portugal 182, 193, 195, 199

CCC (Civilian Conservation Corps) 10, 11, 12, 13, 14

Central Park 40

Channel 13 112

Charles River, Boston 20

Cheaha Mountain, Alabama 138

Chess 74, 75, 95, 202, 216, 226, 289

Chile 93, 95

Chubbuck, Earl 177, 179, 180, 181, 191

Churchill, Winston 44, 45, 56, 95, 106

Civil War 16, 54, 245, 278

Clay, General Lucius 106, 107

CNN (Cable News Network) 258, 261

Coast Guard, US 8, 16, 19, 66

Colchester, England 69, 72

Cold War xiii, 95, 99, 106, 107, 129, 130, 168, 171, 198, 212, 229, 234, 248, 254, 255, 259

Colin, MV 28, 29, 30, 36, 39

Conaughty, Capt. 142, 144, 151, 152, 154, 155, 157, 160, 161

Convoy 37, 79, 80

Cotton, Bob 6, 177, 186, 201

Cox, Dad 6

Cox, Jewel 3, 6

Cullman, Alabama xi, 2, 5, 186, 209, 217, 229, 231, 238, 239, 243, 244, 245, 246, 247, 248, 250, 251, 254, 255, 257, 258, 268, 270, 272, 278, 279, 285, 287, 290

Cullman Times 229, 257

Czechoslovakia 92, 95, 110, 178

D

D-Day 60

Dachau, Germany 223, 228, 229

Daniel 179, 181, 204

Danielsen, Per 78, 275, 276

Darlington Street, Birmingham 137, 141

Darmstadt, Germany 210, 211, 212, 213, 214, 216, 217, 218, 219

Davis, Paul 37

Dentler, Irmgard 212

Denver, Colorado xiii, 241, 248, 260, 269, 274, 280, 283, 287

DEW Drop (Distant Early Warning) 144, 147, 148, 156, 157

Digesu, Fred 9, 10, 12, 21, 22, 24

Double Springs, Alabama 25, 53, 92, 103, 113, 163, 197, 217

Drain, Sonny & Libby xi, 290

Drouets 290
Durkee 201, 218, 228

E

Eastwood, Dick & Pat 190, 210
Edinburgh, Scotland 55, 56, 230, 271, 272, 274
Eisenhower, Dwight 60, 95, 141
Eldridge, Alabama ix, 1
England ix, 7, 24, 46, 53, 55, 58, 59, 75, 78, 98, 209, 272, 275
Englisher Garten, Munich 185
Eniwetok xii, 120, 121, 122, 126, 128, 129, 130, 131, 134, 138, 142, 150, 153, 154, 174, 193, 242, 247
Esten, Perry & Ida 171, 172, 184, 189, 191, 198, 201, 209, 212, 215, 218, 219, 220, 221, 222, 223, 226, 247
Estes, Dallas 280
Estes, Jim & Bea 280
Estoril Golf Club 177, 186, 187
Europe ix, xii, 7, 11, 25, 26, 38, 50, 58, 60, 71, 92, 93, 94, 95, 98, 106, 109, 115, 171, 173, 175, 180, 182, 187, 191, 192, 202, 206, 209, 212, 213, 214, 215, 221, 226, 229, 239, 243, 245, 250, 272, 279
Evans, Frank 3, 6
Evans, Myrl 3, 6

F

Fado 209
Fairfax, Virginia 168, 169, 172, 174, 191, 199
Fallis, Hugh 239, 243
Federal Communications Commission 17, 100, 101
Felipe de Neve, SS 39
Ferguson, Glen 232, 233, 234, 235, 237, 238, 239, 243
Fernandes, Aleixo 180, 191, 192, 238

Fields, Cortis 6
Finnmark, Norway 77
Fischer, Hans 185, 192, 226
Flying Club 172, 183
Foreign Legion, French 57
Foxvog, Donald xii, 78, 279, 280, 287
France 10, 45, 60, 94, 99, 187, 188, 210, 242, 243
Franz, Werner 238
Frey, Clint & Marion 291
Frommeyer, Dr. 139, 143
Fuller, Doris & Bill xiii, 65

G

Gallop, Capt. John 16
Gallups Island x, xi, 10, 12, 16, 17, 21, 22, 24, 25, 26, 28, 29, 39, 51, 66, 69, 121, 123, 176, 252, 269
Gaze, Ralph 148
Geiger, Russ 184, 186, 198, 247, 252
Georgia Tech 206, 208, 213, 217
Germany 26, 45, 88, 92, 94, 99, 106, 107, 171, 185, 188, 209, 211, 212, 213, 214, 215, 216, 217, 218, 223, 231, 233, 234, 238, 243
Gibraltar 46, 49, 60, 204
GIRA (Gallups Island Radio Association) xi, 22
Glasgow, Scotland 72, 76, 88
Gloria, Portugal 179, 181, 182, 183, 184, 185, 189, 190, 191, 192, 198, 201, 202, 203, 204, 209, 211, 212, 216, 219, 220, 223, 232, 233, 234, 235, 238, 242
God 4, 24, 30, 40, 43, 101, 109, 116, 286
Golf ix, xiii, 2, 177, 184, 186, 187, 197, 216, 217, 223, 228, 229, 230, 232, 236, 246, 247, 248, 255, 257, 258, 268, 269, 271, 272, 290
Grace Episcopal Church 247, 268
Graham, Lew 55, 57

Grandmother Bearden 93
Grand Banks 42
Greenland 143, 144, 145, 148, 149, 150, 156, 157, 166
Guantanamo, Cuba 33
Guardian Angel 32, 34, 43, 52, 82, 101, 123, 291
Gurr, John 186

H

Haakon, King 78
Hairston, Carolyn 217
Hammerfest, Norway 77, 259, 260, 261, 263, 264, 266, 276
Hamner, Barney 6, 90
Hamner, Billie xiii, 3, 6
Hamner, Brent 247
Harald, King 260, 262, 263
Harbison/Lott 247
Harrison, Jack xii, 271, 272, 273, 274, 278
Harrison, Peter xii, 273, 274
Hart, Henry 215
Haugland, Baard xii
Haviland, Chief Engineer 87
Hawley, Bob 290
Helicon, Alabama 6
Hendriksen, Harald xii, 270, 271, 275, 276, 277
Henry Bacon, SS ix, xi, xii, 64, 66, 78, 79, 84, 86, 88, 92, 123, 156, 159, 250, 256, 257, 258, 259, 260, 262, 266, 268, 270, 271, 273, 276, 277, 278, 279, 283, 286, 287
Herrmann, Bill & Judy xii, 81, 86, 88, 89, 258
Hetzler, Frank xi
Hiroshima, Japan 97, 112, 121, 128
Hitler, Adolf 7, 10, 11, 29, 38, 44, 58, 60, 185, 275
Holmes & Narver 118, 120, 121, 142
Holzkirchen, Germany 216, 234, 235, 238, 239, 240
Horne, Jan 275, 276, 277, 278

Howell Jackson, SS 55
Hungary 92, 110, 178
Hunt, Alma 92
Hunt, Bob 69, 71, 72, 75, 77, 83, 86, 87, 261, 273
Hunter, Bruce & Gertrude 190, 195, 206, 207

I

Iron Curtain 106, 192, 193, 212, 215, 216, 223, 233, 237, 240, 242, 245, 252
Ishee, Bill xi, 14, 21
Italy 26, 45, 48, 235
"Ivan" 226
Izvestia 237

J

Jacksonville, Florida x, 13, 14, 15, 32, 33, 252
Jacobs, George 236, 290
Jacobsen, Ulf & Heldur 264, 265, 266, 276, 277, 287
Jaguar 198, 204, 222
Jamming 185, 215, 216, 219, 225, 233, 237, 240, 245, 250
Jennings, Stan xi, 22, 24
Johnson, Lyndon 198, 205
Johnson, Pat & Joyce 36, 54, 103, 106, 203, 236, 252, 253, 290

K

Kane, Harold & Lilo 252
Kelly, Mary & Ralph 3, 23, 35, 107, 109, 203, 236
Kennedy, John 165, 167, 184, 194, 214
Kershner and Wright 173, 235
Ketcham 104
Kiwanis Club 254, 268, 270, 271, 272, 278, 291
Kluehe, Willi 186, 209, 211, 219, 235, 238
Kola Inlet, Russia 79

Krahe, Eddie 212, 219, 238

L

Lake Charles, Louisiana 64
Lammon, Allan & Holcomb, Jr. 71, 87, 92
Lampertheim, Germany 238
Lansford, Jack & Janet 247
Lark, HMS 79
Lathlean, Sid 122, 125, 128, 129, 130
Latvia 75
Leinwoll, Stan 216, 228, 245
Liberty Ship 26, 55
Liddle, JR & Mary 113
Lifeboat 32, 69, 82, 83, 84, 86, 87, 92, 164, 258, 259, 261, 264, 277
Little League 139, 141, 157, 161, 163
Liverpool, England 44, 45, 100
Loch Ewe, Scotland xii, 72, 73, 271, 272, 273
Lolliot, Henry 175, 177, 178, 201
London, England 29, 44, 45, 59, 60, 100, 163, 209, 218, 272, 274, 275
Lull, Mary Carlton & Tim 283

M

Maia, Senhor 181
Mama 2, 9, 23, 37, 141
Manchester, England 44
Mansfield, Doug 243
Marchetti, Michael 245
Maritime Service 16
Martens, Carl 8
Maxwell 113
McCullar, Clara & Henry 103, 154, 169, 170, 242, 248
McCullar, Don 54, 105, 163, 169, 191, 248, 269, 279
McCullar, Nell 53, 69, 70, 106, 154, 168, 169, 197, 243, 279, 280
McKenna, Anthony 194, 196, 198, 206

Mediterranean 30, 38, 45, 46, 47, 52, 56, 58, 59, 64
Meek, Alabama 1, 2, 3, 6, 251, 267
Melear, Hollis 6
Merchant Marine, US ix, xi, 8, 33, 86, 98, 250, 253, 271
Metello, Col. 189
Millar xi, 256, 257, 258
Miller 252
Montando, Doug & Ruth 248, 269
Morocco 38, 45, 204, 205
Morse code 8, 19, 20, 27, 31, 41, 70
Mortensen 78, 259, 261, 277
Moscow, Russia xi, 58, 95, 226, 237, 256
Mulvey 55, 59, 61, 62
Murmansk, Russia xi, 37, 67, 70, 73, 74, 76, 78, 185, 212, 215, 216, 226, 253, 256, 259, 265, 266
Murphy, John 235, 236
Murphy, Wyatt 3, 6
Mussolini, Benito 29

N

Naples, Italy 56
Navy, US 18, 37, 39, 44, 45, 48, 55, 59, 69, 87, 88, 96, 135, 142, 147, 253, 271, 278, 286, 287
Nazi xi, 30, 59, 256, 257, 262, 275
Nedregard, Magne 260
Neto, Horacio 180, 191, 192, 202, 209, 233, 238
Neto, Horatio 180
Neubiberg, Germany 219, 220
Newcastle, England 55
Newton, Hubert 20, 21, 24
New Deal 11
New Iberia, Louisiana 14
New Jersey 20, 31, 41, 87, 175, 197, 221, 244
New Orleans 36, 37, 55, 57, 162
New York, New York xii, 15, 17, 19, 20, 27, 28, 31, 39, 40, 42, 48, 49, 51, 54, 58, 68, 69, 70, 71, 75, 87, 88, 89, 93, 100, 139,

171, 172, 173, 175, 176, 194, 196, 218, 228, 243, 245, 280
Norris, Brent 290
North, Paul 228, 233
North Africa 38, 44, 47, 53
North Cape, Norway 74, 79, 267
Norway ix, xi, xii, 37, 55, 67, 77, 156, 258, 262, 267, 268, 270, 272, 275, 286
Notaro, Sam xi, 19, 270
NYA (National Youth Administration) 8, 11, 12, 13, 14

O

O'Brien, Bernie 152, 161
O'Neal, Bob & Clarice 282
O'Neal, Nan ix, x, xiii, 213, 217, 218, 243, 248, 254, 259, 260, 263, 268, 269, 280, 282, 283
Oebbecke, Marty 177, 186, 194, 201, 219, 220, 223, 226, 228
Olaf, Prince 78
Old Howard Theatre 21
OMB (Office of Management and Budget) 221, 234, 235, 238
Opera 207, 234, 235
Opportune, HMS xii, 85, 86, 258, 271, 287
Oran, Algeria 46, 47, 56, 57
Oslo, Norway 260, 263, 267, 270, 271, 275, 277
Owens, Marc 213, 214

P

Page Communications Engineers 142, 144, 184
Palmer, Chief Mate 76, 87
Pals, Spain 228, 233, 242
Panama Canal 93, 99
Papa 7, 9, 37, 38
Parede, Portugal 178, 181, 182, 183, 184, 189, 193
Paris, France 188, 196, 197, 202, 203, 205, 277

Parry Island 121, 122, 128, 129, 130, 135
Patterson, Ralph & Mary Lou 186
Pearl Harbor 26, 251, 257
Pease, Lynn & Martha 219, 233
Pedersen, Elbjorg 78
Pedersen, Henrik 78
Pedersen, Inger 78, 264, 276
Pedersen, Monrad 84, 264, 276, 286, 287
Pedersen, Sophie 78, 258, 261, 264
Pedersen, Torild 264
Peinhardt, Bill 258
Phillips, Len xii, 258, 271, 287
P Mountain, Greenland 145, 147, 151, 152, 158, 166
Poland 10, 92, 110, 178, 240, 259
Pompeii 56
Poole, Russ & Renate xii, 185, 215, 219, 227, 241, 247, 251, 252, 259, 268, 285, 290
Poolewe, Scotland 73, 271, 273, 274
Porter, Dave 194, 198
Portugal 45, 171, 172, 173, 176, 178, 179, 180, 182, 184, 186, 187, 188, 190, 191, 192, 194, 195, 197, 198, 199, 203, 205, 206, 207, 208, 209, 211, 212, 213, 215, 222, 238, 242
Potomac River 15, 161, 165

R

Radio ix, x, xi, xii, 13, 22, 28, 30, 107, 109, 126, 171, 173, 178, 192, 212, 221, 226, 230, 237, 239, 241
Rampy, C. W. 21, 270
RARET (Radio Retransmissão) 178, 192, 201, 238
Reed, Chuck xii, 77, 81, 86, 258, 283, 284, 286, 287
Reigosa, Tony 228, 233
RFE/RL (Radio Free Europe/Radio Liberty) ix, xii, 109, 171, 173, 174, 175, 177, 178, 184, 185,

186, 191, 192, 193, 198, 201,
202, 209, 212, 214, 215, 216,
218, 219, 221, 223, 226, 227,
228, 229, 231, 233, 234, 236,
237, 238, 239, 240, 241, 243,
245, 247, 248, 250, 251, 252,
254, 259, 268, 269, 287
Richardson, John 193, 202
Rocket 60, 135, 189, 190
Rodby, Major 153, 154
Romania 110, 178
Rønbeck, Mayor Kåre 260
Roosevelt, Franklin Delano 26, 45, 93
Russia xii, 73, 144, 152, 250, 251,
270, 271, 286
Russian Embassy 255, 257
Ryals, Joe 142, 144, 157, 161

S

Sailors Haven 25
Salazar, Antonio 178, 206
San Diego, California 96, 101, 102
San Francisco, California 96, 97, 98,
100, 101, 195, 283, 286, 287
Sartain, Arnold & Jackie 104, 105,
124, 134, 163
Schleissheim, Germany 215, 216,
223, 233
Scotland ix, 55, 56, 78, 82, 86, 141,
184, 190, 263, 272, 274, 283
Scott, Herb & Nell 212
Scott, Ken 227, 228, 229
Seattle, Washington 95, 96, 269, 279
Shades Mountain, Alabama 106, 110,
133, 137, 139, 162, 163
Sheddan, Art xi, 13, 21, 24, 33, 252,
270
Sherwood, Fran 252
Sicily 45, 47, 48, 79
Sidi-Bel-Abbes, Algeria 57
Sippola, Lt. 69, 72, 74, 76, 81, 87
Smart, James xi, 270
Smith, Gen. Rodney 185, 201, 290
Sonja, Queen 260, 262, 263, 267

Sørøya, Norway 77, 78, 258, 259,
264, 275, 276, 277
Sørvær, Norway 265
SOS 27, 31, 32, 42, 43, 82, 86
Soviet Union 99, 100, 106, 129, 140,
147, 167, 198, 221, 226, 251
Sparks, Chris ix, 247, 249, 254, 259,
268, 270, 272, 279, 280, 281,
282, 285, 286, 288, 289
Spear, Andy 138, 140, 141, 143, 163
Spud ix, 6, 7, 21, 51, 92, 99, 101, 107,
109, 114, 115, 117, 125, 134,
159, 198, 205, 207, 236, 254,
262, 263, 264, 265, 274, 284
Spurgeon ix, 9, 19
Sputnik 135
St. Raphael, France 61
Stalin 11, 58, 60, 95, 99, 100, 106,
107, 140
Stanford-Benet 7
Staten Island 41, 49
Steele, Varick 186, 226, 228
Stewart, Anita 154, 213
Stewart, Robert, Carol & Will 154,
168, 197, 291
Stewart, Roger 290
Sulphur Springs, Florida 12
Summerfield, Chief 19, 20
Sunday School 19, 190

T

Tallahassee, Florida 11
Tampa, Florida 10, 11, 12, 14, 91
Tanksley, Dick 228, 231
Tatosky, Robert 258
Taylor, Elly xii, 279, 283, 286, 287
Terri Pines 2, 186, 246, 268, 269, 290,
291, 292
Thompson, Roger & Donna 139
Thule, Greenland xii, 140, 142, 144,
145, 146, 148, 149, 150, 152,
153, 154, 155, 156, 157, 158,
159, 160, 161, 164, 166, 193,
247, 261
Times Square 40

TNT 43, 259
Trinidad, British West Indies 33, 34, 37
Trinity 19
Tropospheric Scatter 126, 142, 148, 150
Truman, Presdient 93, 95, 97, 106, 107
TVA (Tennessee Valley Authority) 3
Twilight Immunity 225
Tye, Chris 273, 274
Tyson, Ken 190

V

Vancouver, British Columbia 97, 98, 269
Vichy, France 45, 60
Victoria, British Columbia 99, 269
Virginia 15, 148, 161, 170, 174, 245, 256, 278
VOA (Voice of America) 161, 164, 165, 166, 169, 184, 215, 234, 236, 238
Volker, Dr. 139, 143
Von Braun, Werner 60
Vulcania 174, 176, 177

W

Waldrep, Arvel 8, 36, 38, 203, 282
Waldrep, Betty 8, 10, 36, 38, 52, 203, 282
Waldrep, Evelyn 8, 10, 36, 38, 52, 53, 65, 203, 236, 282
Waldrep, Margaret 203
Walesa, Lech 240, 250, 259
Walker County, Alabama 1
Walter, Ralph 185, 214, 218, 221, 223, 227, 238, 240
Walton, Evelyn & Milo 203
Washington, DC xi, 15, 22, 26, 95, 141, 142, 144, 151, 157, 160, 161, 162, 163, 164, 169, 170, 171, 181, 184, 201, 221, 227, 228, 232, 234, 235, 236, 239, 243, 245, 246, 247, 250, 255, 256, 258, 286, 287
Waugh, Susan 281
WBRC 105
Wetzel, Lee & Nell 279, 280
White, Pat 51
White House 15, 239
Williamson, Howard 278
Winston County, Alabama 1, 13, 53, 54, 113
Wisner, Eric 238
World War II ix, xi, 14, 22, 41, 77, 80, 86, 107, 121, 150, 192, 203, 204, 212, 216, 223, 247, 255, 256, 257, 259, 260, 262, 264, 267, 271, 275, 276, 277, 279, 280, 282, 289
WSGN 105

Y

Yeltsin, Boris 251, 257

About the Author

Growing up on a farm in Alabama, E. Spurgeon Campbell was fascinated listening to voices over his battery radio set, voices beckoning to a wider world. The magical technology of radio became a passage to a lifetime of adventure.

Beginning in cramped cabins of Merchant Marine ships during World War II, signaling through bombardments and once from a lifeboat in the Arctic, Campbell learned radio waves can save lives. His career took him from Eniwetok in the Pacific to the top of the world in Thule, Greenland and then to 20 years with Radio Free Europe, sending news to oppressed societies behind the Iron Curtain.

He and his wife, Bea, are retired in Cullman, Alabama.

Printed in the United States
74782LV00004BA/10